CONTROVERSIES

KARL KEATING

CONTROVERSIES

High-Level Catholic Apologetics

IGNATIUS PRESS   SAN FRANCISCO

Cover design by Roxanne Mei Lum

ISBN 0–89870–828–1
Library of Congress control number 2001088856
Printed in the United States of America ∞

In grateful memory of
Isaac Don Levine

CONTENTS

PREFACE

Toward the end of my undergraduate years, a prominent defector from the Soviet Union spoke on campus. I arrived at the hall early and found a seat near the front, two places away from an elderly man and his wife. I brought along a fat book to occupy myself until the start of the lecture. After a few minutes, the man spoke across the empty seat between us. "May I ask the title of that book?" I said it was Whittaker Chambers' *Witness*. "What do you think of it?" I answered by saying I was on my second reading. He smiled knowingly. "Permit me to introduce myself to you." He reached for the book and opened it to the index. From his suit pocket he fished out a stubby pencil and made a check mark next to the entry "Levine, Isaac Don". That is how I met one of the participants in the Hiss-Chambers case and a man who had been a prominent foreign correspondent for more than half a century.

Over the next three years I periodically visited Don and Ruth Levine at their winter home some miles north of the university. Although long past retirement age, he had not retired from writing. He remained an active journalist until the end. Born in 1891 northwest of Kiev, in the town of Mozyr (which, he noted, was mainly Jewish but included two thousand Catholics), he did not seem to be a religious man, but he had a heart for truth. He had seen much of the world and had tried to learn from what he had seen.

An immigrant to the United States, Levine returned to Russia during the Revolution to report on events for American newspapers. He accompanied Trotsky to the front and went to Ekaterinburg to investigate the murder of the imperial family. He reported the confused events following Lenin's death and the struggle between Trotsky and Stalin. He became close friends with Alexander Kerensky, whose short-lived government had been overthrown by Lenin. With Lincoln Steffens and Ernest Hemingway he observed Benito Mussolini's debut as a statesman at the Lausanne Peace Conference. In later years he came to know Albert Einstein and Joseph McCarthy, and he traveled throughout the Middle East and saw firsthand the political volatility of Iran when it was under the Shah. Levine was a repository of facts, dates, and quotations.

One of the last times I saw him was at the university library. He was attended by his wife, who steadied him as he walked. He said he was finishing up a book and had been downstairs in the microfilm room, where he had looked up a single headline that had appeared in *The New York Times* around World War I. He wanted to make sure he had remembered the wording correctly. I was taken by his devotion to precision. At his age, in his condition, he could have made worthy excuses for not engaging in any but the most necessary research. He could have sent off the manuscript with a headline that possibly was misremembered—who would have checked up on him? It did not matter that no one would have bothered to do so. He went to the microfilm room not so much for his future readers as for himself. He was devoted to accurate reporting because he was devoted to truth.

Levine's search for truth—in his case, historical truth—did not endear him to everyone. "More than once", he wrote in his autobiographical *Eyewitness to History*, "I found myself described as a controversial personality." The appellation was not always meant as a compliment. Not everyone appreciated his digging beneath accepted opinions and, worse, challenging them. Some people shy away from controversy and from those engaged in it, but I found Levine all the more attractive for having lived a life of intellectual tension. He wanted to know, and his search for knowledge sometimes rankled others. No matter. "To thine own self be true", counseled Polonius.

If it can be said that a man's personality is reflected in the reading he enjoys, then my own personality tends toward the controversial, for I enjoy works that defend a position strongly held. This is especially true regarding religion, the most important subject of all. Religious controversy is considered by many to be a relic of a triumphalistic past. Worse, it is socially obtuse. As recently as a lifetime ago a controversial exchange was understood to be one in which two parties expressed decided but gentlemanly disagreement. The truth mattered to them, and they thought it worth fighting over, even though their only weapons were words. They thought that good things arose from a grasp of truth and evil things from a rejection of truth. Today reasoned controversy is unfashionable, and a desire for truth has given way to indifferentism. It no longer matters if such-and-so is true: "There is a truth for you and a truth for me." There is nothing to argue about if everyone is right, if all beliefs are true, if all opinions are "valid". If modern culture has a patron saint, it is Pontius Pilate, who ironically inquired, "What is truth?"— ironically, because the poor man did not realize that he had Truth staring him in the face.

In the following pages are offered eight examples of high-level controversial writing, culled from some of my favorite books. Each selection is a forceful exposition of Catholic truth. Most of them are from the 1930s, all of them come from British Catholics, and all of them are aimed at a single antagonist, with the public invited to look over the writer's shoulder. Four are taken from book-length exchanges of correspondence, a format that lets the reader view the weaknesses and occasional mistakes even of his own champion. In all of the pieces the reader finds vivid personalities. These were men who knew the Catholic faith and could explain it to others. The individuals to whom or against whom they wrote may not have been converted—one or two were, in the long run—but any number of readers of these now-forgotten masterpieces must have found their faith bolstered and their doubts assuaged.

The first selection is from John Henry Newman's *Apologia pro Vita Sua*. It is a rhetorical flourish that was excised from the second and later editions of that justly famous work. There follow two short essays by Hilaire Belloc, he of the cool logic, one replying to J. B. S. Haldane, the other to Dean Inge. Then Ronald Knox writes to Arnold Lunn, who, at the time of writing, was not yet a Catholic. Next are three pieces by the Catholic Lunn and one by Herbert Thurston, a Jesuit historian well known in his time but almost completely forgotten in ours. The eight selections are arranged chronologically—the first appeared in 1865, the last in 1946, and the rest from 1931 to 1937—and, in a preface to each, I introduce the characters and set the stage.

In one-on-one exchanges such as these there is, unavoidably and desirably, a personal element. Newman says of Charles Kingsley that "though I am writing with all my heart against what he has said of me, I am not conscious of personal unkindness towards himself." The intensity of Newman's writing does not detract from its politeness. Belloc explains that a "personal tone" suffuses his remarks: "I can write no other way", and his writing is the stronger for it. Historian G. G. Coulton tests Thurston's and Lunn's patience, but neither Catholic strays from apologetical rectitude. Lunn tells the agnostic C. E. M. Joad that "though we differ on fundamental issues, we are not personally antipathetic"—after all, he notes, "There is always hope for a man, however perverse his views, who prefers Van Eyck to the post-impressionists." Good-natured repartee joins with sharp argumentation. The stakes are high in these essays, but so is the courtesy.

Particularly striking in each piece is the clarity of the thought. Belloc notes that "clear thinking is always an advantage when one is attempting to discover the nature of things." This is the hallmark of each selection, whether it is Newman defending the priesthood, Lunn the rationality of Christianity, or Knox the history of the Church. I find this clarity immensely attractive—and immensely lacking in most modern writing on religion. It is the difference between wading across a crystalline stream and slogging through muck.

A few words about format. Orthography, punctuation, and capitalization have not been made uniform or regularized but have been preserved as in the originals. There occasionally is inconsistency even within individual selections, and even that inconsistency has been retained. The writers used few footnotes—fewer than fifty altogether—with most of them being found in Herbert Thurston's piece. The modern reader might wish for more. He might be at a loss to identify some of the characters and references (who was this "Bishop Barnes", who seems not to have had a first name but whom everyone was expected to know?), so I have added well over three hundred footnotes of my own, identified by "—ED." I hope they do not burden the reading but make reading these selections easier.

K. K.

John Henry Newman vs. Charles Kingsley

The January 1864 issue of *Macmillan's Magazine* included a review of the seventh and eighth volumes of J. A. Froude's *History of England*. The review was signed only with the initials "C. K." The identity of the reviewer might have remained unknown to the general public if the writer had not included two sentences that were to ensure his lasting fame. Were it not for thirty words, Charles Kingsley—professor of history at Cambridge, popular novelist, opponent of the Oxford Movement, and an anti-Catholic—would be known today only by specialists in Victorian studies. He had the personal misfortune (for us, a *felix culpa*) of penning a charge that was to induce the greatest work of its kind since Augustine's *Confessions*. He imprudently wrote, "Truth, for its own sake, had never been a virtue with the Roman clergy. Father Newman informs us that it need not, and on the whole ought not to be." [1] The reply came in the form of John Henry Newman's *Apologia pro Vita Sua*.

Kingsley's father had been "bred as a country gentleman; but, from the carelessness of his guardians during a long

---

[1] *Macmillan's Magazine*, January 1864, 216–17.

minority, had been forced to adopt a profession, and had taken orders after thirty".[2] It might be understandable that such a man, resident with some reluctance in a parsonage, would turn introspective and bookish and would produce a son who was "a precocious child, writing sermons and poems at the age of four". Charles Kingsley (1819–1875) studied at King's College, London, and at Cambridge—where he later taught—and became known as "a good pedestrian", once having walked to London in a day.

He developed a strong dislike of the Oxford Movement, with which Newman was so closely identified—he thought it "represented sacerdotalism, asceticism, and Manichaeism"—and confessed to his future wife that in the late 1830s he was tormented by religious doubts. By 1842 the doubts were allayed sufficiently, and Kingsley was ordained and was appointed curate of a country parish. There he wrote a drama on the life of Saint Elizabeth of Hungary, and that helped him to become acquainted with prominent literary and political figures. His interest in social problems led to an involvement with Christian socialism, and the term *muscular Christianity* came to be applied to his thinking. He styled himself a Platonist and unreservedly endorsed Darwinism, which he found compatible with his theology. High-strung and restless (he found it difficult to sit still through a meal), Kingsley "neither thought nor studied systematically, and his beliefs were more matters of instinct than of reason". It was certain of his instincts, the anti-Catholic, that were to betray him in his controversy with Newman.

Like Kingsley, John Henry Newman (1801–1890) had a sensitive temperament. Unlike Kingsley, he never found

---

[2] The quotations describing Kingsley in this paragraph and the next are taken from *The Dictionary of National Biography*, Leslie Stephen and Sidney Lee, eds., vol. XI (Oxford: Oxford University Press, 1921) 175–81. —ED.

himself plagued by religious doubts. At age fifteen he un-
derwent not so much a conversion, in the current Evangelical sense of the term, as a rapid maturation in his
thinking and beliefs. He discovered Church history and the
Fathers and adopted as the motto of his future religious
investigations "growth the only evidence of life". The line
came from Thomas Scott's autobiography, *The Force of
Truth*,[3] which showed how Scott, an Evangelical commen-
tator on the Bible, had "followed truth wherever it led him,
beginning with Unitarianism, and ending in a zealous faith
in the Holy Trinity".[4] The motto encapsulates Newman's
approach to the Christian faith: authentic Christian truths
are alive, as the Church is alive, and they develop over time
without changing their essence. Errors stagnate; they are
theological dead ends. Truths grow. Growth in doctrine,
both extensively and intensively, is a sign of a vibrant and
therefore real Christianity. One who traces that growth
throughout history will discover the Church established by
Christ.

Newman went on to a successful career at Oxford, teaching at Oriel College and serving as the vicar of Saint
Mary's, from the pulpit of which he gave memorable sermons. He wrote extensively and was a leader of the Oxford
Movement, which sought to bring a more liturgical and
patristic sense to Anglicanism. The culmination of Newman's early investigations appeared in 1845 as *An Essay on
the Development of Christian Doctrine*. During the writing of
that book he found himself convinced of the necessity of
joining the Catholic Church. He said he "recognized in
himself a conviction of the truth of the conclusion to

[3] Thomas Scott, *The Force of Truth* (London: Keith, 1779). —ED.

[4] John Henry Newman, *Apologia pro Vita Sua* (New York: Random
House, 1950 [1864]), 36. —ED.

which the discussion leads, so clear as to supersede further deliberation".[5] His pursuit of the truth had taken him to Rome.

In later years, as a Catholic, Newman defended the Church against the uproar that ensued when the hierarchy was reestablished in England,[6] he wrote novels,[7] and he produced seminal works on Christian education and how one comes to assent to the faith.[8] But his best known work was his *Apologia pro Vita Sua*. Its publication, in response to Kingsley's attack, did much to resuscitate Newman's reputation among Protestants—he had been condemned roundly for becoming a Catholic, even accused of moral laxness for having done so—and reinforced his standing as the foremost defender of the faith in England.

Kingsley's review in *Macmillan's Magazine* precipitated a lengthy correspondence: Newman writing first to the publisher; Kingsley answering him and identifying himself as the reviewer; Newman telling Kingsley that he "was amazed" that a man of his reputation should make such a charge against the Catholic clergy; Kingsley replying that he appreciated the "tone" of Newman's letter, which "make[s] me feel, to my very deep pleasure, that my opinion of the

[5] John Henry Newman, *An Essay on the Development of Christian Doctrine* (London: Pickering, 1878), xi. —ED.

[6] Newman's *Lectures on the Present Position of Catholics in England* (1851) is one of his least-read books but is a masterful and often satirical defense of the Church against anti-Catholic attacks. —ED.

[7] *Callista* (London: Burns and Lambert, 1856), set in the third century, appeared in 1856. *Loss and Gain* (London: Burns, 1848), "the story of a convert" (who in more than a few ways mirrored Newman), was published in 1848; it is one of only three of his works that Newman counted as "controversial", the others being *Present Position* (London: Burns and Lambert, 1851) and *Difficulties of Anglicans* (London: Burns and Lambert, 1850). —ED.

[8] *The Idea of a University* (London: Pickering, 1873) and *An Essay in Aid of a Grammar of Assent* (London: Burns, Oates, 1870). —ED.

meaning of your words was a mistaken one", and back-handedly apologizing in a proposed letter to the editor in which he expressed his "hearty pleasure at finding [Newman] on the side of Truth, in this, or any other, matter".[9] So it continued, with Kingsley conspicuously failing to substantiate his charge.

As Anton C. Pegis noted in his introduction to the *Apologia pro Vita Sua*, "Kingsley's evasive replies to Newman's challenge that his critic advance proof of his assertions forced Newman to edit and publish the correspondence."[10] The correspondence appeared in pamphlet form, with this satirical rephrasing of the exchange appended:[11]

REFLECTIONS ON THE ABOVE

I shall attempt a brief analysis of the foregoing correspondence; and I trust that the wording which I shall adopt will not offend against the gravity due both to myself and to the occasion. It is impossible to do justice to the course of thought evolved in it without some familiarity of expression.

Mr. Kingsley begins then by exclaiming,—"O the chicanery, the wholesale fraud, the vile hypocrisy, the conscience-killing tyranny of Rome! We have not far to seek for an evidence of it. There's Father Newman to wit: one living specimen is worth a hundred dead ones. He, a Priest writing of Priests, tells us that lying is never any harm."

I interpose: "You are taking a most extraordinary liberty with my name. If I have said this, tell me when and where."

Mr. Kingsley replies: "You said it, Reverend Sir, in a Sermon which you preached, when a Protestant, as Vicar of

---

[9] *Apologia* (1950), 382–83.
[10] Ibid., xi. —ED.
[11] Ibid., 388–90. —ED.

St. Mary's, and published in 1844; and I could read you a
very salutary lecture on the effects which that Sermon had at
the time on my own opinion of you."

I make answer: "Oh . . . *Not*, it seems, as a Priest speaking
of Priests;—but let us have the passage."

Mr. Kingsley relaxes: "Do you know, I like your *tone*.
From your tone I rejoice, greatly rejoice, to be able to believe
that you did not mean what you said."

I rejoin: "*Mean* it! I maintain I never *said* it, whether as a
Protestant or as a Catholic."

Mr. Kingsley replies: "I waive that point."

I object: "Is it possible! What? waive the main question! I
either said it or I didn't. You have made a monstrous charge
against me; direct, distinct, public. You are bound to prove it
as directly, as distinctly, as publicly;—or to own you can't."

"Well," says Mr. Kingsley, "if you are quite sure you did
not say it, I'll take your word for it; I really will."

My *word!* I am dumb. Somehow I thought that it was my
word that happened to be on trial. The *word* of a Professor of
Lying, that he does not lie!

But Mr. Kingsley re-assures me: "We are both gentle-
men," he says: "I have done as much as one English gentleman can expect from another."

I begin to see: he thought me a gentleman at the very time
that he said I taught lying on system. After all, it is not I, but
it is Mr. Kingsley who did not mean what he said. "*Habemus
confitentem reum.*" [12]

So we have confessedly come round to this, preaching
without practising; the common theme of satirists from
Juvenal to Walter Scott! "I left Baby Charles and Steenie
laying his duty before him," says King James of the reprobate

---

[12] "We have a self-confessed criminal", Cicero, *Pro Q. Ligario*, sec. 2. —ED.

Dalgarno: "O Geordie, jingling Geordie, it was grand to hear Baby Charles laying down the guilt of dissimulation, and Steenie lecturing on the turpitude of incontinence." [13]

While I feel then that Mr. Kingsley's February explanation is miserably insufficient in itself for his January enormity, still I feel also that the Correspondence, which lies between these two acts of his, constitutes a real satisfaction to those principles of historical and literary justice to which he has given so rude a shock.

Accordingly, I have put it into print, and make no further criticism on Mr. Kingsley.

J. H. N.

Stung, Kingsley responded with a pamphlet of his own: "What, Then, Does Dr. Newman Mean?" At forty-eight pages it was more than twice the length of the correspondence and began with a sentence that was to prove more wrong than Kingsley ever could have feared: "Dr. Newman has made a great mistake." The mistake was to be Kingsley's; he had chosen the wrong opponent. He thought his pamphlet would end the dispute, but it only induced the *Apologia*.

"My object had been throughout to avoid war, because I thought Dr. Newman wished for peace", Kingsley said, a few paragraphs into his pamphlet:

> But whether Dr. Newman lost his temper, or whether he thought that he had gained an advantage over me, or whether he wanted a more complete apology than I chose to give, whatever, I say, may have been his reasons, he suddenly changed his tone of courtesy and dignity for one of which I shall only say that it shows sadly how the atmosphere of the

[13] Sir Walter Scott, *The Fortunes of Nigel* (Lincoln, Neb.: University of Nebraska, 1965 [1822]), 394. —ED.

Romish priesthood had degraded his notions of what is due to himself; and when he published (as I am much obliged to him for doing) the whole correspondence, he appended to it certain reflexions, in which he attempted to convict me of not having believed the accusations which I had made.[14]

Not content with this, Kingsley erred again in saying, "I have declared Dr. Newman to have been an honest man up to the 1st of February, 1864. It was, as I shall show, only Dr. Newman's fault that I ever thought him to be anything else. It depends entirely on Dr. Newman whether he shall sustain the reputation which he has so recently acquired." [15]

Kingsley laced his essay with ad hominem remarks. Among them was this, which referred to sermons Newman gave as the Anglican vicar of Saint Mary's parish in Oxford: "I know that men used to suspect Dr. Newman—I have been inclined to do so myself—of writing a whole sermon, not for the sake of the text or of the matter, but for the sake of one single passing hint—one phrase, one epithet, one little barbed arrow which, as he swept magnificently past in the stream of his calm eloquence, seemingly unconscious of all presences, save those unseen, he delivered unheeded, as with his finger-tip, to the very heart of an initiated hearer, never to be withdrawn again." [16] Newman the religious pied piper.

In the final chapter of the *Apologia*, Newman was to write, of his Anglican sermons, "Can there be a plainer testimony borne to the practical character of my Sermons at St. Mary's than this gratuitous insinuation? Many a preacher of Tractarian doctrine has been accused of not letting his parishioners alone, and of teasing them with his private theological

[14] *Apologia* (1950), 393. —ED.
[15] Ibid., 393–94. —ED.
[16] Ibid., 399. —ED.

notions. You would gather from the general tone of this Writer [this is how he refers to Kingsley in the body of the *Apologia*] that that was my way. Every one who was in the habit of hearing me, knows that it wasn't. This Writer either knows nothing about it, and then he ought to be silent; or he does know, and then he ought to speak the truth." [17]

Kingsley had declined to be silent, wrapping up his pamphlet with lines such as "I am henceforth in doubt and fear, as much as an honest man can be, concerning every word Dr. Newman may write" [18] and "Yes—I am afraid that I must say it once more—Truth is not honoured among these men [Catholic priests] for its own sake." [19] But Kingsley was outclassed. [20] He gave "a complete victory to a powerful antagonist. With all his merits as an imaginative writer, Kingsley never showed any genuine dialectical ability." [21]

Between April 21 and June 2, 1864, Newman issued his "history of his religious opinions", [22] as he subtitled his book. One part appeared each Thursday. "The success of the *Apologia* was instantaneous," said Pegis, "and that is a remarkable fact, and also a remarkable tribute to Newman, when we

[17] Ibid., 283–84. —ED.

[18] Ibid., 426. —ED.

[19] Ibid., 428. —ED.

[20] In the sermon given at Kingsley's funeral, held at Westminster Abbey, Dean Stanley said that Kingsley's "righteous indignation . . . betrayed him into the only personal controversy in which he was ever entangled, and in which, matched in unequal conflict with the most subtle and dexterous controversialist of modern times, it is not surprising that for the moment he was apparently worsted". *Letters and Memories*, ed. Fanny Kingsley (New York: Taylor, 1899), vol. II, 185. —ED.

[21] *The Dictionary of National Biography*, vol. XI, 179–80. —ED.

[22] "It is significant that nowhere does Newman call his work an autobiography and it is not included in his autobiographical writings, which are very different in kind from the *Apologia*." John R. Griffin, *A Historical Commentary on the Major Catholic Works of Cardinal Newman* (New York: Peter Lang, 1993), 97. —ED.

remember the unpopularity of the Catholic cause in England. Long after he had crushed Kingsley, Newman captured the English world by the clear and impassioned honesty of the personal history which he bared to public gaze." [23]

The second edition of the *Apologia*, nearly a hundred pages shorter than the first, appeared just a year later, in 1865. Gone were all of the first and most of the second parts of the 1864 edition, "Mr. Kingsley's Method of Disputation" and "True Mode of Meeting Mr. Kingsley". Gone was the seventh and final part of the main manuscript, "General Answer to Mr. Kingsley".[24] Gone also was the appendix, consisting of the correspondence and Kingsley's pamphlet. Newman thought these "to be of merely ephemeral importance".[25] He acted on the advice of his publisher, William Longmans, who wanted to reissue the book "in a smaller form, omitting, perhaps, such passages or parts of the work as derive their interest from the controversy. I cannot but think that this would be the best course." [26]

---

[23] *Apologia*, xii. —Ed.

[24] This section includes a passage especially consoling to those whose apprehension of the faith is less than solid: "Ten thousand difficulties do not make one doubt, as I understand the subject; difficulty and doubt are incommensurate. There of course may be difficulties in the evidence; but I am speaking of difficulties intrinsic to the doctrines, or to their compatibility with each other. A man may be annoyed that he cannot work out a mathematical problem, of which the answer is or is not given to him, without doubting that it admits of an answer, or that a particular answer is the true one" (ibid., 237–38). Catholics need not abandon their faith on realizing they cannot explain all of it to their opponents' or their own satisfaction; each question has a satisfactory answer, but some answers, for some people, are difficult to find or understand. —Ed.

[25] John Henry Newman, *Apologia pro Vita Sua*, 2nd ed (London: Longmans, 1879 [1865]), iv. —Ed.

[26] Letter to Newman, Nov. 12, 1864, cited in Vincent Blehl, *John Henry Newman: A Bibliographic Catalogue of His Writings* (Charlottesville: University Press of Virginia, 1978), xxxv–xxxvi. —Ed.

In an enlarged preface for the final edition of 1873, Newman briefly recounted the quarrel, without mentioning his opponent by name. On seeing Kingsley's pamphlet, "I recognized what I had to do, though I shrank from both the task and the exposure which it would entail. I must, I said, give the true key to my whole life; I must show what I am, that it may be seen what I am not, and that the phantom may be extinguished which gibbers instead of me. I wish to be known as a living man, and not as a scarecrow which is dressed up in my clothes. False ideas may be refuted indeed by argument, but by true ideas alone are they expelled." [27]

Many who read the *Apologia* in its revised edition are unaware of the elisions and so have no opportunity to read Newman at his biting best. His is a high level of personal disputation. Of the omitted introductory parts, Ian Ker has said they contain "some superb invective which may grate on modern religious ears but which ought to appeal to anyone with an ear for the English language and a taste for the literature of controversy".[28] The following selection, which is Part I of the original edition, demonstrates the truth of this observation.

MR. KINGSLEY'S METHOD OF DISPUTATION

I cannot be sorry to have forced Mr. Kingsley to bring out in fullness his charges against me. It is far better that he should discharge his thoughts upon me in my lifetime, than after I am dead. Under the circumstances I am happy in having the opportunity of reading the worst that can be said of me by a

[27] *Apologia*, 2nd ed., xix. —ED.
[28] Ian Ker, *The Achievement of John Henry Newman* (Notre Dame, Ind.: University of Notre Dame Press, 1990), 158. —ED.

writer who has taken pains with his work and is well satisfied
with it. I account it a gain to be surveyed from without by
one who hates the principles which are nearest to my heart,
has no personal knowledge of me to set right his misconcep-
tions of my doctrine, and who has some motive or other to
be as severe with me as he can possibly be.

And first of all, I beg to compliment him on the motto in
his Title-page; it is felicitous. A motto should contain, as in a
nutshell, the contents, or the character, or the drift, or the
animus of the writing to which it is prefixed. The words
which he has taken from me[29] are so apposite as to be almost
prophetical. There cannot be a better illustration than he
thereby affords of the aphorism which I intended them to
convey. I said that it is not more than an hyperbolical expression to say that in certain cases a lie is the nearest approach to
truth. Mr. Kingsley's pamphlet is emphatically one of such
cases as are contemplated in that proposition. I really believe,
that his view of me is about as near an approach to the truth
about my writings and doings, as he is capable of taking. He
has done his worst towards me; but he has also done his best.
So far well; but, while I impute to him no malice, I un-
feignedly think, on the other hand, that, in his invective
against me, he as faithfully fulfils the other half of the
proposition also.

This is not a mere sharp retort upon Mr. Kingsley, as will
be seen, when I come to consider directly the subject, to
which the words of his motto relate. I have enlarged on that
subject in various passages of my publications; I have said that
minds in different states and circumstances cannot understand one another, and that in all cases they must be in-

---

[29] "It is not more than a hyperbole to say that, in certain cases, a lie is the
nearest approach to truth", *University Sermons* (London: Rivingtons, 1872),
341. —ED.

structed according to their capacity, and, if not taught step by step, they learn only so much the less; that children do not apprehend the thoughts of grown people, nor savages the instincts of civilization, nor blind men the perceptions of sight, nor pagans the doctrines of Christianity, nor men the experiences of Angels. In the same way, there are people of matter-of-fact, prosaic minds, who cannot take in the fancies of poets; and others of shallow, inaccurate minds, who cannot take in the ideas of philosophical inquirers. In a Lecture of mine I have illustrated this phenomenon by the supposed instance of a foreigner, who, after reading a commentary on the principles of English Law, does not get nearer to a real apprehension of them than to be led to accuse Englishmen of considering that the Queen is impeccable and infallible, and that the Parliament is omnipotent. Mr. Kingsley has read me from beginning to end in the fashion in which the hypothetical Russian read Blackstone; not, I repeat, from malice, but because of his intellectual build. He appears to be so constituted as to have no notion of what goes on in minds very different from his own, and moreover to be stone-blind to his ignorance. A modest man or a philosopher would have scrupled to treat with scorn and scoffing, as Mr. Kingsley does in my own instance, principles and convictions, even if he did not acquiesce in them himself, which had been held so widely and for so long,—the beliefs and devotions and customs which have been the religious life of millions upon millions of Christians for nearly twenty centuries,—for this in fact is the task on which he is spending his pains. Had he been a man of large or cautious mind, he would not have taken it for granted that cultivation must lead every one to see things precisely as he sees them himself. But the narrow-minded are the more prejudiced by very reason of their narrowness. The Apostle bids us "in malice be children, but

Lewis

in understanding be men." [30] I am glad to recognize in Mr. Kingsley an illustration of the first half of this precept; but I should not be honest, if I ascribed to him any sort of fulfilment of the second.

I wish I could speak as favourably either of his drift or of his method of arguing, as I can of his convictions. As to his drift, I think its ultimate point is an attack upon the Catholic Religion. It is I indeed, whom he is immediately insulting,—still, he views me only as a representative, and on the whole a fair one, of a class or caste of men, to whom, conscious as I am of my own integrity, I ascribe an excellence superior to mine. He desires to impress upon the public mind the conviction that I am a crafty, scheming man, simply untrustworthy; that, in becoming a Catholic, I have just found my right place; that I do but justify and am properly interpreted by the common English notion of Roman casuists and confessors; that I was secretly a Catholic when I was openly professing to be a clergyman of the Established Church; that so far from bringing, by means of my conversion, when at length it openly took place, any strength to the Catholic cause, I am really a burden to it,—an additional evidence of the fact, that to be a pure, german, genuine Catholic, a man must be either a knave or a fool.

These last words bring me to Mr. Kingsley's method of disputation, which I must criticize with much severity,—in his drift he does but follow the ordinary beat of controversy, but in his mode of arguing he is actually dishonest.

He says that I am either a knave or a fool, and (as we shall see by and by) he is not quite sure which, probably both. He tells his readers that on one occasion he said that he had fears I should "end in one or other of two misfortunes." "He

---

[30] 1 Cor 14:20. —Ed.

would either," he continues, "destroy his own sense of honesty, i.e. conscious truthfulness—and become a dishonest person; or he would destroy his common sense, i.e. unconscious truthfulness, and become the slave and puppet seemingly of his own logic, really of his own fancy. . . . I thought for years past that he had become the former; I now see that he has become the latter." Again, "When I read these outrages upon common sense, what wonder if I said to myself, 'This man cannot believe what he is saying?'" Such has been Mr. Kingsley's state of mind till lately, but now he considers that I am possessed with a spirit of "almost boundless silliness," of "simple credulity, the child of scepticism," of "absurdity," of a "self-deception which has become a sort of frantic honesty." And as to his fundamental reason for this change, he tells us, he really does not know what it is. However, let the reason be what it will, its upshot is intelligible enough. He is enabled at once, by this professed change of judgment about me, to put forward one of these alternatives, yet to keep the other in reserve;—and this he actually does. He need not commit himself to a definite accusation against me, such as requires definite proof and admits of definite refutation; for he has two strings to his bow;—when he is thrown off his balance on the one leg, he can recover himself by the use of the other. If I demonstrate that I am not a knave, he may exclaim, "Oh, but you are a fool!" and when I demonstrate that I am not a fool, he may turn round and retort, "Well, then, you are a knave." I have no objection to reply to his arguments in behalf of either alternative, but I should have been better pleased to have been allowed to take them one at a time.

But I have not yet done full justice to the method of disputation, which Mr. Kingsley thinks it right to adopt. Observe this first:—He means by a man who is "silly" not a man who is to be pitied, but a man who is to be *abhorred*. He means a man who is not simply weak and incapable, but a moral leper; a man who, if not a knave, has every thing bad about him except knavery; nay, rather, has together with every other worse vice, a spice of knavery to boot. *His* simpleton is one who has become such, in judgment for his having once been a knave. *His* simpleton is not a born fool, but a self-made idiot, one who has drugged and abused himself into a shameless depravity, one who, without any misgiving or remorse, is guilty of drivelling superstition, of reckless violation of sacred things, of fanatical excesses, of passionate inanities, of unmanly audacious tyranny over the weak, meriting the wrath of fathers and brothers. This is that milder judgment, which he seems to pride himself upon as so much charity; and, as he expresses it, he "does not know" why. This is what he really meant in his letter to me of January 14, when he withdrew his charge of my being dishonest. He said, "The *tone* of your letters, even more than their language makes me feel, *to my very deep pleasure*,"— what? that you have gambled away your reason, that you are an intellectual sot, that you are a fool in a frenzy. And in his Pamphlet, he gives us this explanation why he did not say this to my face, viz. that he had been told that I was "in weak health," and was "averse to controversy." He "felt some regret for having disturbed me."

But I pass on from these multiform imputations, and confine myself to this one consideration, viz. that he has made any fresh imputation upon me at all. He gave up the charge of knavery; well and good: but where was the logical necessity of his bringing another? I am sitting at home without a thought of Mr. Kingsley; he wantonly breaks in upon me with the charge that I had *"informed"* the world "that Truth for its own sake need not and on the whole *ought not to be* a virtue with the Roman clergy." When challenged on the point he cannot bring a fragment of evidence in proof of his assertion, and he is convicted of false witness by the voice of the world. Well, I should have thought that he had now nothing whatever more to do. "Vain man!" he seems to make answer, "what simplicity in you to think so! If you have not broken one commandment, let us see whether we cannot convict you of the breach of another. If you are not a swindler or forger, you are guilty of arson or burglary. By hook or by crook you shall not escape. Are *you* to suffer or *I*? What does it matter to you who are going off the stage, to receive a slight additional daub upon a character so deeply stained already? But think of me, the immaculate lover of Truth, so observant (as I have told you) of '*hault courage* and strict honour,'—and (aside)—'and not as this publican'—do you think I can let you go scot free instead of myself? No; *noblesse oblige.* Go to the shades, old man, and boast that Achilles sent you thither."

But I have not even yet done with Mr. Kingsley's method of disputation. Observe secondly:—when a man is said to be a knave or a fool, it is commonly meant that he is *either* the one *or* the other; and that,—either in the sense that the hypothesis of his being a fool is too absurd to be entertained; or, again, as a sort of contemptuous acquittal of one, who after all has not wit enough to be wicked. But this is not at all what Mr. Kingsley proposes to himself in the antithesis which he suggests to his readers. Though he speaks of me as an utter dotard and fanatic, yet all along, from the beginning of his Pamphlet to the end, he insinuates, he proves from my writings, and at length in his last pages he openly pronounces, that after all he was right at first, in thinking me a conscious liar and deceiver.

Now I wish to dwell on this point. It cannot be doubted,

I say, that, in spite of his professing to consider me as a dotard and driveller, on the ground of his having given up the notion of my being a knave, yet it is the very staple of his Pamphlet that a knave after all I must be. By insinuation, or by implication, or by question, or by irony, or by sneer, or by parable, he enforces again and again a conclusion which he does not categorically enunciate.

For instance (1) "I know that men *used to suspect Dr. Newman*, I have been inclined to do so myself, of writing a whole sermon . . . for the sake of one single passing hint, one phrase, one epithet, one little barbed arrow which . . . he delivered unheeded, as with his finger tip, to the very heart of an initiated hearer, *never to be withdrawn again.*"

(2) "How *was* I to know that the preacher, who had the reputation of being the most *acute* man of his generation, and of having a specially intimate acquaintance with the weaknesses of the human heart, was utterly blind to the broad meaning and the plain practical result of a sermon like this, delivered before fanatic and hot-headed young men, who hung upon his every word? That he did not *foresee* that they would think that they obeyed him, *by becoming affected, artificial, sly, shifty, ready for concealments and equivocations?*"

(3) "No one *would have* suspected him to be a dishonest man, if he had not perversely chosen *to assume a style* which (as he himself confesses) the world always associates with dishonesty."

(4) "*If* he will indulge in subtle paradoxes, in rhetorical exaggerations; if, *whenever he touches on the question of truth and honesty*, he will take a perverse pleasure in saying something shocking to plain English notions, he *must take the consequences of his own eccentricities.*"

(5) "At which most of my readers will be inclined to cry: 'Let Dr. Newman alone, after that. . . . He had a human

reason once, no doubt: but he has gambled it away.' . . . True: so true, &c."

(6) He continues: "I should never have written these pages save because it was my duty to show the world, if not Dr. Newman, how the mistake (!) of his *not caring* for truth *arose*."

(7) "And this is the man, who when accused of countenancing falsehood, puts on first a tone of *plaintive* (!) and startled innocence, and then one of smug self-satisfaction— as who should ask, 'What have I said? What have I done? Why am I on my trial?' "

(8) "What Dr. Newman teaches is clear at last, and *I see now how deeply I have wronged him*. So far from thinking truth for its own sake to be no virtue, *he considers it a virtue so lofty as to be unattainable by man*."

(9) "There is no use in wasting words on this 'economical' statement of Dr. Newman's. I shall only say that there are people in the world whom it is very difficult to *help*. As soon as they are got out of one scrape, they walk straight into another."

(10) "Dr. Newman has shown 'wisdom' enough of that *serpentine* type which is his professed ideal. . . . Yes, Dr. Newman is a very economical person."

(11) "Dr. Newman *tries*, by *cunning sleight-of-hand logic*, to prove that I did not believe the accusation when I made it."

(12) "These are hard words. If Dr. Newman shall complain of them, I can only remind him of the fate which befell the stork caught among the cranes, *even though* the stork had *not* done all he could to make himself like a crane,[31] *as Dr.*

---

[31] A reference to Aesop's fable "The Farmer and the Stork": "A farmer placed nets on his newly-sown plowlands and caught a number of Cranes, which came to pick up his seed. With them he trapped a Stork that had fractured his leg in the net and was earnestly beseeching the Farmer to spare his life. 'Pray save me, Master,' he said, 'and let me go free this once. My

Newman has, by 'economising' on the very title-page of his pamphlet."

These last words bring us to another and far worse instance of these slanderous assaults upon me, but its place is in a subsequent page.

Now it may be asked of me, "Well, why should not Mr. Kingsley take a course such as this? It was his original assertion that Dr. Newman was a professed liar, and a patron of lies; he spoke somewhat at random; granted; but now he has got up his references and he is proving, not perhaps the very thing which he said at first, but something very like it, and to say the least quite as bad. He is now only aiming to justify morally his original assertion; why is he not at liberty to do so?"

Why should he *not* now insinuate that I am a liar and a knave! he had of course a perfect right to make such a charge, if he chose; he might have said, "I was virtually right, and here is the proof of it," but this he has not done, but on the contrary has professed that he no longer draws from my works, as he did before, the inference of my dishonesty. He says distinctly, "When I read these outrages upon common sense, what wonder if I said to myself, 'This man cannot believe what he is saying?' *I believe I was wrong*." And, "I said, This man has no real care for truth. Truth for its own sake is no virtue in his eyes, and he teaches that it need not be. *I do not say that now*." And, "I do not call this conscious

---

broken limb should excite your pity. Besides, I am no Crane, I am a Stork, a bird of excellent character; and see how I love and slave for my father and mother. Look too, at my feathers—they are not the least like those of a Crane.' The Farmer laughed aloud and said, 'It may be all as you say, I only know this: I have taken you with these robbers, the Cranes, and you must die in their company.' Moral: Birds of a feather flock together" (George Tyler Townsend, *Three Hundred Aesop Fables* (Philadelphia: McKay, n.d.) 14. —ED.

dishonesty; the man who wrote that sermon *was already past the possibility* of such a sin."

Why should he *not*! because it is on the ground of my not being a knave that he calls me a fool; adding to the words just quoted, "[My readers] have fallen perhaps into the prevailing superstition that cleverness is synonymous with wisdom. They cannot believe that (as is too certain) great literary and even barristerial ability may co-exist with almost boundless silliness."

Why should he *not*! because he has taken credit to himself for that high feeling of honour which refuses to withdraw a concession which once has been made; though, (wonderful to say!) at the very time that he is recording this magnanimous resolution, he lets it out of the bag that his relinquishment of it is only a profession and a pretence; for he says, "I have accepted Dr. Newman's denial that [the Sermon] means what I thought it did; and *heaven forbid*" (oh!) "that I should withdraw my word once given, *at whatever disadvantage to myself.*" Disadvantage! but nothing can be advantageous to him which is *untrue*; therefore in proclaiming that the concession of my honesty is a disadvantage to him, he thereby implies unequivocally that there is some probability still, that I am *dis*honest. He goes on, "I am informed by those from whose judgment on such points there is no appeal, that '*en hault courage,*' and strict honour, I am also *precluded,* by the *terms* of my explanation, from using any other of Dr. Newman's past writings to prove my assertion." And then, "I have declared Dr. Newman to have been an honest man up to the 1st of February, 1864; it was, as I shall show, only Dr. Newman's fault that I ever thought him to be any thing else. It depends entirely on Dr. Newman whether he shall *sustain* the reputation which he has so recently acquired," (by diploma of course from Mr. Kingsley.) "If I give him thereby a fresh advantage in this argument, he is *most welcome* to it. He needs, it seems to me, *as many advantages as possible.*"

What a princely mind! How loyal to his rash promise, how delicate towards the subject of it, how conscientious in his interpretation of it! I have no thought of irreverence towards a Scripture Saint, who was actuated by a very different spirit from Mr. Kingsley's, but somehow since I read his Pamphlet words have been running in my head, which I find in the Douay version thus; "Thou hast also with thee Semei the son of Gera, who cursed me with a grievous curse when I went to the camp, but I swore to him, saying, I will not kill thee with the sword. Do not thou hold him guiltless. But thou art a wise man and knowest what to do with him, and thou shalt bring down his grey hairs with blood to hell." [32]

Now I ask, Why could not Mr. Kingsley be open? If he intended still to arraign me on the charge of lying, why could he not say so as a man? Why must he insinuate, question, imply, and use sneering and irony, as if longing to touch a forbidden fruit, which still he was afraid would burn his fingers, if he did so? Why must he "palter in a double sense," [33] and blow hot and cold in one breath? He first said he considered me a patron of lying; well, he changed his opinion; and as to the logical ground of this change, he said that, if any one asked him what it was, he could only answer that *he really did not know.* Why could not he change back again, and say he did not know why? He had quite a right to do so; and then his conduct would have been so far straightforward and unexceptionable. But no;—in the very act of professing to believe in my sincerity, he takes care to show the world that it is a profession and nothing more. That very proceeding which he lays to my charge, (whereas I detest it,)

[32] 1 Kings 2:8–9. —ED.
[33] *Macbeth*, act 5, sc. 8, l. 20. —ED.

of avowing one thing and thinking another, that proceeding he here exemplifies himself; and yet, while indulging in practices as offensive as this, he ventures to speak of his sensitive admiration of "*hault courage* and strict honour!" "I forgive you, Sir Knight," says the heroine in the Romance;[34] "forgive you as a Christian." "That means," said Wamba, "that she does not forgive him at all." Mr. Kingsley's word of honour is about as valuable as in the jester's opinion was the Christian charity of Rowena. But here we are brought to a further specimen of Mr. Kingsley's method of disputation, and having duly exhibited it, I shall have done with him.

It is his last, and he has intentionally reserved it for his last. Let it be recollected that he professed to absolve me from his original charge of dishonesty up to February 1. And further, he implies that, *at the time when he was writing*, I had not *yet* involved myself in any fresh acts suggestive of that sin. He says that I have had a great *escape* of conviction, that he hopes I shall take warning, and act more cautiously. "It depends entirely," he says, "on *Dr. Newman, whether* he shall *sustain* the reputation which he has so recently acquired." Thus, in Mr. Kingsley's judgment, I was *then*, when he wrote these words, *still* innocent of dishonesty, for a man cannot sustain what he actually has not got; *only he could not be sure of my future.* Could not be sure! Why at this very time he had already noted down valid proofs, as he thought them, that I had already forfeited the character which he contemptuously accorded to me. He had cautiously said "*up* to February 1st," *in order* to reserve the Title-page and last three pages of my Pamphlet, which were not published till February 12th, and out of these four pages, which he had *not* whitewashed, he had *already* forged charges against me of dishonesty at the

---

[34] Sir Walter Scott, *Ivanhoe*, chap. 32. —ED.

very time that he implied that as yet there was nothing against me. When he gave me that plenary condonation, as it seemed to be, he had already done his best that I should never enjoy it. He knew well what he meant to say. At best indeed I was only out upon ticket of leave; but the ticket was a pretence; he had made it forfeit when he gave it. But he did not say so at once, first, because he meant to talk a great deal about my idiotcy and my frenzy, which would have been simply out of place, had he proved me too soon to be a knave again; and next, because he meant to exhaust all those insinuations about my knavery in the past, which "strict honour" did not permit him to countenance, in order thereby to give colour and force to his direct charges of knavery in the present, which "strict honour" *did* permit him to handsel. So in the fifth act he gave a start, and found to his horror that, in my miserable four pages, I had committed the "enormity" of an "economy," which in matter of fact he had got by heart before he began the play. Nay, he suddenly found two, three, and (for what he knew) as many as four profligate economies in that Title-page and those Reflections, and he uses the language of distress and perplexity at this appalling discovery.

Now why this *coup de théatre*? The reason soon breaks on us. Up to February 1, he could not categorically arraign me for lying, and therefore could not involve me, (as was so necessary for his case,) in the popular abhorrence which is felt for the casuists of Rome: but, as soon as ever he could openly and directly pronounce (saving his "*hault courage* and strict honour*") that I am guilty of three or four new economies, then at once I am made to bear, not only my own sins, but the sins of other people also, and, though I have been condoned the knavery of my antecedents, I am guilty of the knavery of a whole priesthood instead. So the hour of doom for Semei is come, and the wise man knows what to do with him;—he is down upon me with the odious names of "St. Alfonso da Liguori," and "Scavini" and "Neyraguet," [35] and "the Romish moralists," and their "compeers and pupils," and I am at once merged and whirled away in the gulph of notorious quibblers, and hypocrites, and rogues.

But we have not even yet got at the real object of the stroke, thus reserved for his *finale*. I really feel sad for what I am obliged now to say. I am in warfare with him, but I wish him no ill;—it is very difficult to get up resentment towards persons whom one has never seen. It is easy enough to be irritated with friends or foes, *vis-à-vis*; but, though I am writing with all my heart against what he has said of me, I am not conscious of personal unkindness towards himself. I think it necessary to write as I am writing, for my own sake, and for the sake of the Catholic Priesthood; but I wish to impute nothing worse to Mr. Kingsley than that he has been furiously carried away by his feelings. But what shall I say of the upshot of all this talk of my economies and equivocations and the like? What is the precise *work* which it is directed to effect? I am at war with him; but there is such a thing as legitimate warfare: war has its laws; there are things which may fairly be done, and things which may not be done. I say it with shame and with stern sorrow;—he has attempted a great transgression; he has attempted (as I may call it) to *poison the wells*. I will quote him and explain what I mean.

"Dr. Newman tries, by cunning sleight-of-hand logic, to

[35] Kingsley, in his pamphlet "What, Then, Does Dr. Newman Mean?" when writing of St. Alphonsus Liguori included this footnote, which apparently was intended to seem ominous: "I quote from Scavini, tom. ii. page 232, of the Paris edition, and from Neyraguet, page 141, two compendiums of Liguori which are (or were lately) used, so I have every reason to believe—one at Oscott, the other at Maynooth", Catholic seminaries. *Apologia*, 426. —ED.

prove that I did not believe the accusation when I made it. Therein he is mistaken. I did believe it, and I believed also his indignant denial. But when he goes on to ask with sneers, why I should believe his denial, if I did not consider him trustworthy in the first instance? I can only answer, I really do not know. There is a *great deal* to be said for *that* view, *now that* Dr. Newman has become (one must needs suppose) *suddenly* and *since* the 1st of February, 1864, a convert to the *economic* views of St. Alfonso da Liguori and his compeers. I am *henceforth* in doubt and *fear*, as much as any honest man can be, concerning every word Dr. Newman may write. *How can I tell that I shall not be the dupe of some cunning equivocation*, of one of the three kinds laid down as permissible by the blessed Alfonso da Liguori and his pupils, even when confirmed by an oath, because 'then we do not deceive our neighbour, but allow him to deceive himself?' . . . It is admissible, therefore, to use words and sentences which have a double signification, and leave the hapless hearer to take which of them he may choose. *What proof have I, then, that by 'mean it? I never said it!' Dr. Newman does not signify*, 'I did not say it, but I did mean it?' "

Now these insinuations and questions shall be answered in their proper places; here I will but say that I scorn and detest lying, and quibbling, and double-tongued practice, and slyness, and cunning, and smoothness, and cant, and pretence quite as much as any Protestants hate them; and I pray to be kept from the snare of them. But all this is just now by the bye; my present subject is Mr. Kingsley; what I insist upon here, now that I am bringing this portion of my discussion to a close, is this unmanly attempt of his, in his concluding pages, to cut the ground from under my feet;—to poison by anticipation the public mind against me, John Henry Newman, and to infuse into the imaginations of my readers, suspicion and mistrust of every thing that I may say in reply to him. *This I call poisoning the wells.*

"I am henceforth in *doubt and fear,*" he says, "as much as any *honest* man can be, *concerning every word* Dr. Newman may write. *How can I tell that I shall not be the dupe of some cunning equivocation?* . . . What proof have I, that by 'mean it? I never said it!' Dr. Newman does not signify, 'I did not say it, but I did mean it?' "

Well, I can only say, that, if his taunt is to take effect, I am but wasting my time in saying a word in answer to his foul calumnies; and this is precisely what he knows and intends to be its fruit. I can hardly get myself to protest against a method of controversy so base and cruel, lest in doing so, I should be violating my self-respect and self-possession; but most base and most cruel it is. We all know how our imagination runs away with us, how suddenly and at what a pace;—the saying, "Caesar's wife should not be suspected," [36] is an instance of what I mean. The habitual prejudice, the humour of the moment, is the turning-point which leads us to read a defence in a good sense or a bad. We interpret it by our antecedent impressions. The very same sentiments, according as our jealousy is or is not awake, or our aversion stimulated, are tokens of truth or of dissimulation and pretence. There is a story of a sane person being by mistake shut up in the wards of a Lunatic Asylum, and that, when he pleaded his cause to some strangers visiting the establishment, the only remark he elicited in answer was, "How naturally he talks! you would think he was in his senses." Controversies should be decided by the reason; is it legitimate warfare to appeal to the misgivings of the public mind and to its dislikings? Any how, if Mr. Kingsley is able thus to

---

[36] A traditional saying derived from Plutarch's *Caesar*, sec. 10. —ED.

practice upon my readers, the more I succeed, the less will be my success. If I am natural, he will tell them, *"Ars est celare artem;"* [37] if I am convincing, he will suggest that I am an able logician; if I show warmth, I am acting the indignant innocent; if I am calm, I am thereby detected as a smooth hypocrite; if I clear up difficulties, I am too plausible and perfect to be true. The more triumphant are my statements, the more certain will be my defeat.

So will it be if Mr. Kingsley succeeds in his manoeuvre; but I do not for an instant believe that he will. Whatever judgment my readers may eventually form of me from these pages, I am confident that they will believe me in what I shall say in the course of them. I have no misgiving at all, that they will be ungenerous or harsh with a man who has been so long before the eyes of the world; who has so many to speak of him from personal knowledge; whose natural impulse it has ever been to speak out; who has ever spoken too much rather than too little; who would have saved himself many a scrape, if he had been wise enough to hold his tongue; who has ever been fair to the doctrines and arguments of his opponents; who has never slurred over facts and reasonings which told against himself; who has never given his name or authority to proofs which he thought unsound, or to testimony which he did not think at least plausible; who has never shrunk from confessing a fault when he felt that he had committed one; who has ever consulted for others more than for himself; who has given up much that he loved and prized and could have retained, but that he loved honesty better than name, and Truth better than dear friends.

And now I am in a train of thought higher and more serene than any which slanders can disturb. Away with you,

[37] "Art lies in concealing art." —ED.

Mr. Kingsley, and fly into space. Your name shall occur again as little as I can help, in the course of these pages. I shall henceforth occupy myself not with you, but with your charges.

2

Hilaire Belloc vs. J. B. S. Haldane

In his last years Newman oversaw the Oratory School at Edgbaston in Birmingham. In 1880 a new pupil, aged ten, arrived. It is unknown what impression he made upon the elderly cardinal, but we have some indication of Newman's impression on Hilaire Belloc (1870–1953), whose "active religion was moulded more by Cardinal Manning—'much the greatest Englishman of his time'—than by Cardinal Newman[1] (both of whom figured in his youth): Manning having had a very strong theory of the Church, and a siege mentality, while emphasizing the Church's responsibility to

[1] One should not conclude that Belloc had little appreciation of Newman. Fifty years after entering the Oratory School, Belloc wrote the foreword to Daniel M. O'Connell's edition of Newman's *Apologia pro Vita Sua* (Chicago: Loyola University Press, 1930). He noted (p. xi) that "the *Apologia* was written against a man, Kingsley, who had made an accusation which would not have galled in any other surrounding as it did in those surroundings [Oxford]. He had accused Newman of falsehood and insincerity. A Catholic from almost anywhere else in Europe than from Oxford would have laughed aloud at accusations of insincerity from the peculiar atmosphere of the English Church. Not so Newman. Newman well understood the penetrative power of that accusation in England. He knew to the quick the impact against which he must defend himself. We know what the re-action was. It produced the great, the strongly founded book, standing stronger after so many years, which the reader has here before him." —ED.

the poor."[2] Belloc reflected that siege mentality—even reveled in it—in his many polemical writings, and sometimes the mentality got the better of him. Once he was "having a controversy with that *engagé* Cambridge champion of truth, Dr. [G. G.] Coulton; to close it Belloc came out with something devastating. [Douglas] Woodruff asked him, 'But is it true?' Belloc replied blithely, 'Oh, not at all. But won't it annoy Coulton?' I thought and still think that rather wicked."[3] It was Woodruff who was to write, years later, Belloc's entry in *The Dictionary of National Biography*. There he noted that "even those who most strongly disagreed with his general conclusions respected his immense integrity, that of a man who never stopped to think what it was politic to write, but only what was the truth to be stated"—pranks notwithstanding.[4]

While his friend G. K. Chesterton came to be known for gentleness and jocularity, Belloc achieved a reputation for clean syllogisms and pugnaciousness, the latter being hinted at, perhaps, in the epigraph chosen for the title page of *Essays of a Catholic*, from which the essays in this and the next chapter are taken: "Truth comes by conflict."[5]

In the preface to that book Belloc apologizes for the "personal tone in each of the papers here printed: I can write in no other way, and, indeed, I prefer in reading the writings of others to discover a similar note myself. . . . I do not know whether I ought to apologize for the fact that all of these papers deal only with what may be called the externals of religion, are even in great part political, and without excep-

---

[2] Kevin L. Morris, *Hilaire Belloc: A Catholic Prophet* (London: Catholic Truth Society, 1995), 13. —ED.

[3] A. L. Rowse, *Portraits & Views* (London: Macmillan, 1979), 72. —ED.

[4] *The Dictionary of National Biography*, suppl. 1951–1960, 88. —ED.

[5] Hilaire Belloc, *Essays of a Catholic* (New York: Macmillan, 1931), 3. —ED.

tion controversial. I have perhaps no faculty for dealing on
paper with the more essential, the all-important, interior
things of Catholic life.[6]

The same year that saw *Essays of a Catholic* saw also the
publication of *1066 and All That*, a spoof history of England.[7]
On the dust jacket Alexander Woollcott was quoted as calling the book "a dazzling guess at what remains in the average
Englishman's mind of all the history he studied at school".
That muddled history had coexisted, for several decades,
with press accounts of the antics of Chesterton, Belloc, and
George Bernard Shaw's fire-breathing concoction, the Ches-
terbelloc. It is little wonder that in *1066 and All That* the story
of Thomas à Becket ended up reading like this: "It was at this
time that Thomas à Belloc, a great religious leader, claimed
that clergymen, whatever crimes they might commit, could
not be punished at all; this privilege, which was for some
reason known as Benefit of Clergy, was in full accord with
the devout spirit of the age. Henry II, however, exclaimed to
some of his Knights one day, 'Who will rid me of this
Chesterton beast?' Whereupon the Knights pursued Belloc
and murdered him in the organ at Canterbury Cathedral.
Belloc was therefore made a Saint and the Knights came to
be called the Canterbury Pilgrims. Shortly afterwards Henry
died of despair on receiving news that his sons were all
revolting." [8] Belloc, by age sixty, had become a literary and
religious fixture, ripe for caricature.

Forever on the verge of penury, he had made his living
through writing and long must have had a keen appreciate
for Dr. Johnson's dictum that "no man but a blockhead ever

[6] Ibid., 10. —ED.
[7] W. C. Sellar and R. J. Yeatman, *1066 and All That* (New York: Dutton,
1931). —ED.
[8] Ibid., 22. —ED.

wrote, except for money." [9] Belloc authored more than a hundred books, many of them collections of essays that first appeared in newspapers. His better-crafted writings tended to have been written before World War I. During the next quarter century, until his pen was halted by a stroke in 1942, he turned out a large mass of material, little of it as finely styled as his earlier works, the most popular of which being *The Path to Rome* (1902). Nevertheless, there remained power in his words, and he was a conspicuous figure in English journalism through the 1930s.

His adversary in the following selection, J. B. S. Haldane (1892–1964), was a noted geneticist, known particularly for trying to unite Darwinian evolution and Mendelian genetics. In the 1920s he was influential in reestablishing natural selection, the reputation of which had suffered a decline, as the agreed-upon mechanism of evolutionary change. "His great strengths as a scientist were an ability to reduce complex systems to simple mathematical equations, an extraordinarily wide range of interests which enabled him to see connections missed by others, and a gift for lucid and vivid exposition." [10]

Haldane's skills in science, however well developed they may have been, did not seem to overflow into matters of politics—or religion. Beginning in the 1930s he wrote weekly articles for the *Daily Worker*, the newspaper of the Communist Party, and in 1940 he became chairman of the publication's editorial board, a post he held for ten years. Ever the party man, Haldane defended much of the work of the Soviet agronomist Trofim Lysenko, who adopted the doctrine of acquired characteristics over against Mendelian genetics and whose ideas were taken as Marxist orthodoxy

---

[9] James Boswell, *The Life of Johnson* (London: Dent, 1906), 2:16. —ED.
[10] *The Dictionary of National Biography*, suppl. 1961–1970, 474. —ED.

until Stalin's death. After that they were criticized roundly, Lysenko's name becoming emblematic of bad science. Around 1950 Haldane, without any public announcement, dropped out of the Communist Party, later explaining that he had become disaffected with "Stalin's interference with science". *Bush admin, similar esp. in environmental science, global warming etc.*

Whereas Haldane's politics caused him to focus his later writings on the class struggle, in his earlier essays he was "more interested in taking a swipe at God than at the ruling class".[11] It was in response to one such essay that Belloc wrote. His reply was prefaced with this note: "A biologist of high distinction, by implication or affirmation, touches upon those points where the Catholic Faith is at issue with the great bulk of men of his profession. The nature of this issue should be examined and the validity of the affirmations or implications tested, for work from such a pen is a good and typical instance of the conflict between Catholicism and the agnostic 'scientific' world."[12] *I suppose Dawkins & his God Delusion '07 would occupy Haldane's position now. He is best known because of his polemical style. Hard to imagine a civil debate.*

AN ARTICLE OF MR. HALDANE'S

In my daily paper of the morning on which I write these words I read an article of some length which is by far the most interesting thing in the sheet. It proceeds from the pen of Mr. Haldane, the deservedly distinguished biologist who stands in the very front rank of the generation junior to my own. It is because Mr. Haldane holds such a position, but also because his name stands for such a great tradition in England, that I have taken what he has written for the text of what follows. It is amusing, and sometimes profitable, to

[11] Ibid. —ED.
[12] Belloc, *Essays*, 265. —ED.

Now also Lysenkos of junk science today, see Kaminer's books

consider or to refute one of the host who are unequipped for
dealing with the great theological problems, and who yet fill
our time with silly repetitions of errors which have been
exposed during hundreds of years. Their adventures in the
obvious, their simple pride in discovering as novelties what
men have discussed for thirty centuries are the absurdity of
our time. There is quite a different interest in reading and
considering the work of a man so really eminent as Mr.
Haldane. His father,[13] amid a mass of public work of the
highest value, produced that essay on Vitalism[14] (not yet, I
hope, forgotten) which helped to change the thought of our
time. His uncle[15] was a statesman of the first rank, and more
than any other man made possible the strength of England by
land in the Great War. He was also among the greatest of
English lawyers. Mr. Haldane's sister[16] has an increasing name
in literature, and his own achievement is one which every
man of intelligence respects and admires.

It is on account of all this that I take a particular interest in
dealing with certain points in Mr. Haldane's article which, by
implication, challenge the Catholic position, and which also
present at their best the attitude opposed to ours in modern
intellectual life.

I do not propose to deal with the article as a whole,
because it does not as a whole challenge conclusions of the
Faith. It is concerned with modern life in general, and only

[13] J. S. Haldane (1860–1936), a physiologist with an interest in the religious
implications of science; his views were generally sympathetic to religion,
unlike his son's. —ED.

[14] The doctrine that the functions of a living organism are due to a vital
principle distinct from mere physical or chemical processes. —ED.

[15] R. B. Haldane (1856–1928), later Viscount Haldane, was the Liberal
Minister for War in World War I. As Lord Chancellor, he was driven from
office by a newspaper campaign. —ED.

[16] Naomi Mitchison (1897–1999), early feminist and freethinker, author of
more than seventy novels, biographies, and works of poetry. —ED.

in three significant passages touches upon that point of vital
interest to myself (and I think to the writer)[,] the quarrel
between the best intelligences within the two camps; the
camp. of the Faith, the camp of those opposed to it. To
consider work from such a pen is of real value, for, indeed,
there is no equality of armament or method between the
Catholic and any other opponent of his save the high sceptic.
Our other opponents are lesser people with whom it is a
pastime to deal, but the high sceptics are serious antagonists.
For there are to-day but two essential attitudes possible: the
sceptical and the Catholic.

The points I select as being of special interest to me in
Professor Haldane's article are these:

First. The writer speaks of a fellow Catholic and literary
colleague of mine, Mr. J. B. Morton[17] ("Beachcomber," of
the *Daily Express*) as being one of those fighting "a rear-
guard action against the advance of science." It is a phrase
which may be extended to the whole frame of mind which
it implies. It is a phrase implying the statement that those
who are of the Faith are falling back reluctantly from position to position, retreating before the triumphant and inevitable advance of something which can but destroy the Faith
and which is labelled "Science." *Robert Coles calls it the Secular Mind '99 mantra of recent scientific atheists in 08*

Second. The writer, in what is perhaps the most interesting
of all the sentences of this interesting article, expresses his
intellectual preoccupation with a certain problem—which
he puts thus, "Why millions of men have been persuaded
that there is spiritual advantage in bathing in the water of the

[17] J. B. Morton (1893–1979), essayist, humorist, and versifier. He joined
the *Daily Express* in 1922, taking over from Wyndham Lewis the humorous
column "By the Way", which he renamed "Beachcomber" and wrote from
1924 to 1975. After Belloc's death he wrote *Hilaire Belloc: A Memoir* (New
York: Sheed and Ward, 1955). —Ed.

Ganges, or in believing in the doctrine of the Immaculate Conception." Mr. Haldane is quite rightly moved by the chief question facing mankind. It has been put in a very concise and striking form in the Gospels, "Is religion from God or from man?" [18]

Third. Mr. Haldane in this very passage, using the phrase "Immaculate Conception," uses it for the doctrine known to Catholics as the Incarnation of God as man and his birth from a pure Virgin. I hope I am not misrepresenting him. I think I am rightly interpreting his intention, for as was the case with Mr. Wells[19] and almost every other modern English writer on these affairs, that technical term of Catholic theology "The Immaculate Conception" is thought to be identical with the term "Nativity"; that is, the doctrine that Jesus Christ who was very God was incarnate as man by divine generation through the Virgin Mary.[20]

Now let us consider those three points in their order.

First of all, what about the "rear-guard action" against science? Long before Brunetière[21] (I think) launched that famous epigram, "The bankruptcy of science" a lifetime ago, the idea implied in the epigram has spread widely. During all

[18] Apparently a reference to Matthew 21:25: "The baptism of John, whence was it? from heaven or from men?" (Douay-Rheims). —ED.

[19] H. G. Wells (1866–1946), an inveterate and often acrimonious anti-Catholic, as demonstrated in his book *Crux Ansata* (1944), which advocated the Allied bombing of Rome so as to eliminate the cultural influence of the Catholic Church. Belloc took on Wells in a series of articles in 1926, the year after Wells' *Outline of History* (New York: Agora Publishing, 1925), in revised form, was issued in fortnightly parts. —ED.

[20] As it turned out, Belloc did misunderstand Haldane on this point. See Arnold Lunn and J. B. S. Haldane, *Science and the Supernatural* (New York: Sheed and Ward, 1935), 32. —ED.

[21] Ferdinand Brunetière (1849–1906), French literary critic and one-time materialist who converted to the Catholic faith after studying Jacques-Bénigne Bossuet's sermons. —ED.

our time there has been a latent and often open war between
those who defend the Faith and those who tell us that they
base themselves upon the impregnable conclusions of physical science: that is, the body of acquired demonstrable
knowledge, tested by experiment, and not to be denied by
the human reason.

On the nature of this quarrel I have written elsewhere in
this book. What I am concerned with here is the operative
word "rear-guard."

There is no doubt that those who defend the Faith are
fighting with more and more vigour, and in increasing numbers, and with a rapidly accumulating wealth of illustration
and argument, the old academic position of the nineteenth
century, which in a dozen ways believed itself to have triumphed over Catholicism, or (as they preferred to call it) the
more guarded of them "Dogma," the more sincere, "Christianity." But the word "Catholicism" is the accurate word in
this regard, for there is no meaning in "Christianity" unless it
imply at least some fragment or distortion of the Catholic
scheme. Of the intellectual vigour displayed by Catholicism
to-day, I say, there is no doubt at all, even in England; in the
larger air of Europe it is a commonplace. To deny the new
activity of Catholicism as compared with its old timidity
would be as foolish as to deny the change in men's attitude
towards Parliaments, or towards the conception of "Progress," or any other sign of the awakening from ideas which
were taken for granted a generation ago.

But is this activity the fighting of a rear-guard action? Is
the Catholic effort losing ground?

I should have said that a general conspectus of Europe
would lead to the exactly contrary conclusion. I am not here
concerned with the truth or falsehood of the opposing
philosophies. I am concerned with the question: "Which of

the two sides, Catholic and Anti-Catholic, is occupying new ground? Which of them is giving way before the other?" A completely indifferent and detached mind, surveying Europe as a whole, can only conclude that the Catholic side is advancing. It may be regrettable. The Catholic advance may be, as Mivart[22] said in old age, one more reaction of unintelligence against intelligence, comparable to the swamping of Buddhism by Brahmanism in the East. It may be the deplorable accompaniment of a decline in civilisation comparable to the decline in art and letters at the end of the Roman Empire. It may be but one aspect of that deplorable fatigue which ruins high civilisations at their highest achievement—but *there it is*.

You may see it in any one of a dozen fields. Let me return to two I have touched on elsewhere. Half a lifetime ago everyone took it for granted that "scientific" criticism had destroyed the authenticity of the Fourth Gospel. It was not the testimony of an eye witness. It was not due to St. John's experience of Jesus Christ. It was put together long after the date when the last of the contemporaries of Christ must have been dead. The traditional author, John the son of Zebedee, thus dethroned could not have been the Beloved Disciple—and so forth. Where is all that mass of hypothesis and guess-work to-day? I do not say that it is disproved because fashion has changed. I do not here make fashion a criterion of truth. All I am saying is that fashion on this point has changed. The rejection of the Fourth Gospel "dates." The arguments used to destroy its value belong to the age of hansom cabs. Where in this matter is there a sign of "rear-guard action"?

You must not use the words "a rear-guard action" as the

[22] George A. Mivart (1823–1900), biologist and chief opponent of Darwinism. In his last years several of his writings were put on the Index, and he died without ecclesiastical rites. —ED.

description of men who continually advance. Their advance may be a tragic example of intellectual decline in our civilisation, just as the German breaking of the Allied line at St. Quentin in 1918, was tragic in our eyes. To us it was the deplorable success of what was worse against what was better. But not the wildest of patriots could have described the German advance upon Amiens during that Easter week as "a rear-guard action."

Take a parallel example in the field of what was called "Scientific" Criticism. What about the attitude on St. Luke's authorship of the Acts of the Apostles? Harnack[23] in famous pages, destroyed that criticism.

There was nothing Catholic about him. I do not think it unjust to a famous name to say that he did not understand what the Catholic Church was, nor, for that matter, is it Catholic doctrine to my knowledge that St. Luke wrote the Acts. It is certainly tradition, and may be common sense; it is not dogma, so far as I know. But no one can say that Harnack was "fighting a rear-guard action," still less that those of us, great Catholic scholars, or ignorant Catholic laymen like myself, are now taking part in a rear-guard action when we defend the claims of tradition. We were heavily pressed when Plancus[24] was Consul, but to-day the pressure is the other way round. I say again, this change does not prove that we are right. The wrong side may be advancing and the right side retreating; but there is no doubt as to the direction of movement.

Or take Dom Chapman's [25] *Studies in the Early Papacy*; is

[23] Adolph von Harnack (1851–1930), German Protestant theologian and church historian, noted especially for the four-volume *Handbook of the History of Dogmas* (1886–1890). —ED.

[24] Lucius Munatius Plancus, consul in 42 B.C. At his instigation the people set fire to the Roman senate. —ED.

[25] John Chapman, O.S.B. (1865–1933), *Studies in the Early Papacy* (London: Sheed and Ward, 1925). —ED.

that a "rear-guard action"? It reads much more like a bombardment before attack.

Take another department in this same type of criticism, where Andrew Lang[26] and others fought, in the old days, what was then called a rear-guard action: the nature of the *Iliad* and the *Odyssey*. Within living memory it was difficult to maintain that those two bodies of verse were the work of an individual poet. They were tribal songs strung together. They were nature myths. They were anonymous barbaric rhapsodies. Even if there had been a conscious recension of the one, it was not from the same hand as the conscious recension of the other. The *Iliad* and the *Odyssey* were every conceivable thing in turn, except poems by a poet; and those who knew what poetry was, having written it themselves, or having a sane taste on the subject, were thought to be out of court. There never was any Homer,[27] and the *Iliad* and the *Odyssey*, arising popularly in a primitive society grew up in any way you will, but not from the creative inspiration of one poetic genius.

Where are all those theories now? They are still held by many. I should be rash indeed were I in my ignorance to challenge those who still hold them; but it would be silly to pretend that the intellectual fashion in this matter has not changed. Can anyone say that Bérard[28] is fighting "a rear-guard action"?

At this point I may be told that my examples are beside

---

[26] Andrew Lang (1844–1912), Scottish poet, man of letters, adapter of children's stories, scholar, and translator of *The Odyssey* (1879) and *The Iliad* (1883). —ED.

[27] As many humorists, including Mark Twain and Richard Lederer, have put it, "Homer was not written by Homer but by another man of the same name." —ED.

[28] Victor Bérard (1864–1931), translator of *The Odyssey* and professor at L'École des Haute Études. —ED.

the mark. The traditionalist is not identical with the Catholic, nor are the methods of the old criticism, even when they are applied to the Canon of Scripture, necessarily an attack upon the Faith. All this is true; but the examples I have given illustrate the spirits of two camps in opposition. The Catholic temper is Traditionalist. Individual Catholics may indulge in almost any modern or belated vagary, so long as it does not contradict defined doctrine or specific moral commandment. But the Catholic temper as a whole reacts against that other temper which produced the old-fashioned methods once called scientific criticism, now so heavily discounted. It opposes them because it feels them to be at issue with reason. But whether it be right or wrong in opposing them, no one may doubt that such opposition has been going forward all through our time, and the other side going back.

Take another department where actual doctrine is concerned; the main body of non-Catholic learning in the past generation denied the will; we affirm the will. The great body of non-Catholic physical scientists was fatalist. Well, in this department also it is the reaction which has been winning. The old-fashioned materialistic Monism which was so widely spread half a lifetime ago is to-day nearly dead. The few people who still maintain it are surviving veterans, revered as antiquities. Indeed, the opposite tendency is actually exaggerated, and men are beginning to accept on far too slender evidence all manner of stories, supernatural or quasi-supernatural; anyhow, it is not the old materialism which has been winning; or the old fatalism either. The world is full to-day of voices, those of deluded men, of quacks, and of imperfect philosophers who give the will inordinate power; while others, more sincere, are proudly announcing it as a new discovery—absolutely modern—that if you resolutely direct your thoughts in the right direction you will improve your character. Only the other day I read two columns of this from the pen of a popular novelist in the very same paper which contained Mr. Haldane's article. The popular novelist, not only thought himself ultra-modern, but said so emphatically and over and over again. His attitude was: "Oh, that people would only appreciate the great results of recent research! Then they would learn the startling truth that we can improve ourselves by thinking about the right things and harm ourselves by thinking about the wrong ones." It certainly does not look as though in this department—will versus mechanics—Catholic doctrine were fighting a rearguard action. I should say that it was rather time for us Catholics to put the brakes on, and check the spiritualists and faith-healers.

Now let me turn to the second point of those I have selected as typical in this piece of writing. Mr. Haldane professes his interest in that social phenomenon, the acceptation by millions of men of doctrines not based upon, and (in his view) contradictory to, demonstrable experience. He professes an eager interest in finding out how and why men fall under what its opponents call the religious illusion.

Now, Mr. Haldane's interest in this is an excellent proof of his high intelligence. One of the main marks of stupidity is the impatient rejection of mystery; one of the first marks of good judgment, combined with good reasoning power, is the appetite for examining mystery. Mr. Haldane takes for his examples the belief of masses of orientals that bathing in the waters of the Ganges is of an effect beneficial to the soul of man, and the belief in the Incarnation—the belief that a Galilean who lived and died nearly two thousand years ago was, not only the man he certainly was, but also, born of a miraculous birth, the Omnipotent and Infinite God who made the universe. He wants to know "How men persuade themselves of such things?"—the implication being that all such ideas must be illusions.

Well, let us begin by thinking clearly in the matter; clear thinking is always of advantage when one is attempting to discover the nature of things.

There are here two distinct categories of implied affirmation. The first implied affirmation is that a relation between a seen, visible, natural world wherein truths are demonstrable by repeated physical experiment, and an unseen, immaterial, spiritual world (if any such exist) cannot be a real relation and can only be an imaginary one. Supposing there were a man in Galilee, presenting all the characteristics which we know from experience to inhere to the known object—a man; then it can but be an illusion to predicate of that man other characteristics which are not known by the senses or demonstrable by experience. And the greater the undemonstrable, unexperienced, unseen characteristics you predicate, the less credible your predication.

On the sanctity of the Ganges a parallel affirmation is implied. There is a tract of country over which flows a stream of water, and to this stream, though itself has no real unity, the mind of man gives unity and calls it by a name— the Ganges. The water has certain qualities demonstrable by experience. We all know what water is physically and what it will do and what it will not do physically. We can test by experiment what this particular water may be in its physical composition. To predicate over and above these known physical characters of a particular stream of water a number of unseen, immaterial spiritual attributes, is to nourish an illusion.

There you have the first affirmation implied in the statement I am examining. It is all of a piece with the general affirmation which denies the validity of a sacramental system, of shrines, in general of spiritual influence acting in, or being connected with, natural things.

The second implied affirmation is, that as this sort of illusion seems to crop up at random and to fix upon all manner of disconnected objects, it must proceed from the self-deceiving mind and corresponds to no external reality. In this specific instance you have myriads accepting the sanctity of the Ganges water, and other myriads accepting the divinity and miraculous generation of a particular, limited historical human being. The one is worth as much as the other and both are worthless.

Now let us examine these two affirmations. The first, the denial that there can be a connection between a spiritual world (if it exists) and a natural one is gratuitous; it relies upon no law of thought; still less upon any piece of experimental knowledge.

If you say: "This medal has the virtue of protecting men from bullets in a battle. So long as a man wears it he cannot be hit," that proposition can be subjected to experiment. You can distribute such medals to every soldier in a brigade going into action; you can see to it under the severe discipline of modern armies that the men actually wear the medals; and you can then see whether the singular unseen powers ascribed to the medals are real or not. But if it is affirmed that the medal has an influence of holiness, has an unseen effect upon the unseen and spiritual part of man (supposing there be anything immaterial) then you can believe or disbelieve the statement, but you cannot disprove it. To affirm that there can be no sacramental connection between the physical and the spiritual, that therefore the worship paid to every shrine, to every god inhabiting every grove, is an example of illusion, is an affirmation and nothing more.

If you say the thing is an illusion because it is not subject to some sort of test that would apply to physical processes, your affirmation is not only gratuitous, but against reason; for you are applying to one category what is proper to another. It is as though I were to say that Velázquez[29] was not a good painter because no chemical analysis of the pigments used by him proved a sense of beauty in him.

The second affirmation, the affirmation that all such things are illusions because they are so separate, sometimes so contradictory, so numerous and sometimes so demonstrably false (as in the case of the medal that is said to be a charm against being killed in battle) relies upon false reasoning.

A good grasp of the logical principles involved should show this clearly. Because of ten similar conceptions nine are proved false it does not follow that the tenth is false. For instance a man hears that there are ten very different pictures each said to be the portrait of his dead father, whom he remembers well. He travels about to inspect each in its place, and says of nine, one after the other: "That is not my father." He may then get weary of the process and say: "All these rumours are erroneous": but if he gives up the search on that account he is acting from emotion and not from reason; he is urged by fatigue or disgust, and not by the process of intelligence. For it may well be that the tenth which he has not examined will turn out to be indeed the portrait of his father which he was seeking.

Another way of putting it is the reply to the very true and forcible sentence: "Man is the only animal who makes gods." In that sentence most who use it mean to imply further: "And as one can show that many of these gods are man-made only, therefore every God is man-made." But the true

[29] Diego Rodríguez de Silva y Velázquez (1599–1660), court painter to Philip IV. —ED.

reply is: "This 'therefore' is unwarrantable. It may be that men make gods precisely because the instinct of worship is an instinct corresponding to a reality. And even though it were demonstrable (which it is not) that none of these twenty or a hundred gods you mention were real, but each and all of them figments of the imagination, it does not follow that some one other God may not be real—may not be that which the soul was seeking."

It seems to me of the first importance that this plain piece of reasoning should be correctly stated, followed and repeated whenever the controversy arises.

Let us take the particular example here given. The implication was: "We are all agreed that the water of the Ganges has no spiritual effect, and we may therefore be all agreed that the doctrine of the Virgin Birth is false." But in the first place, who knows whether the waters of the Ganges have or have not any spiritual effect? By what right do you affirm that it has none? If there are spirits, if there be a spiritual world, why may not a spiritual influence, good or evil, or neither good nor evil, be found working through a physical means or interconnected with a material object? You cannot prove by your reason that the thing is *not* so. You can *feel* that it is not so. You may be led by your *emotions* to sneer at the conception; but do not mistake your emotions for your reason. If it comes to mere emotions, my emotions are the other way about. I incline to the sanctity of shrines and to the presence of the unseen in groves and fountains, *More majorum,*[30] as all our fathers did, Pagan and Catholic. You don't feel any such thing? That proves nothing. My emotions do not disprove yours, but then, your emotions do not disprove mine. That the thing is logically

---

[30] "According to the custom of the fathers." —ED.

possible, granted the two worlds spiritual and physical, cannot be denied.

To sum up; it is our business, I think, to clear the ground in this great debate and to make our modern opponents comprehend what our position is—and how they are but affirming a faith contrary to ours when they think they are disproving it by a process which they take to be the use of the reason, but which, on analysis, proves to be the very negation of the use of the reason.

Now let me conclude with the third point I have chosen—the use of the term "Immaculate Conception" to mean "Incarnation through a miraculous birth."

It may seem a point too insignificant to be taken. After all (I may be told), it is but an error on a technicality. No one outside the secluded little world of Catholic theologians uses their technical terms or can give you the exact definitions of such terms. The swarm of modern English writers who are perpetually using the term "Immaculate Conception," wrongly imagining it to mean "Incarnation through a Virgin," are guilty only of a little slip in a quite unessential and ex-centric department of the discussion. The writers who have misused the terms have only to correct their proofs and write "Virgin Birth" where, by a piece of very natural ignorance, they had written "Immaculate Conception," and all will be well. It is (I may be told) as though a Catholic defending the authenticity of the Johannine comma[31] (which by the way has not been defined as authentic) were to spell it

---

[31] Probably an uncanonical additional to John's first epistle, consisting of the words "in heaven: the Father, the Word, and the Holy Spirit: and these are one. And there are three who bear witness on earth" (1 Jn 5:7b–8a, Douay-Rheims translation). The words do not appear in the most ancient manuscripts and may have been inserted as a marginal notation by a copyist, the notation later being incorporated into the text in error by a later copyist. —Ed.

"coma" instead of "comma." It would show him ignorant of Greek spelling, but Greek spelling is not the essence of the affair.

But wait a moment. The term "Immaculate Conception" means all this: "That the race of man suffers from an hereditary taint, proceeding from some action at its origin in which the will of man rebelled against the will of God, and this original taint is called Original Sin. But of the human race" (says the Catholic definition promulgated in the nineteenth century) "there is one exception to this rule, to wit, the Mother of Jesus Christ." *That* is the doctrine of the Immaculate Conception.

The doctrine of the Incarnation is something quite different; it is the doctrine that Jesus Christ was not only man, but also the Infinite God incarnate in that Man and was born of a divine and miraculous Maternity. To confuse the two doctrines is like confusing the atomic hypothesis with the series of atomic weights, or the term "vitalism" with the term "vital statistics." It is, then, a startling error in a point of fact. And is it so unimportant after all—an error of this kind?

Does it not rather betray the fact that even the most eminent men in the camp opposed to us, and even those most readily prepared to consider this strange phenomenon called religion, do not know what men of average education ought to know? Does not so widespread an error as this, though it only concerns two technical terms in the particular department of theology, argue that our opponents have lost, in some degree, their sense of historical proportion and, in that degree, their power of appreciating truth?

The doctrine of Original Sin has been of the first consequence to the world. It has vitally affected the formation of all our culture. It largely explains the political history of

Europe since Europe first became Christian. The worship[32] of our Blessed Lady also, and its culmination in the doctrine of the Immaculate Conception, has been of immeasurable effect upon that culture. However thoroughly one may be convinced that both these things are nonsense, one cannot pass them by as immaterial, as being something on which there is no need to have even general knowledge; for no European can know the past of his race, nor understand how he came to be what he is, who has not some general conception of that Religion which formed us.

When Monsieur Briand[33] alluded a short time ago to the Council of Trent as "The Council of Thirty Men," the slip was quite rightly pointed out by his opponents as a proof that he was not competent to deal with European diplomacy. The word "Trente" in French means both the town of Trent and the number thirty; but the man who knew so little of the formation of Europe as not to know that there had been a Council held at Trent certainly could not understand from what roots the present international complications spring.

He was like a man who should be discussing modern English politics and attempting a solution of our industrial troubles under the impression that the word "statute" meant "statue"—and anyone making that mistake in his efforts at the reconciliation of capitalist and proletarian would not be taken seriously.

[32] Belloc here employs what in 1931 was already an archaic sense of the term *worship*, by which was meant "honor" rather than "adoration". (In British courts some magistrates traditionally are called "Your Worship" instead of "Your Honor", the terms being synonymous.) Orestes Brownson (1803–1876), an American convert to Catholicism from Unitarianism, used *worship* similarly to Belloc when he titled an 1853 essay about the veneration of the Virgin "The Worship of Mary". —ED.

[33] Aristide Briand (1862–1932), French statesman, ten times Premier between 1909 and 1921, later foreign minister and recipient of the 1926 Nobel Peace Prize. —ED.

I do not sneer at those who (in this country and America alone, I think) fall into the elementary error of mistaking the Immaculate Conception for the Miraculous Birth, any more than I should sneer at a distinguished Chinaman, who, not having travelled in Europe thought (like a recent Prime Minister of England) that the Dalmatian coast was on the Baltic, or, like another Cabinet Minister, that the Dardanelles were at the Gibraltar end of the Mediterranean. The Chinaman might be a very great figure in his own country and might reply with justice that the particular position of the Dalmatian coast left him cold. But I do say that to discuss Catholic ideas and in doing so to mix up the Immaculate Conception with the Incarnation through a miraculous birth is to show oneself unacquainted with the subject one is criticising. It is an error which the more often it is made, the better proves that our opponents have not yet learnt the alphabet of that which they think they are about to destroy.

3

Hilaire Belloc vs. W. R. Inge

Belloc next turned his attention to an article that appeared in the *Evening Standard* of London. The writer, William Ralph Inge (1860–1954), had been brought up a Tractarian but had abandoned that tradition for a more sceptical posture. He had an aloof personality—apparently exacerbated by bouts of melancholia and progressive deafness—and, during and after his time as a tutor at Oxford, he had become well known for writings on religion. Later he taught at Cambridge and was surprised at his selection, in 1911, as dean of Saint Paul's Cathedral. The general public was surprised too, since he was known as a theological liberal.

Inge was reluctant to give up his academic career, and he accepted the appointment with some hesitation. His tenure as dean was not all that he might have hoped. Among other things, the canons associated with Saint Paul's were more conservative theologically than he was and did not always cooperate with him. Over time, Inge turned more and more to his writing. It is said that "his chief service to the cathedral was his preaching, which attracted increasing congregations up to the date of his retirement" in 1934. "He preached as he had lectured, with no oratorical art and with his eyes fixed upon his manuscript. His power lay in the impression of his personality, his originality of thought, and his gift of startling epigram. Men recognized that he was a preacher who was always thinking for himself and speaking the truth that he had found."[1] Such, anyway, was the opinion of W. R. Matthews, writing a biographical sketch of Inge. However original the dean's thinking may have been in some fields, he seems to have been conventional in his thinking about the Catholic faith, and Belloc repeatedly complained about Inge's lack of appreciation for things Catholic.

Inge's liberalism was of a dour sort. His weekly articles in the *Evening Standard*, published from 1921 to 1946, earned him the nickname of "the gloomy dean". He attacked religious and political views that he thought were superstitious, and he had an evident contempt for democracy. He retired as dean in 1934 but continued to write, mainly popular books but also some scholarly works. Throughout his long career he had an aversion to Catholicism, and it would not be unfair to say that he often enough, in his writings, acted the part of the anti-Catholic. So far was he from the faith that Arnold Lunn, himself not yet a Catholic, could use as an illustration of omnipotence that, if he so chose, God could convert "Dean Inge to Catholicism by an instantaneous revelation".[2]

The gloomy dean's attitude toward Rome rankled Belloc, who prefaced his essay with these words: "The hatred of the Catholic Church, when it is expressed by a man of high culture, is at issue with that culture. It forbids him to say what he really thinks and it breeds in him a misapprehension of that from which this very culture proceeded."[3] Belloc con-

---

[1] *The Dictionary of National Biography*, suppl. 1951–1960, 531. —ED.

[2] Ronald Knox and Arnold Lunn, *Difficulties* (London: Eyre and Spottis-woode, 1952 [1932]), 137. —ED.

[3] Hilaire Belloc, *Essays of a Catholic* (New York: Macmillan, 1931), 299. —ED.

cluded his essay with a paragraph that often has been quoted and perhaps as often put to memory.

A LETTER TO DEAN INGE

You have often attacked (and defamed) the Catholic Church in your pages. In that effort you have introduced, among others, my own less significant name. I propose to answer you.

The task is the easier because your animosity leads you to open declaration of your hatred, and, unlike too many of your kind, you are sometimes led by exasperation to be sincere.

Your indictment against the Faith (which you have also called "A bloody and treacherous corporation") is in these articles: that it is foreign, that it is disciplined, and that it is false—or (as you have written) "an imposture." The first is puerile, the second misconceived, the last momentous and the issue. I will take them in their order.

The Faith, you say, is foreign. Certainly it has been alienated by force and fraud from the English—but since how long? You know that it made England, and in particular re-made England out of barbarism as no other province of our civilisation was restored.

You are a man cultured and acquainted with the sources. You know well enough that England only is because the Church made England after the chaos of the fifth and sixth centuries. You know also—as your readers do not—that all about us, axe and ladder and saw, pillar and arch, and verse and law, and reasoning, are from that Mediterranean antiquity which the Church barely saved, and having saved, nourished into Christendom.

This done, England so recovered, the Faith presided over all her being for a thousand years. It was not till three hundred years ago that the half of England doubted. It is not two hundred since the last body of Englishmen loyal to the ancient national Faith of Englishmen were crushed out. A hideous official persecution, violent beyond example, and carried out in the interest of men newly enriched by the plunder of sacred things, took three lifetimes before it succeeded.

more true [handwritten margin note]
of an American [handwritten margin note]

I find a contradiction in you here. An Englishman (you say) cannot be English unless he has in him some Manichean poison of the Puritans. So Chaucer, Alfred, Bede are not English? But next I hear that this Puritanism is a product of Englishry, so those thousand years were English after all— but, took their thousand years to bear the Protestant fruit,

Pearce's new [handwritten margin note]
book on [handwritten margin note]
Shakespeare [handwritten margin note]

which blossomed suddenly three hundred years ago. When Shakespeare wrote, England was manifestly Catholic; when Milton, no longer. Yet you would abandon Shakespeare— with regret. You define an Englishman by his religion—no true Englishman can be of Shakespeare's mood, you say, only of Milton's. An Englishman of Shakespeare's mood, or Chaucer's, or More's, was no true Englishman.

The Englishman, groping for the light, shall no longer be English for you if he attains it. He shall only be English in your eyes on the condition of groping still. Certitude and the light upon eternal things are a bar to your granting a certificate of English essence.

What is more, the answer to the most universal (and most important) of questions must, you tell us, be local: and truth must be provincial to be true. If it oversteps national boundaries it is false. Was there ever such nonsense!

I have called it puerile—and so it is: a schoolboy's folly, to which all things not familiar seem ridiculous; for how can truth have local boundaries?

Your second objection is weightier. We of the Faith are not universal, but segregated. The world notes (as do you) that we stand together, making one regiment. You mistake that unity for mere servitude, and that bond for a chain. There is none of us but can assure you that only in the Faith does the reason reach a plenitude of freedom, nor any of us that has searched into ideas but will further tell you that we of the Faith may doubtfully admit some sceptics for our equals, but certainly no sentimentalists or men of merely emotional religion.

You say that we are within walls. So we are. But they are the walls of a city. It is the secure City of God. You resent our unity. Without it how would the structure of revelation be preserved, or of that Christian society which we made, which is Europe, and the dissolution of which would be the death of all? You are offended at our central command. But are we not under siege?

In truth it is not the constitution of the Church you abhor, but the thing itself—little though you know that thing: just as men hate some strange country though they know not a word of its language. When such decry the tyranny or the licence of some polity, it is not Monarchy nor the Republic which troubles them, but the very texture of a detested nation. With you it is not the Captaincy of Peter that offends—though that is holy, necessary, and aboriginal—it is his Ship: the Ship itself: life on shipboard: the manner of the sea.

Wherein also resides your chief, and only grave, indeed your one grievance: that what the Catholic faith lays down, this you do not believe.

You have written "The Catholic Church is an Imposture," thereby provoking all the past of Europe, and challenging Ignatius of Antioch and Augustine of Hippo no less than the least of our fellowship to-day.

I forbear to pin you to a strict explanation, whether that "imposture" be the Incarnation, the Eucharist, or any other of our structural mysteries.

Your office forbids you to reply. You take money paid you to teach and maintain some, at least, of the Christian doctrines and the creeds. Therefore you cannot speak your mind openly, or tell us whether at heart you do not agree with the half-instructed millions around you who make no doubt that religion is of man: a figment.

I will content myself by concluding with this: that there wholly escapes you the character of the Catholic Church. You judge it by indications dead and valueless; you have not—for all your detestation of it—experienced its life, not known it for what it is. You are like one examining the windows of Chartres from within by candle-light, and marvelling how any man can find glory in them; but we have the sun shining through. You are like one curious to note the canvas-marks on the back of a Raeburn,[4] and marvelling to hear its obverse called the true picture of a man. For what is the Catholic Church? It is that which replies, co-ordinates, establishes.

It is that within which is right order, outside, the puerilities and the despairs. It is the possession of perspective in the survey of the world. It is a grasp upon reality. Here alone is promise, and here alone a foundation.

Those of us who boast so stable an endowment make no claim thereby to personal peace; we are not saved thereby alone. But we are of so glorious a company that we receive support, and have communion. The Mother of God is also ours. Our dead are with us. Even in these our earthly miseries we always hear the distant something of an eternal

[4] Henry Raeburn (1756–1823), Scottish portrait painter, who painted more than seven hundred portraits. —ED.

music, and smell a native air. There is a standard set for us whereto our whole selves respond, which is that of an inherited and endless life, quite full, in our own country.

You may say, "All this is rhetoric." You would be wrong, for it is rather vision, recognition, and testimony. But take it for rhetoric. Have you any such? Be it but rhetoric, whence does that stream flow? Or what reserve is that which can fill even such a man as myself with fire? Can your opinion (or doubt, or gymnastics) do the same? I think not!

One thing in this world is different from all other. It has a personality and a force. It is recognised, and (when recognised) most violently loved or hated. It is the Catholic Church. Within that household the human spirit has roof and hearth. Outside it, is the Night.

4

Ronald Knox vs. Arnold Lunn

In the first half of the twentieth century perhaps no Catholic apologist engaged more frequently in debates with prominent opponents of Catholicism—and of Christianity in general—than did Arnold Lunn, but Lunn did not begin his religious debates as a defender of the Catholic faith. His first important exchange found him arguing against Catholicism. His opponent was Ronald Knox.

The most distinguished English convert to Catholicism since Newman, Ronald Knox (1888–1957) was the son of an Anglican bishop. He excelled at Eton and Oxford and at eighteen published a fine volume of English, Latin, and Greek verse. Although his father was a leader of the Low Church Party, Knox early adopted the Anglo-Catholic position, and he vigorously wrote in its favor. Of particular note are "Absolute and Abitofhell",[1] a parody of Dryden in which Knox criticized modern theology, and "Reunion All Around",[2] a satirical look at ill-conceived attempts at religious unity and an essay that remains instructive today. These works received considerable acclaim—and notoriety—and were written while their author was in his midtwenties.

[1] Ronald Knox, *Essays in Satire* (New York: Dutton, 1930), 79–90. —ED.
[2] Ibid., 45–78. —ED.

Knox converted to the Catholic faith in 1917 and offered a justification for his switch of allegiance in *A Spiritual Aeneid*.[3] The next year he was ordained a Catholic priest. After teaching at Saint Edmund's College for eight years, he was appointed chaplain to the Catholic undergraduates at his beloved Oxford, a post he held until 1939. While there he produced a substantial body of work, including sermons, retreats, detective stories,[4] and his best-known book, *The Belief of Catholics*.[5]

During World War II Knox lived in Aldenham Park in Shropshire, where he worked on his translation of the Bible and as chaplain to girls whose school had been moved there at the outbreak of hostilities. To them he gave simple apologetical and exegetical sermons that were collected as *The Mass in Slow Motion*,[6] *The Creed in Slow Motion*,[7] and *The Gospel in Slow Motion*.[8] A decade later, as his life neared an untimely end, Knox again turned seriously to apologetics, having come to feel that a new approach was needed if the

<hr />

[3] Ronald Knox, *A Spiritual Aeneid* (London: Longmans, Green, 1919). —ED.

[4] Knox's six detective novels were *The Viaduct Murder* (London: Methuen, 1925), *The Three Taps* (London: Methuen, 1927), *Footsteps at the Lock* (London: Methuen, 1928), *The Body in the Silo* (London: Hodder and Stoughton, 1933), *Still Dead* (London: Hodder and Stoughton, 1934), and *Double Cross Purposes* (London: Hodder and Stoughton, 1937). Evelyn Waugh observed, regarding Knox's detective books, "None was more ingenious than he, more scrupulous in the provision of clues, more logically complete in his solutions. Very few women have ever enjoyed them." *Monsignor Ronald Knox* (Boston: Little, Brown, 1959), 189. —ED.

[5] Ronald Knox, *The Belief of Catholics* (London: Sheed and Ward, 1927; San Francisco: Ignatius Press, 2000). —ED.

[6] Ronald Knox, *The Mass in Slow Motion* (London: Sheed and Ward, 1948). —ED.

[7] Ronald Knox, *The Creed in Slow Motion* (London: Sheed and Ward, 1949). —ED.

[8] Ronald Knox, *The Gospel in Slow Motion* (London: Sheed and Ward, 1950). —ED.

faith were to make an impression on midcentury readers. The result was the unfinished and posthumously published *Proving God: A New Apologetic.*[9]

In the first chapter Knox avers that "religion, except in its crudest form, has to make room for apologetics, not merely for doctrinal theology; a rough estimate of history, a rudimentary process of inference, are demanded of the simplest mind before it can say 'I believe.' Thus the presentation of the divine fact to the human mind calls for persuasion; and if you would persuade, you must have some knowledge of how people's minds work, of the ideals which move them and the prejudices which enchain them." He goes on to say, "I think that our Catholic apologetic, nearly all of it, strikes the modern reader as inhuman. Just because it is worked out with such mathematical precision, just because a suitable answer comes pat to every question, just because it always seems to face you with a dilemma from which there is no logical escape, it afflicts our contemporaries with a sense of *malaise.*"[10] This may explain, in part, the collapse of apologetics following Vatican II, which convened five years after Knox's death amid the atmosphere of this "*malaise*". There was something impersonal and thus unattractive about postwar apologetics—the golden age of twentieth-century Catholic apologetics had run its course by 1940—and Knox was trying to find a way around that problem.

His translation of the New Testament was published in 1945. The Old Testament appeared in two volumes, the first in 1948, the second in 1950. He translated from the Vulgate rather than the Hebrew and Greek because, he said, the Vulgate was the official Bible of the Church. This decision

[9] Ronald Knox, *Proving God: A New Apologetic* (London: *The Month*, 1959). —ED.

[10] Ibid., 11. —ED.

may account in part for the short life span of his rendering; after Vatican II there seemed to be an urgency to get back to the original languages, and versions translated from the Vulgate fell into desuetude.

Knox tried to achieve what he termed a "timeless English", and for some years his Bible was accepted for use in the liturgy in England and Wales. Not all commentators liked the Knox version. In a collection of essays written in explanation, if not exactly in defense, of his decisions, Knox said, "I have long since given up protesting when controversialists misquote me, or newspaper columnists credit me with the authorship of Limericks that are none of mine. But if you question a rendering of mine in the New Testament, you come up against a parental instinct hardly less ferocious than that of the mother-bear. I shall smile it off, no doubt, in conversation, but you have lost marks." [11]

An example of his thinking—one quite useful in apologetical work today—concerns the *scandalum Pharisaeorum*. What does it mean to say that something our Lord has said "scandalizes the Pharisees"? "What was the trouble with the Pharisees?" asked Knox. "Not that they were shocked, exactly—that is a modern connotation of the term; not that they were indignant—that is a false inference from the Authorized Version's 'offended'. To be scandalized is, rather, to be 'put off'; if only slang were not so much more expressive than English! . . . You have been going along, so far, quite happy and undisturbed in your religious beliefs, your spiritual loyalties, and then *suddenly* something crops up, something seen or heard, which throws you out of your course; you have the feelings of a man who has tripped over some

[11] Ronald Knox, *Trials of a Translator* (New York: Sheed and Ward, 1949), viii. This book was published in England under the title *On Englishing the Bible* (London: Burns, Oates, 1949). —ED.

unseen obstacles and stumbled off the pathway into rough ground; that is to be scandalized." [12]

We might say that Knox was to scandalize Arnold Lunn (1888–1974), tripping him up in his opposition to the Catholic faith. The two were exact contemporaries, though Knox was a year ahead of Lunn at Oxford. Each in turn edited *The Isis*, the undergraduate journal, and each was prominent in the Oxford Union, Knox as president and Lunn as secretary. At that time they were traveling on different trajectories, Knox adhering ever more assiduously to the Anglo-Catholic position, Lunn embracing a studied agnosticism. They would match wits years later in an exchange of letters, published as *Difficulties*.[13] In the preface to the first edition Lunn remarked of Knox, "I awaited his letters with far greater eagerness than the moves of my chess opponents. My efforts to entangle him in a mating net have failed; the Roman Bishop has not yet been forked by the Protestant Knight, and the game, which remains unfinished at the call of time, must therefore be submitted for adjudication to the reader." [14] A year later Lunn made his own adjudication obvious by joining the Catholic Church. Lunn apparently had not been as far from the Church as he had thought. "Indeed," noted Robert Speaight, "none of the difficulties adduced by Arnold Lunn in his exchange of letters with Ronald Knox is so nearly insuperable as the difficulty in believing that he himself ever disbelieved in Catholicism. In that respect, as in some others, the book has a certain period charm." [15]

Lunn led two lives. The Lunn best known to Catholics is

[12] Ibid., 67–68. —Ed.

[13] Ronald Knox and Arnold Lunn, *Difficulties* (London: Eyre and Spottiswoode, 1952 [1932]). —Ed.

[14] Ibid., xi. —Ed.

[15] Thomas Corbishley and Robert Speaight, *Ronald Knox* (New York: Sheed and Ward, 1965), 186. —Ed.

the Catholic apologist, but to many people he became known not for his writings on religion but for his writings on mountaineering and for his promotion of Olympic skiing. His father, Sir Henry Lunn, was a medical missionary and travel agent who in 1910 established Mürren as a resort popular for winter sports. It was at that Swiss hamlet that Arnold Lunn invented the slalom ski race in 1922. For many years he was an active mountain climber, even though in 1909 he had suffered a fall that resulted in one leg being shortened by three inches. He wrote numerous books on skiing and mountaineering and from 1919 to 1971 edited the *British Ski Year Book*. In 1952 he was knighted for his services to British skiing and to Anglo-Swiss relations.

Of Lunn's sixty-three books, sixteen concern religion. The first was *Roman Converts*,[16] an examination of John Henry Newman, Henry Edward Manning, George Tyrrell, G. K. Chesterton, and Ronald Knox. At the time of writing Lunn was a Christian (with a remaining agnostic streak) but not a Catholic, and his portrait of Knox was not entirely complimentary. He said, for example, "The trouble with Knox is that he is a Catholic, but only nominally a Christian. He is much more interested in the Church than in the founder of that Church"[17]—a complaint that was not entirely untrue but that could have been lodged more effectively against Hilaire Belloc, who wrote much on the Church but hardly a word on Christ.

Despite his criticisms of Knox's religious positions, Lunn had to acknowledge the former's literary gifts: "'Absolute and Abitofhell,' which first appeared in the pages of the *Oxford Magazine*, is perhaps the finest satiric poem which theological controversy has ever produced. . . . The style of

[16] Arnold Lunn, *Roman Converts* (London: Chapman and Hall, 1924). —ED.
[17] Ibid., 199. —ED.

Dryden is caught to perfection; the epigrams are magnificent, the wit unforced and brilliant. Controversy, whether theological or political, has seldom produced a more scintillating sally." [18] Lunn's first critique of Knox had come earlier, in a review of *A Spiritual Aeneid*. That review illustrated Lunn's "fascination of, and exasperation at" [19] a Church that promoted seemingly irrational doctrines and yet attracted converts known for their intellectual gifts. It was this fascination that would lead him to meet Knox in the literary exchange that would prompt Lunn's conversion.

At the end of *Roman Converts* Lunn gave Knox unsolicited advice: "But he must learn to temper his wit with some sympathy and some understanding of his opponent. At present he seems in danger of imitating the weakest tactics of too many Catholic controversialists. Roman Catholics are credited, justly credited, with more worldly wisdom and with more astuteness than most of their Anglican brethren, but they seldom realize the worldly wisdom of treating an opponent with reasonable generosity. Father Benson's novels,[20] for instance, were effective propaganda, but they would have been doubly effective had he found it possible to depict an Anglican parson who was neither a knave nor a fool." [21] Lunn and Knox began their exchange of letters only six years after the appearance of *Roman Converts*, and years later Lunn would acknowledge that Knox's

[18] Ibid., 189. —ED.

[19] Karl G. Schmude, *Sir Arnold Lunn: Mountaineer of Faith* (Melbourne: A.C.T.S. Publications, 1976), 7. —ED.

[20] Robert Hugh Benson (1871–1914), Catholic priest and author of such historical novels as *The King's Achievement* (New York: Kenedy, 1905) and *Come Rack! Come Rope!* (New York: Kenedy, 1912). The definitive biography, in two volumes, is C. C. Martindale's *The Life of Monsignor Robert Hugh Benson* (London: Longmans, Green, 1916). —ED.

[21] Lunn, *Roman Converts*, 203. —ED.

restraint and his application of "reasonable generosity" made an indelible impression on him and brought him the last way toward Catholicism.[22] In 1933 Knox received Lunn into the Church.

Lunn, who wrote no fewer than five books of memoirs that related elements of his conversion,[23] in 1951 gave a broadcast on Vatican Radio, shortly after he and Knox had contributed an extra letter apiece to a new edition of *Difficulties*. In the broadcast he summarized how he became a Catholic. "It was not easy to think myself back into the state of mind when I had written with such conviction about the difficulties which kept me out of the Church. Not that these difficulties were fictitious or that Father Knox's answers were always completely convincing. I became a Catholic not because there was a slick and easy answer to every objection but because I was tired of remaining suspended like Mahomet's coffin between heaven and earth. The Catholic key certainly unlocked most locks, and if the key stuck in a few locks perhaps the fault was not in the key but in my use of it. To enter the Church was a gamble. To remain outside the Church was an even deadlier risk. I decided to gamble on the hope that the practice of Catholicism might slowly transform the water of uneasy conviction into the wine of unquestioning faith."[24] It did.

Halfway through the correspondence that was to be published as *Difficulties*, in his letter of August 16, 1931, Lunn declared that he wanted "to discuss in some detail the cardi-

---

[22] Knox and Lunn, *Difficulties*, 245–46, 257. —ED.

[23] Arnold Lunn, *Now I See* (New York: Sheed and Ward, 1937), *Within That City* (New York: Sheed and Ward, 1937), *Come What May* (Boston: Little, Brown, 1941), *Memory to Memory* (London: Hollis and Carter, 1956), and *Unkilled for So Long* (London: Allen and Unwin, 1968). —ED.

[24] *The Beda Book*, no editor given (London: Sands, 1957), 219. —ED.

nal point of this discussion—the claim of the Roman Catholic Church to infallibility".[25] This would be done in terms of the papacy. He identified eight points of preliminary focus:[26]

1. "The Scripture evidence to which the Catholics appeal in support of the Papal claims is based in the main on three texts", Matthew 16:18–19, Luke 22:32, and John 21:15–17.
2. Whether "this rock" refers to Peter, Peter's confession of faith, or Christ himself.
3. Whether Peter claimed to be infallible or the apostles credited him with infallibility.
4. The incident at Antioch, in which Paul corrected Peter (Gal 1:12).
5. Papal succession: Even if Jesus gave Peter certain prerogatives, is there evidence they were transmitted to successors?
6. The claims that Peter was in Rome and served as bishop there. (Lunn said yes to the first, no to the second.)
7. The apparent fact that popes have been on wrong sides of controversies over the centuries, "and orthodoxy has only been saved by the bishops in opposition to the Pope".
8. The posthumous condemnation of Pope Honorius by an ecumenical council.

After briefly addressing each of these points, Lunn examined papal infallibility head on, roving from Vatican I to *Providentissimus Deus*,[27] from Nicholas I writing to the

---

[25] Knox and Lunn, *Difficulties*, 112. —ED.

[26] Ibid., 112–16. —ED.

[27] *Providentissimus Deus* (1893), an encyclical on biblical studies. In it Leo XIII defended inspiration and encouraged the study of ancillary sciences. —ED.

Bulgarians[28] to Innocent VIII writing on witches,[29] from the Spanish Inquisition to Galileo. Then it was Knox's turn. In his reply he addressed most of Lunn's arguments, though not in strict sequence. What he wrote is as useful in current apologetic discussions as it was in his correspondence with Lunn. Every sustained argument against the papacy by today's Evangelicals and Fundamentalists will include the points listed by Lunn (who was neither an Evangelical nor a Fundamentalist), and today's apologists could do far worse than to mimic Knox's good-natured reply.

Aug. 20, 1931

Dear Lunn,

I am rather sorry you do not want to argue more about the meaning of the Petrine texts. Your modest claim that the

---

[28] In response to an inquiry about baptism administered by pagans or Jews, Nicholas I wrote confusingly about whether the baptismal formula had to be "in the name of the Father, and of the Son, and of the Holy Spirit" or "in the name of Jesus". —ED.

[29] In 1484 Innocent VIII issued the bull *Summis Desiderantes Affectibus*, which incorrectly has been held responsible for the "witch mania" of the following two centuries. In fact, the bull attempted to codify procedures in the already long-established campaign against various forms of sorcery. Lunn's particular interest was with what many interpreted to be Innocent's belief in witches' "intercourse with incubi and succubi, their interference with the parturition of women and animals, the damage they did to cattle and the fruits of the earth, their power and malice in the infliction of pain and disease" (*Catholic Encyclopedia*, vol. XV, 676). By listing the charges levied against supposed witches, Innocent appeared to endorse the factuality of the charges. It may have been the case that he indeed believed in their factuality. Even if that were so, the bull is irrelevant to the issue of papal infallibility inasmuch as it made no attempt to issue a dogmatic definition. Nothing in the bull indicates that Innocent expected his readers to believe anything beyond what Scripture had to say about sorcery. —ED.

three texts do not constitute a "legal charter" for the Papacy might surely be paralleled by saying that the words "As the Father hath sent me, even so send I you . . . whosoever sins ye remit," [30] etc. etc., are not a *legal charter* for the episcopate. In both cases, you have to read the texts in the light of what actually followed as a matter of history; the tradition that the apostolic ministry is continued by bishops, the tradition that the Bishop of Rome succeeds to the pre-eminent position of Peter. If in either case the tradition was a matter of usurpation in the first instance, show us (we say) where you have record of any protest against it. And if there are no protests, or if (as in the case of St. Cyprian) you find that the protests were made in a moment of excitement by a man whose views elsewhere can be quoted in favour of the tradition, then it is natural to interpret the texts in the light of the tradition. Personally, I have never seen any Protestant exposition of the texts which gave me the smallest satisfaction, even when I was a Protestant; but I think it is important to insist that the Bible should be interpreted in the light of Christian tradition, not in isolation from it.

By the way, your quotations are not quite accurate. In the last chapter of St. John there is a possibly important variation of verb, *poimaino* instead of *bosko*.[31]

I agree with you that in the Acts St. Peter does not claim to be infallible when speaking *ex cathedra*. Nor does St. Paul mention Transubstantiation in the Corinthians. But if you suppose that St. Peter, in using arguments to support his view about the Gentiles, was disclaiming the right to interpret the mind of the Church on the subject, you are strangely unfamiliar with Pius IX's decree about the Immaculate

---

[30] Jn 20:21–23. —ED.

[31] The reference is to John 21:16, "tend my sheep", as distinguished from 21:17, "feed my sheep". —ED.

Conception.[32] As we priests know (for we have to read all
through it in the breviary) he produced arguments from
history and from tradition at interminable length before he
came to his conclusion. And naturally. Let me insist from the
first that Infallibility does not mean what almost all non-
Catholics think it does. They seem to think that the Pope,
like the high priest in the Old Testament, keeps a kind of
Urim and Thummim somewhere in the Vatican; and that if
he wants to know the answer to a vexed question he just
applies to this oracle, and the answer is miraculously given
him. Every Pope, in every decision, makes up his mind as
best he can as to the true doctrine of the Church, using every
effort to consider the full history of Catholic traditions on
the subject. He makes up his mind as anybody else does; the
difference is that the Pope, in certain circumstances, is providentially directed so that he makes up his mind right. Hence
both St. Peter and Pius IX were prepared to "argue the case
on its merits."

What happened, it seems, was that there was much disput-
ing; then St. Peter, exercising his primacy by speaking first,
got up, and after his speech all the multitude held their peace.
Then St. James, who is generally supposed to have been
inclined to the Judaizing party, got up and agreed with St.
Peter. Not perhaps in the tone of Bishop Dupanloup[33] sub-
mitting to the Vatican decrees; but then (1) St. James was an
apostle, and the Apostles were jointly witnesses of our Lord's
teaching—conflicts about the *tradition* of the Church do not
arise while the eye-witnesses are alive; and (2) the whole

---

[32] *Ineffabilis Deus* (1854). —ED.

[33] Félix-Antoine-Philibert Dupanloup (1802–1878), Bishop of Orléans,
France, leader of the minority at Vatican I, opposed to the promulgation of
the dogma of papal infallibility. Once the dogma was defined, he quickly and
not half-heartedly endorsed it. —ED.

subject of the decree was rather a matter of discipline than of faith or morals.

I think *The Layman's New Testament*[34] is certainly right in saying that the Antioch interview[35] happened before the Council. And of course the question at Antioch was simply whether St. Peter should sit at the Jewish table or at the Gentile table; presumably there must have been two because of kosher meat. I have always felt that St. Peter was following the prescriptions laid down by St. Paul in Romans 14:15. But I don't quite agree with you about St. Paul not recognizing the pre-eminent position (at any rate) of St. Peter. The phrase "I withstood him to his face" always reads to me as if it were the assertion of an unwontedly bold action; I mean, it suggests that it wasn't a thing you ordinarily did, talking to the Chief of the Apostles like that. But it is a thing that can be done in an emergency, when you think the Pope is showing weakness; St. Catherine of Siena[36] knew that.

I think it is a forced argument to imply that because the gospel of the circumcision was committed to St. Peter, and that of the uncircumcision to St. Paul, there were really two Popes, one for the Jews and one for the Gentiles. The division is one of missionary spheres (St. Peter up to that time having apparently confined himself to the Dispersion), not of administrative areas. Your phrase "St. Paul never guessed that St. Peter possessed the prerogatives that modern Catholics attribute to him" is one that needs more precision if it is to be answered in detail. Nobody thinks

[34] Hugh Pope, *The Layman's New Testament* (London: Sheed and Ward, 1934), 643. —ED.

[35] Gal 2:11–14. —ED.

[36] Catherine of Siena (1347–1380) received in 1370 a vision that prompted her to enter public life. She implored Gregory XI to leave Avignon and return to Rome, there to reform the clergy and the administration of the Papal States. —ED.

that St. Peter had fans and silver trumpets; and there are obviously a whole lot of ways—not merely confined to externals—in which the Pope's position *vis-à-vis* his brother bishops is very different from what St. Peter's was *vis-à-vis* his brother apostles. Especially, as I say, because of the living witness; I expect you know Newman's comments on the point in *The Development of Christian Doctrine*,[37] also because the Church was still too small to need much organization. Yet wherever St. Peter does appear in the Acts, he is always the leading actor in the scene.

The question whether St. Peter was ever Bishop of Rome has always seemed to me an odd equivocation introduced by controversialists. Was St. John ever Bishop of Ephesus? I should not have thought that there was any sense in using the word "Bishop" as applied to an apostle; surely the episcopate came into being to replace the Apostles, and the Apostles themselves included the episcopate in their powers as the greater includes the less, as the episcopate includes the priesthood. This, surely, was in Eusebius' mind when he talked about Linus being appointed the first bishop of the Romans.[38] The whole question, I should say, is simply one of names. Wherever an apostle was, in the first age of the Church, he was a bishop and something more than a bishop. Even if Linus was "bishop" of Rome while the two apostles were still alive, you do not surely suppose that he was St. Peter's superior? He may have been thus appointed, though I doubt if Irenaeus implies it; but he would surely be in the position of the Cardinal who actually looks after the churches in Rome—I forget his title.[39]

---

[37] John Henry Newman, *Essay on the Development of Christian Doctrine* (London: Pickering, 1878), 148–65. —ED.

[38] Eusebius, *Ecclesiastical History* (Cambridge: Harvard, 1926), III, iv, 8. —ED.

[39] The title is Vicar General of His Holiness for the City of the Vatican. —ED.

If St. Peter was not, at the end of his life, exercising his apostolic functions with Rome as their centre, why did not the Bishops of Antioch get hold of this fact, and run it for all it was worth? They were constantly jealous for the privileges of their see; and it was common tradition that St. Peter had, at one time, his see at Antioch. No, I think that argument is altogether rather played out. The theory of the early Church, as far as I understand it, is this. A tradition of doctrine has been handed down by the Apostles, centred at various geographical points. Each bishop hands on the tradition to his successors (even now, as you know, there is a custom that a bishop should publicly testify his faith on his death-bed); and the traditions of those cities, like Ephesus, where apostles took up their headquarters, are particularly valuable, because there the tradition is likely to have survived in its purest form. But Rome stands altogether by itself; for Rome has the tradition of that apostle who was commanded to "confirm his brethren." [40] Its Bishop has a tradition of doctrine which is, by divine guarantee, immune from error as is the general tradition of doctrine collectively given to the Church. Hence when heresies begin to arise, the attitude of the Roman Bishop is all-important. I do not mean this is all the early Papacy meant; but that, I imagine, must have been its salient aspect.

I think I must refer you back to the ordinary books of controversy for Liberius and Honorius.[41] I was always taught (as a Protestant) that Liberius acted under *force majeure*, and that clearly invalidates his expressions of opinion, which he withdrew when at liberty. Nobody claims for the Pope a gift of invincible fortitude. And Honorius, so far from

---

[40] Lk 22:32. —ED.

[41] For a discussion of these popes, see Karl Keating, *Catholicism and Fundamentalism* (San Francisco: Ignatius Press, 1988), 227–29. —ED.

pronouncing an infallible opinion in the Monothelite controversy, was "quite extraordinarily not" (as Gore[42] used to
say) pronouncing a decision at all. To the best of his human
wisdom, he thought that the controversy ought to be left
unsettled, for the greater peace of the Church. In fact, he was
an inopportunist. We, wise after the event, say that he was
wrong. But nobody, I think, has ever claimed that the Pope is
infallible in *not* defining a doctrine. Your remark, by the way,
that it was Athanasius rather than Liberius who saved the
Church in the Arian controversy is not in the least offensive
to pious ears. It is quite possible for the Pope to be remiss
about his duty, and for God to raise up a saint—witness St.
Catherine of Siena again—to hold him to it.

Now, may I turn your point inside out? Has it ever
occurred to you how few are the alleged "failures of infallibility"? I mean, if somebody propounded in your presence
the thesis that all the kings of England have been impeccable,
you would not find yourself murmuring, "Oh, well, people
said rather unpleasant things about Jane Shore[43] . . . and the
best historians seem to think that Charles II spent too much
of his time with Nell Gwynn."[44] Here have these Popes
been, fulminating anathema after anathema for centuries—
certain in all human probability to contradict themselves or
one another over again. Instead of which you get this measly
crop of two or three alleged failures! I don't say that proves
infallibility; that would be claiming too much. But surely it
suggests there has always been a tradition in the Church—call
it an instinct if you like—that what has been laid down by a

[42] Charles Gore (1853–1932), Anglican bishop and theologian. —ED.

[43] Jane Shore (died 1527), mistress of Edward IV of England. Accused in
1483 of sorcery by Richard III, she was placed in the Tower. —ED.

[44] Nell (Eleanor) Gwynn (1650–1687), English actress and, from 1669,
Charles II's mistress. —ED.

previous Pope is of itself irreformable. And that is the Vatican doctrine against which these criticisms are really directed. One Pope who yielded, when he was much in the position of Tikhon[45] with the Bolshevists; one who thought it would be nice if the question of the two Wills (much complicated because nobody had yet invented the blessed words "form" and "content") were left an open question—and then you have to fish round wildly and even dig out poor old Galileo to make up a party!

On the infallibility decree itself, apart from the matter of the "ruling decisions," I do not think that your objections are very formidable. You repeat, without much apparent enthusiasm, the logical dilemma, so beloved of controversialists, about the infallible Pope needing a second infallible authority to decide when he is and when he is not infallible. I expect you are familiar with the speculation, hardly more impressive, "How are we to be certain that the reigning Pope was ever baptized?" (We can only have human certainty of this; and if he was never baptized, then his orders were invalid and consequently he is no Pope!) What is asserted in the decree is that *ex cathedra* definitions are infallible, objectively; it does not follow that they can always be detected as such. And I cannot understand why we Catholics should need a second infallible authority to guide us on this point; surely here a certainty which excludes all reasonable doubt is sufficient for our purposes? And such a certainty can be obtained, say, in the matter of the Immaculate Conception decree, either by one's own common sense or by the "common sense" of the theologians. I will not labour this point until I know how it strikes you. But if you read any formal manual of theology

[45] Tikhon (1865–1925), patriarch of the Russian Orthodox Church after 1917, imprisoned 1922–1923 on charges of opposing the Communist regime. —ED.

you will come across heaps of points which, without being *de fide*, are labelled "certain," because the whole tradition of Catholic theology is agreed on them; and no preacher (for example) would dream of teaching the contrary. It is this kind of certainty we should have to fall back on, if we could not decide for ourselves, from the very terms of a definition, whether it was meant to be infallible or not.

But a more serious point arises—the fact that only three or four decisions are recognized as infallible on this reckoning. Your comment is "Infallible decisions are so rare that they have had virtually no effect on the Church's teaching on faith or morals." I agree. After all, there are several organs of infallibility—the recognized General Councils, the unanimous consent of the Fathers, the ordinary magisterium (as it is called) of the Church. Thus there are very few subjects on which it would be possible for the Pope to make an infallible decision without covering ground which has already been covered by infallible pronouncements from other quarters. The Vatican decree was meant to decide a point of principle rather than to institute a practice. Otherwise, you would expect all the Popes since 1870 to have been making pronouncements with violent anathemas attached; we find the exact contrary. The main point is to assert the principle that the inerrancy which belongs to the Roman Church is independent, in theory, of the inerrancy which belongs to the Universal Church; that the truths which have been defined by General Councils would have been *de fide* none the less if in each case a Pope and not a Council had defined them.

About the "ruling decisions," I think I had better make a short answer which, if you challenge me, I will try to amplify. This letter is already too long. Your instances contain a sort of innuendo which really reopens questions we have already discussed about persecution, etc.; I will confine

myself to answering the argument in which you sum them
up. You ask how we can be certain that the present ruling
decisions of the Church on Biblical criticism, on divorce,
and on birth control may not later be altered, as the Church
has already altered her decisions on doubtful rites, on
Copernicus, on witchcraft, and on the right to persecute.
My answer is this—that it is easy to see at a glance when
these ruling decisions are simply reiterating what has been
the general tone of Catholic teaching in the past about points
in which theology is directly concerned. Birth prevention,
apart from its explicit condemnation in Scripture (Gen.
38:10), has always been treated as a mortal sin by theologians;
it is not a new idea; it was being propagated a century ago,
when Cobbett[46] wrote against it, and I fancy also two centuries ago. No new facts can come to light which could alter
the malice of the sin. It is therefore quite certain that the line
now taken up by the Holy Father is one which would be
reasserted in a formally *ex cathedra* pronouncement, if such a
pronouncement were required. The same is to be said of
divorce, with an even longer history behind it; there are one
or two "freak" references in medieval literature, but nobody
can doubt what the Church's mind has always been. Modern
pronouncements are in line with her past tradition, and the
idea of a change is out of the question. You can say the same
of her attitude towards the interpretation of the Bible in its
main outlines (which are, I think you will agree, sharply
distinguished from the modern Protestant attitude on the
subject); I do not think it is impossible that in matters of
detail teaching which is now suspect should receive recognition, because in this department it is always possible for new
facts to come to light.

[46] William Cobbett (1763?–1835), British journalist, champion of agrarian-
ism, and reformer. —ED.

This is what happened in Galileo's case: the congregations condemned his teaching while it was, in their view, still unproved; when satisfactory proofs were forthcoming, the opposition ceased. In the case of witchcraft, and in the matter of inflicting cruel punishments on heretics, official pronouncements asserted a policy which was in accordance with the notions of the time; there was Catholic tradition enshrined in them, in so far as they asserted the existence of diabolic powers or the Church's power in general to deal with heretics, but the application of those principles, which led to such regrettable results, depended, evidently, on the manners of an age. Nicholas I's reply[47] is not interpreted in your sense by our theologians (see the *Catholic Encyclopaedia*, under the word Baptism). Your quotation from Cardinal Perrone,[48] not being in any way a Papal document, does not really belong to this subject. The point is a very interesting one, and I have tried to deal with this in *The Belief of Catholics*. I hope this brief answer has made clear the line of distinction I wish to draw; if not, say so.

Yours ever,

R. A. Knox

In his next letter, Lunn asked Knox's "patience and consideration for a few private heresies on the nature of God".[49] He said he believed "that it is possible to prove the existence of God and the existence of a supernatural world", but he had

[47] Nicholas I (died 867) was sent 106 questions on Church teaching and disciplines by Prince Boris, ruler of the Bulgarians. The Pope answered exhaustively in "*Responsa Nicolai ad consulta Bulgarorum*". Response 104 noted that baptism by a Jew or a pagan is valid. —Ed.

[48] Giovanni Perrone (1794–1876), Jesuit theologian, for many years instructor at the Roman College. —Ed.

[49] Knox and Lunn, *Difficulties*, 132. —Ed.

"no compulsion to believe in an infinite, omnipotent, and omniscient deity". He cited the universal acknowledgment that not even an omnipotent God "could alter the past" or "make two and two equal five". Quoting Jacques Maritain, he brought up the fate of the Spanish Armada: "A most Catholic King, all Spain at prayer, the defence and promotion of God's cause in the world, the extirpation of heresy"—and yet the Armada was defeated.[50] He pointed to the problem of evil and the inadequacy of attempts to deal with the issue. Then came a consideration of the reconciliation of man's free will and God's omniscience. Knox replied, covering much other ground besides, and Lunn countered by enumerating twelve topics Knox addressed. Then came the following letter.

Sept. 8, 1931

Dear Lunn,

Thank you for your second letter on the free will and omniscience question. I just want to add a little, more by way of defining our respective positions than with any hope of making you alter yours. I am not philosopher enough, heaven knows, to help you over this time question. At least, I am not sure that even a philosopher could. Let me assure you at once that all the relativity talk is mere Hebrew to me; to tell me that time is a dimension of space enlightens me no more than if you told me that pink is a function of altruism. But that is probably because I am stupid; whereas the notion of timeless existence is one which neither I nor, I suppose, any other man can fully comprehend; any more than we can comprehend (say) the union of mind with matter in the composition of Man. There we are all in the same position as yourself; and

---

[50] Ibid., 136. —ED.

an existence outside space is an equal difficulty. We only
claim that it must be so, because time and space, although
they condition all our experience and all our imagination,
are not necessities of thought like the law of contradiction;
therefore they are part of God's Creation, and can have no
power to limit him. I am not trying to make time "subjec-
tive," any more than space, and I think you have misunder-
stood my allusion to the churchyard, which was meant to be
purely spatial; the bunkers on a golf course will illustrate my
point equally well.[51]

Before I proceed to discuss your numbered points, let me
answer one or two of your casual queries as best I can. The
saints in heaven are surely (somehow) in time, although, of
course, it is probable that time itself must *feel* very different
when it is experienced as endless.[52] But the timelessness of
God is not shared by his creatures. . . .[53] About suffering in
creation before the Fall I am only, of course, speculating. But
then, I do not think we really know the answer to the question
why animals suffer. Let me restate my suggestion in this way,
so as to lessen the difficulty about anticipatory punishment: it
may be that if God had been preparing the world for a
humanity which, he foresaw, would not fall, he would have
made it a more comfortable place for rabbits to live in. I do
not know. . . . The consequences of the Fall consist not so
much in the infliction of certain punishments as in the with-
drawal of certain privileges, which privileges were from the
first more than man had any strict right to expect. We are not

[51] Knox attempted to illustrate what it means to say that "God is outside of
time" by contrasting a sequential view of tombstones, as seen horizontally
from ground level, with an all-at-once view, as seen from a plane. Ibid.,
149. —ED.

[52] Knox refers here to aeviternity, the state of saints in heaven, which is to
be distinguished from eternity, God's state. —ED.

[53] This and the following ellipsis are in the original. —ED.

being punished for Adam's sin, but for a race-sinfulness common to him and us. Now for the numbered points.

1. I do *not* agree that God is limited. God is Pure Act, and has no passivity; I am not going to put him into the passive voice like that. Only that is "impossible" to him, and that not in the strict sense of the word, which contradicts his own Nature (which is himself). If the coexistence of foreknowledge and free will were a contradiction of his own nature, as being unthinkable, then it would be "impossible" for him to make them coexist. But that is not the issue between us at all. The issue is that you regard the coexistence of foreknowledge with free will as unthinkable; whereas I, quite apart from theology, find no sort of difficulty in thinking it, though any amount of difficulty in imagining it (a quite different thing), because I find it possible to think (though not to imagine) God outside time.

2. I do not admit that my criticism of your position, about prayer, is equally applicable to my own. According to you, prayer can only ask God to influence human wills, unless, indeed, it be a prayer for a miracle. For the course of events, apart from the effect human wills have on it, will, according to you, be already predetermined. So it is according to me; but I claim that, since God foresees our prayers, the course of events can be, and is, predetermined in view of those prayers. However, if you believe in a plurality of minor miracles (contrary to the scholastic canon that miracles are not to be multiplied unnecessarily), that, of course, justifies you in expecting an answer to most kinds of prayer. What about praying for fine weather, though?

3. I know.[54] And the strict Dominican would think you little, if at all, better than a Pelagian.

[54] In his letter of August 28, 1931, Knox wrote, "A strict Dominican would, I think, agree with you about the close connection between fore-

4. "Fact" is, of course, a bad word for my purpose, because by derivation it should mean something that has already happened. Let me say, then, that the future victory of Cambridge (or, let us hope, Oxford)[55] is a thing, and God knows all things. If he only knew possibilities as possibilities, he would be very much in the same position as ourselves.

5. I do not find anything in the quotation from Maritain,[56] as you give it, which suggests that God's Power is limited by external circumstances. But if it does he is wrong.

6. Phrases like "Grieve not the Holy Spirit of God" are regularly interpreted by the Church in a non-proper sense, just like phrases about God's right Hand, his Ear, etc. The sense is that we are troublesome to the Holy Spirit, not that the Third Person of the Blessed Trinity can experience unhappiness. Nor could the Second Person of the Blessed Trinity have done so, or do so, in his Divine Nature. He took a Human Nature upon him in order that he might be able to suffer. That is, largely, the point of the Incarnation. After his Resurrection, he has ceased to experience suffering in his Human Nature; and the rhetorical or pulpit phrases which

---

knowledge and predestination; only, whereas your argument is that God predestines events because he foresees them, the Dominican would say that he foresees them because he predestines them. He sees the future, such a philosopher would tell you, mirrored in his own Will." Knox and Lunn, *Difficulties*, 149. In his reply of September 4, 1931, Lunn remarked, as the third point in a list, "Your strict Dominican seems to me very little better than a Calvinist." Ibid., 164. —ED.

[55] In athletic events. —ED.

[56] In his August 23, 1931, letter, Lunn remarked that he had "been reading a little book, *Religion and Culture*, by that stimulating French Catholic, Jacques Maritain" (1882–1973). The passage concerned the fate of the Spanish Armada. If God had favored the "Catholic side" in history, why had he permitted the Armada to fail so disastrously? Lunn wondered whether Maritain was suggesting that this implied a limitation in God's power to mold history. Knox and Lunn, *Difficulties*, 136–37. —ED.

speak of him as sad, wounded, etc., must be referred back to the time of his Life on earth, when he did suffer for our sins, which he foresaw.

7. I do not agree with your phrase about difference in degree. The main issue between us, as I see it, is whether the non-interference of God at certain points in history is due to his unwillingness or to his inability to interfere. If the latter, then his power is circumscribed, and I cannot rest until I find out the nature of that superior Power which circumscribed it.

8. I think the difference between our points of view is here correctly stated. But you do not seem to me to have met my point, which is that the performance of miracles is, and is meant to be, an advertisement to us of the fact that God's Power is unlimited. In your last letter you seem more inclined to confine that limitation to the action of human wills; and here, of course, there is no question of God's showing his Power by a miracle, for even if he did miraculously override a human will we should not know that it was miraculous.

9. My argument is an *argumentum ad hominem*. You believe in eternity as an endless time-series, for God as for ourselves; therefore you must either think of Creation as having existed from all eternity (which is surely nonsense), or else think of it as having had an origin at a point in the time-series. In the latter event, you have to think of all the endless years before that point as a retrospective eternity during which God's existence was incomplete. Neither I nor any Catholic author would pretend to explain why the act of creation happened when it did; nor can you.

10. Of course the Incarnation was anthropomorphic; it consisted precisely in God taking upon him the *morphe* of an *anthropos*. Where I consider you anthropomorphic in your

view is that you attribute limitations to the Divine Nature itself. That God could suffer, grieve, etc., as Man, could, *as Man*, exist in time and suffer physical death, is the whole nerve of that mystery.

11. The kenotic theory claims that God suspended his own Powers when he became Man. I am not sure that on your theory he needed to. But I have no quarrel with your definition of the issue.

12. I admit that your god fulfils at least, *prima facie*, the conditions you want him to fulfil. That is just why I mistrust him; he is so suspiciously adequate. He looks to me like a super-Lunn, enlarged to scale. But I do not want to worship a super-Lunn, or a super-Knox. The great adventure of theology, to me, is that the Being who fulfils your conditions does more than that, escapes beyond the reach of our ambitions for him. Whether in natural theology or in revelation he is shown to be something more than a mere convenience for human thought: he dominates it and makes us reconsider all our values. That sense of human contact which you seem to find with God himself I find not in the Divine Nature as such, but in the Incarnate Christ.

I cannot at all agree with you or with William James[57] (though I suppose he was actually writing about determinism) that God's foreknowledge robs human life of its adventure and reduces it to the level of private theatricals, because I do believe in the real freedom of my will and in the power of my actions to affect the course of events. But I believe, as I say, that God, being outside time, can see that which has not yet happened in the time-series. I only feel a puppet in the sense that God could, if he liked, have picked on somebody else to do any job I have ever done or am ever likely to

[57] William James (1842–1910), American philosopher, psychologist, radical empiricist, and advocate of pragmatism. —ED.

do, and enabled him to do it ten times as well. Only he hasn't; so it is up to me.

Your final statement under this head modifies, I think, considerably all you have said hitherto. Because to say that God has "limited his own omnipotence . . . so that he does not override human wills," seems to me nothing other than an acceptance of my position, viz. that we must explain instances of his non-interference by saying that he does not wish to override human wills, not by saying that he has no power to. For, if God has "limited" his own power, then evidently he could, if he would, reverse that process and resume the power which he has laid aside. So that the one position comes to no more than the other. But to say that he has limited his own knowledge—Zeus turning away his eyes from the Lycian plain so as not to witness the death of Sarpedon[58]—is an idea which does not help me at all. For, if he has determined, by an act of will, not to know the future, that means that he could know the future if he wanted to. And that means that the future is knowable, which, on your showing, is a denial of human free will. I suppose you to mean, rather, that God has endowed one creature, man, with the power to act in an unpredictable manner; that, of course, gets us back where we were before.

Yours ever,

R. A. Knox

The correspondence, which had entered its fourteenth month, now drew to a close. Five days after Lunn composed his last letter, Knox wrapped up the discussion with a look at

---

[58] Sarpedon was the son of Zeus, by either Europa or Laodamia (sources differ), and was the King of Lycia during the Trojan War. He was killed at Troy by Patroclus, friend of Achilles. —ED.

authority.[59] Of particular note is his argument concerning religious experience ("I distrust the argument from experience, whether it appeals to one man's experience or to that of many"), something he would address at length two decades later in *Enthusiasm*.[60]

Oct. 5, 1931

Dear Lunn,

I travelled in the train the other day with a pertinaciously enquiring infant, the kind that wants to know what everything is "for". At Banbury, seeing the station clock, it asked what the time was; and here at last, it seemed, was a question that could be met with a conclusive answer. But no; on being told that it was ten minutes to two, the little brute said: "What's it ten minutes to two for?" I begin to think it must have been a relation of yours; whatever answer I try to make, you always start again. However, as this is to be final— definitely Paddington,[61] this time—I will try to make my answer short and clear-cut, leaving it to whoever will to judge between us.

I was not intending to criticize Protestant virtues, but all virtues; and more especially my own, if I am ever credited with any. The only psychology anybody can read, and that imperfectly, is, I claim, his own; and my own, as I say, makes me think all human virtues a pretty mixed grill, as far as motives are concerned. And I am not going to decide whether the average Catholic Mexican is what you call "a better man" than the average Protestant Englishman; I don't know. I know which I would rather take with me on a

---

[59] The last four paragraphs of this final letter have been omitted. —ED.
[60] Ronald Knox, *Enthusiasm* (Oxford: Oxford University Press, 1950). —ED.
[61] Paddington Station, in Westminster, the terminus of the rail line. —ED.

walking tour, but that is not the same thing. I prefer Englishmen to the natives of any other country in the world, but that is not going to do them much good, poor dears, at the Day of Judgment. Among other things, I think I agree that Englishmen on the whole do not tell lies. (I don't think they tell the truth, which is a very difficult thing to do; but their words do not often contradict their minds.) But I wonder how much of that came of being "top nation"?[62] Gilbert Frankau[63] wrote somewhere the other day that until the war you could take an Englishman's word in a business deal, now you can't; I don't know whether this is true. But, you see, even if you proved up to the hilt that nationality had more to say in determining a man's morals than religion, all you would have proved would be that ethnographical considerations are enormously important; and consequently that the effect of various religious beliefs on people's minds is more difficult to determine than ever, with ethnographical considerations constantly coming in to put one's reckoning out. No, to establish your point you would have to compare Catholic with Protestant inhabitants of a single country—your own Switzerland,[64] for example. Perhaps you would claim, like Harris in the *Tramp Abroad*, that "you would never see an untidy glacier like that in a Protestant canton."[65] For me, I am a stay-at-home; and the more I love my fellow-English, the more important do I find it to attempt their conversion.

[62] A term used to describe, facetiously, Britain's historical role as recounted in Sellar and Yeatman, *1066*. —ED.

[63] Gilbert Frankau (1884–1952), English novelist. —ED.

[64] Lunn spent winters at Mürren, Switzerland, where he founded the prestigious Kandahar Ski Club. —ED.

[65] The character Harris actually says, "You never see a speck of dirt on a Protestant glacier." Mark Twain, *A Tramp Abroad* (New York: The Heritage Press, 1966 [1880]), 251. —ED.

Surely the whole point of Mgr. Talbot's[66] dictum was that he was only familiar with a particular type of *English* Catholics, who devoted themselves to hunting, shooting, and entertaining, because, until quite recent memory, the laws of the country had not allowed them to do anything else. But such a criticism would have been impossible coming from a Continental ecclesiastic. But I must not linger over details; I will only deal with your last point—viz. that God ought to have made the claims of the Church as clear as the proofs of his own existence. Personally I think he has, the only difference being in the nature of the proof required. A metaphysical proof does not admit of degrees of probability; if it is valid at all, it makes a claim on the assent which cannot without insincerity be resisted. But the proof of the Church's claim is necessarily one in which historical considerations must play a part; and in an argument from history the best you can reach is a conviction which excludes all prudent doubt; apodeictic demonstration is impossible. You know, you have no idea how far-fetched the arguments against the Church appear to a Catholic! It is a matter of temperament, I suppose; but to me there is far more temptation not to believe in God than not to believe in the Church. For, as St. Thomas admitted, you have the whole fact of evil in Creation apparently against you, when you assert that God exists; and it is only because the proofs you have used are ungetawayablefrom (a pity there is no more technical word for this idea) that you resist the contrary suggestion. Whereas the arguments against the Church always seem to me scraped together; they are like the thousand and one holes which a disgruntled man will find to pick in the character of a man or an institution he has quarrelled with.

[66] Msgr. George Talbot (1816–1886) gave this definition of the duties of the laity: "to hunt, to shoot, to entertain". —Ed.

And now for your main point, about authority. I am in rather a difficulty here, because I don't believe in religious experience. And, if I proceed to attack it, shall I not be false to my own principle, expressed in my last letter but one, that I do not try to destroy the beliefs a man has on the off-chance that he will become a Catholic if I do? In this case, however, you have asked for it. Understand that it is I who speak, not the Church, when I say that to me all this modern talk about religious experience is cant; that is to say, when it is used for apologetic purposes. If a man professes to accept any religious doctrine only or chiefly on that ground, claiming that he or any other man has "verified" it by "experience," meaning that he has tried the experiment of behaving as if that doctrine were true, and has found some kind of spiritual satisfaction in so doing, I say that is cant, and mischievous cant. Cant, because he is transferring a certainty which he only feels about his own states of mind to a reality lying outside of, and corresponding to, those states of mind, which is a vicious process. It proves nothing. You know the old myth of Stesichorus,[67] that Helen never went to Troy at all, it was only a phantom that ran off with Paris? Consider how feeble a disproof it would be of that theory if we argued as follows: "What! Do you think it possible that Hector could have displayed that courage, that Ajax and Diomede should have performed such prodigies of endurance, that Achilles should have laid down his life, for the sake of a phantom?" The argument only proves that the notion of God as existing, the notion that the Catholic Church is divine, the notion that sins are forgiven by a loving trust in our Redeemer, the notion that the Sacred Elements are something more than Bread and Wine, have the power of stirring man's emotional

---

[67] Stesichorus (fl. c. 600 B.C.), Greek lyric poet. —ED.

being to its very depths; not that those notions have any
corresponding content in the world of objective existence.

And I have added "mischievous cant," because all this
psychological ramp of our time, which is just beginning to
be accepted by the man-in-the-street as if it were something
true, instead of the charlatanry it is, will make the "argument
from experience" look even less convincing than it really is.
Julian Huxley's book,[68] which you attacked and I have just
been attacking, derives all the appeal it has from this habit of
Christian apologists, who try to argue the existence of God
from the satisfactory feeling which religion gives them. That
is what I mean, largely, when I say that the Anglo-Catholic
movement is crawling with "modernism." The vice of modernism lies, not in this or that false statement, but in its
general attitude about belief. Catholic modernism claimed,
and modernism outside the Church implies (without putting
it sturdily into words, like Tyrrell),[69] that the defence of
Catholic tradition on historical grounds is useless; we ought
to accept the fact that a tradition may be historically false, yet
spiritually true. For example, I am told (I never saw the
article) that Goudge[70] laughed at Vernon Johnson[71] for writing as if the Apostles, even after the Ascension, realized that
our Lord was God. Now, if the Apostles didn't believe in our
Lord's Divinity, why on earth should I? That he was the

[68] A reference to Julian Huxley's *Religion Without Revelation* (New York:
Harper, 1927), which Knox critiqued in his *Broadcast Minds* (London: Sheed
and Ward, 1932). —ED.

[69] George Tyrrell (1861–1909), English Jesuit and a leading proponent of
modernism. —ED.

[70] Canon H. L. Goudge (1866–1939), coauthor, with W. R. Inge, of *Hebrews*
(London: Cassell, 1924). —ED.

[71] Msgr. Vernon Johnson, a long-time friend of Knox from their university days and, like Knox, a convert from Anglicanism. He served as chaplain
to the Catholic undergraduates of Oxford during and shortly after World
War II. —ED.

accredited Medium of a divine revelation, I believe on merely historical grounds; that he was personally God is a view upon which (at least) I could have no certainty, if it were not part of a continuous tradition handed down by the Apostles themselves. Yet Goudge is a leading and influential High Churchman.

You say, "The doctrines which Rome asks us to receive on her authority have no real bearing on conduct." You would not include among those, I take it, the doctrine of the Real Presence. Now, my belief in the Real Presence is founded on tradition. I believe that it is a view which has always been held in the Church; and it is of course guaranteed by words which I know to have been used by Christ, because the Church has preserved records of the occasion among her official "Scriptures." The only alternative process by which you can defend the doctrine against (say) the Bishop of Birmingham's[72] criticisms is the modernist process, now unhappily much in vogue. You appeal to Christian experience; you point out that multitudes of good people all through the centuries have received the Sacrament under the impression that it was the Body and Blood of Christ; that this belief has been the greatest possible support to them, and has had a salutary effect in their lives; further that they were often conscious, at the moment when they received the Sacrament, of extraordinary sweetness and consolation; their hearts burned within them. And you say "It is impossible that this experience should not have been real."

[72] Ernest William Barnes (1874–1953), clergyman and mathematician. He taught mathematics at Cambridge and in 1924 was appointed Anglican bishop of Birmingham. He was a proponent of theological modernism and wrote *Scientific Theory and Religion* (Cambridge: Cambridge University Press, 1933) and *The Rise of Christianity* (London: Longmans, Green, 1947). —ED.

Well, the experience was no doubt real, so far as this adjective can properly be applied to a mental experience. I think it would be difficult to deny reality, in the same sense, to the devotions of many estimable Buddhists. But, the fact behind the experience—the stimulus, so to say, which provoked it—how is anybody going to prove, from the experience itself, that that was real? At the very best, the doctrine of the Real Presence can only claim, on this understanding, to be a hypothesis which is not excluded by the facts; how are we to maintain that it is verified by the facts? The Bishop of Birmingham, in the paper not long ago, made it clear that he believes all right in the value of those "experiences" which pious persons have when they go to Communion. He believes in that; but he is not bound that I can see, to proceed beyond that, and assert that the Body and Blood of Christ are really present in the sacred Elements. All the worshipper can possibly be conscious of is a change which takes place in himself; he has no earthly right, that I could ever see, to infer from that a change in the Elements. He comes to Communion believing—because it is part of the tradition of his Church—that it is the Body and Blood of Christ he is to receive; and it is in response to that belief that he experiences what he experiences. But this only testifies to the existence of his belief, not to the existence of an objective fact corresponding with it.

In this sense, I think you might call most of the Anglican clergy "experientialists," if you prefer that term to "modernists"; and this applies, it seems to me, quite as much to the High Church ones as to the others. And I believe that it is deeply undermining their influence; though the High Church ones will, perhaps, be the last to feel it, because their churches are partly filled with people from all over the town who do not come from the parish, but "like the service" at

St. Enurchus'. On the other hand, I am not so cynical about ministers of religion as you seem to be; you write of "trial and error," "supply and demand," as if they had all gone modernist because they thought modernism was likely to catch on, and are prepared to go traditionalist again when they find that the experiment has not been justified by the turn-over! I do not believe that they are thus frankly experimentalists, though (as I told them long ago) I think the consideration "How much will Jones swallow?" weighs with them, unconsciously, more than they realize. No, I think they will go on appealing, as you suggest, to reason plus experience, or more likely to experience only (for they are frightened of metaphysics), and will more and more give up the appeal to tradition. And that will weaken the whole basis of their teaching, whose definiteness has, till now, been the chief source of their strength. But I may be prejudiced over this, owing to my own Anglican memories; perhaps I remind you of the strict Tories who are saying, "Ah, if we'd only listened to Joe Chamberlain[73] twenty years ago!" But I think I see there a decline which has not so far been arrested, whereas it seems to me that the Catholic Church goes on as ever, losing on the swings and gaining on the roundabouts.

As you say, it is the doctrinal authority of the Church against which you are kicking all the time. I do not agree with your implication that the doctrine of Hell reflects the fashion of an age now dead, because it seems to me that here the authority of our Lord himself is deeply imbedded in the Catholic tradition; and our Lord's own teaching (according to our claim) cannot have been coloured by the notions of his age. I think it probably is true that the modern Catholic preaches hell with less gusto than his predecessors. I am not

quite clear about your special objection to the word "torture"; to me, torture means the use of force to extract secrets
from an unwilling witness, which is here out of place. But I
think we have been over this ground sufficiently, as also over
the ground of indulgences in general. To your complaint
about the quantitative language in which the doctrine is
preached I should reply that we can only think of what lies
beyond the grave in terms of our experience in this world,
and remind you that when we speak of years, days, or
quarantines in this connection we only mean to indicate the
volume of punishment, however computed, which would
correspond to so many years, days, or quarantines of ecclesiastical penance under the discipline of the early Church. No
doubt it is unsatisfactory to think of merit as if it could be
measured in foot-pounds or kilowatts; but under what other
terms are we, with our present knowledge, to speak of these
things? Our Lord himself said, "Thou shalt not come out
thence till thou hast paid the last mite";[74] surely that is
"artless" enough?

At this point you have branched off in a fresh direction
(Banbury again!) by raising the whole question of Masses
for the dead. As you probably know, when you ask a priest
to offer Mass for a special intention it is etiquette to make
an offering of five shillings, which is supposed to be a
priest's living expenses for the day (hardly a Union wage!).
If you are poor, you give him three and sixpence. It is a
primitive, but not to my mind an ungracious device for
supporting the clergy, who have, in most parts of the world,
no endowments at all. He is strictly forbidden, if he is
saying two Masses, to take an offering for more than one;
the day's wage, you see. Often you ask him to pray for the

[74] Mt 5:26. —ED.

soul of a dead person. And people who want, before they die, to do something on a larger scale will sometimes endow a Mass in perpetuity; they make a permanent contribution to the support of the parish in return for a permanent remembrance. Are they really so much worse than the people who put up a parish hall and write their own names in big letters across the front? Of course, it is their duty before doing this to see that their relatives are provided for, if the relatives are in need and have deserved to be remembered in the will; that goes without saying. To you the whole thing sounds commercial, because the priest who says the Mass does not necessarily know the dead person. But the more you understand the communion of Saints and the efficacy of the Mass, the less you will be scandalized to hear that a Mass "intention" given in Liverpool has been handed on, perhaps, to some priest on an African mission, who gets no salary and no leaves home. You have to remember, too, that an enormous quantity of Masses are said for "the faithful departed" without distinction; and I suppose God sees to it that those who leave no rich relations behind them enjoy full benefit from these.

As for the "old Protestant charge" that priests persuade people on their death-beds to leave money for Masses, it is either so old or so Protestant that I do not remember ever to have heard it. If you will send me the name and parish of any priest who has done this thing I shall be happy to complain to his bishop. They might give us credit for not fooling all the people all the time; do they really think that if such behaviour as that were heard of more than once in a blue moon the priests would enjoy the respect that is paid to them? Of course, if a will is made on a death-bed (I wonder how many are, outside novels?), it is difficult to *prove* that there has been no undue influence from those present; of

course, among Catholics, the priest is one of these; of course
it is common for people who are near their end to want to
make some gift to religion; of course endowing a Mass, and
so helping the funds of the parish, is an easy way of doing it.
(In my experience, I should say Masses are more often
endowed by widows.) And you will get people saying that
there has been undue influence, more especially the disap-
pointed nephews. But have they a shadow of proof, when
they bring such a charge against the priesthood? In the long
run, one can only speak from experience. Let me say, then,
that I once heard a priest jokingly rebuke his parishioners
because nobody had asked for a Mass for his predecessor on
the anniversary of his death. "If you treat me like that," he
said, "I'll haunt you!" Apart from that, I have never heard of
a priest taking the initiative in suggesting that anybody should
pay for, still less endow, a Mass; though, of course, you will
hear them giving out in the Church notices, when November comes round, that there will be a box at the door for such
as want to.

Next to the question of eternal punishment, it is the
interpretation of the Bible that chiefly worries you. I have
said all I wanted to say about Old Testament atrocities. You
have brought in the story of Paradise rather at the last
moment; and it is not easy to deal with your objection in a
few lines. But surely, even if you find any grotesque elements
in the story, it is precisely *not* those elements which are
recapitulated in the reply of the Biblical Commission in
1906, except for the final words "in the form of a serpent."
To what extent those words are "operative" I would not like
to say; but I should have thought you ought to have been
gratified by the way in which the Commission insists on the
doctrinal aspects of the story, rather than the accessories—
ribs, fruit trees, fig leaves, flaming swords, etc. Beyond that I

will not add anything at this late stage; I do not see any likelihood of approaching an agreement.

Your notion of the Catholic Church as a House of Lords, to which Anglican traditionalists can appeal as a Court of Reference, but not as a Supreme Court, is admirably ingenious. I wish I had thought of it first. "Because, with all their faults, we love our House of Peers" [75]—how admirably that hits off the High Anglican attitude towards the Holy See! "The House of Lords throughout the war did nothing in particular"—the old complaint against Benedict XV! [76] If only the Church had been built as a lean-to against the Rock of Peter! But I am afraid (to alter the metaphor rousingly) that Peter's bark is like a punt on the river—all right to be in it, but to have one foot in it and the other on the bank is courting disaster. A man should not found some part of his faith upon an institution which, if it is true at all, is true altogether; it will give way under him. Oh, we are a convenience to the other Christianities, we Catholics; a lightning-conductor to draw the world's criticism away from them; a repository whose furniture they can reproduce without the worm-holes; a standard of theological currency, against which they can balance their rate of exchange. But, in the nature of things, we cannot accept the second-best positions you try to thrust upon us. Our whole witness is stultified if we are not to be the absolute thing we claim to be.

Of course, I think you are in a dilemma; I do not mean of logic, but of facts. You are trying, as you indicated in your last letter, to substitute "experience" for authority, a modern

---

[75] W. S. Gilbert, *The Pirates of Penzance* (1879), act II. The line actually reads, "because, with all our faults, we love our House of Peers". —Ed.

[76] Benedict XV (1854–1922) reigned during World War I, during which he kept the Vatican neutral and strenuously tried to promote peace. —Ed.

form of compensation; but, whereas it might help to salve
conscience if you wanted to find some reason for "staying
where you are," experience is a precious poor light for
anyone who is searching, as you are searching, for religious
truth. And what guidance it gives, for all I could ever see,
brings you straight up against the Catholic Church, whose
doors you find still closed to you. It is all very well to say that
Christians outside our communion have found peace or
consolation in the religion to which they are attached. But
the message which brought them peace or consolation is
something which is common to their system and ours, not
something which divides us. I know much has been said and
written to suggest that Protestantism differs from Catholicism over a positive, not over a negative issue because Protestantism stands for an immediate approach of the soul to God.
But the word "immediate," in itself, is a concealed negation;
nor has it ever been true to say that the Catholic Church
discouraged souls from seeking a direct approach to God,
though doubtless at some times, in some countries, a prevailing laxity of spiritual tone among Catholics has made such an
approach difficult. The argument from experience, therefore, for what it is worth (as I say, I do not think it worth
much), tells in our favour, not against us. For it asserts the
value of the Catholic religion under one aspect, its mystical
aspect; it attacks the claims of a merely "commonsense"
religion such as the eighteenth century loved. Which is why
the eighteenth century, as you know, condemned Wesley-
anism as a kind of approach to Catholicism, and was prepared
to believe that two Wesleyan preachers at Brighton (I think it
was) were Jesuits in disguise.

On the other hand, as you yourself admit, modern symp-
toms suggest that Protestantism does not come well out of
the "trial and error" test. There seems to be, somehow, a law

of diminishing returns about its spiritual energy. At the moment, as you say, it is rather the High Church movement, in England and certain of the Dominions, which seems to be justified by its success. Here that success, such as it is, is plainly due to its insistence on a quite different aspect of the Catholic religion, its institutional aspect. And here, even more obviously, what is attractive about a movement outside the Church is something in which it resembles (not to say "which it borrowed from") the Church. You know how the more fatuous kind of animal lover will tell you that she thinks she really prefers her dog to human beings, because it is so intelligent about opening doors and what not. Wherein she gives herself away; she ought to ground her preference on the dog's power of smell, in which it excels man; instead, she trumpets its relative achievements in a department where man is superior. In something the same way, what men admire about the other Christianities is always something for which, if they would take a longer view, their admiration should rather be attracted towards the Church herself.

Personally, I repeat, I distrust all these arguments. I distrust the argument from experience, whether it appeals to one man's experience or to that of many; mass hallucination is as easily understandable as private hallucination. And I distrust the argument from trial and error; here is religion collapsing in Spain, and it may collapse elsewhere to-morrow; but I hope I have faith enough to be superior to such accidents of time, and if necessary to "go and die with Odin." [77] But you, if these processes of argument mean so much to you, will surely come to admire more and more the history of a Church which has so often righted herself after repeated failures; has thriven in such varied soils, whether of country

[77] Robert Louis Stevenson, *Fables* (New York: Scribner's, 1914), XVII, "Faith, Half Faith and No Faith at All". —Ed.

or of century; has inspired such heroic obedience and survived such lamentable betrayals. But all that will get you no
further as long as you are a stranger to that inner principle, a
principle of authority, which organizes her. The wave of
experience will always dash you up against the rock of
authority, which dashes you back to seek refuge in experience again; "he that wavereth is like a wave of the sea, driven
with the wind and tossed." [78] There have been people—
Mallock[79] is the obvious instance—whose admiration for the
Church seemed to kill in them all appreciation of other
religious approaches, yet who never, at least till death was
upon them, found their way in. I would not have you
undergo that agony of the soul; this, I suppose, is to be a
propagandist.

Yours ever,

R. A. Knox

---

[78] James 1:6. —ED.

[79] William Hurrell Mallock (1848–1923). His *New Republic*, in which a
debate occurs in the setting of a party at a country house, was Knox's
"favourite work of secular literature outside the Classics", according to
Evelyn Waugh in *Monsignor Ronald Knox*, 188. Knox envisioned using a
setting like Mallock's for a never-completed work of apologetics. —ED.

5

Arnold Lunn vs. C. E. M. Joad

Ten days after concluding his exchange with Ronald Knox, Arnold Lunn began an exchange with J. B. S. Haldane, who, after receiving Lunn's second letter, fell unexpectedly—and, for Lunn, exasperatingly—quiet. It would take nine months for Haldane to post his reply, and their correspondence would end up requiring a full three years, compared to fifteen months for the letters that comprise *Difficulties*. Apparently sensing that Haldane would not be replying soon, Lunn accepted C. E. M. Joad's invitation to debate. Their exchange concluded in eight months (by which time Haldane had just sent his third letter to Lunn) and was published in 1933 as *Is Christianity True?* [1]

Like Lunn, Cyril Joad (1891–1953) attended Balliol College, Oxford, which he entered in 1910, where he was three years Lunn's junior. After graduation Joad joined the staff of what later would be named the Ministry of Labour. For a decade and a half he worked as a civil servant and, like not a few civil servants of the time, issued a steady stream of books. In 1930 he was named head of the department of philosophy at Birkbeck College, University of

[1] Arnold Lunn and C. E. M. Joad, *Is Christianity True?* (Philadelphia: Lippincott, 1933). —ED.

London, and he held that appointment until his death. Again like Lunn, Joad had a deep appreciation of the outdoors, and for years he guided climbing expeditions and lent his support to efforts to preserve the English countryside. During World War II he became known to a wider public through his BBC broadcasts. At one point *Punch* carried a cartoon that depicted Joad remarking to a waiter, "It all depends on what you mean by (a) thick and (b) clear", a line not unlike those favored by some American politicians six decades later.

In 1948 Joad's reputation took a nosedive when he was convicted of riding a train without a ticket. That year saw the publication of his book *Decadence*, a complaint that modern philosophical trends had eviscerated the idea of the objectivity of value in morals, ethics, art, epistemology, and political philosophy. Joad "passed through change and development in his views, from pacifism to the belief that some evils must be combated by force, from agnosticism to Christianity".[2] He died a communicant of the Church of England, but, at the time of his exchange with Lunn, he styled himself an unbeliever.

Joad challenged Lunn to debate, in written form, the merits and demerits of Christianity, and Lunn indicated his acceptance in the following letter. He begins with considerable praise for his opponent. "You give and take hard blows, as I have reason to know, with imperturbable good-humour." The fourth paragraph of this letter perhaps came to Lunn's mind fourteen years later, when he began a similar exchange with the curmudgeonly G. G. Coulton, their letters being published as *Is the Catholic Church Anti-Social?*[3] Lunn likely

---

[2] *The Dictionary of National Biography*, suppl. 1951–1960, 547. —Ed.

[3] G. G. Coulton and Arnold Lunn, *Is the Catholic Church Anti-Social?* (London: Burns and Oates, 1946). —Ed.

wished that Coulton had been as agreeable a controversialist as had Joad.

One might expect that Joad the philosopher would be more likely than Lunn the nonphilosopher to be precise in his terminology and rigorous in his logic, but Lunn straight-away—after the initial compliments—takes Joad to task for falling down on both counts, at least when it comes to religion. "In your philosophical work, you are at great pains to think out things for yourself, and your work is, in conse-quence, interesting and original. But any stick is good enough for Christianity." Later in their exchange, on August 19, Lunn would say, "My chief complaint is that your atti-tude toward the Church is lacking in chivalry and generosity. You have never made the least effort to master even in outline the history of the Church or to approach with sympathetic understanding the problems with which the Church has been confronted."[4] Lunn again expressed his exasperation on October 11: "Most of the authors which you mention . . . are on my shelves. I have read both sides, whereas you have spent a few days desperately 'mugging up' the anti-Christian case."[5] Despite these remonstrances, Joad seemed unperturbed. Since Lunn had opened the exchange, Joad closed it, saying, "Now for the bouquets! First of all, I have enjoyed it. We are both of us controversial animals, and I, at least, have had a good many controversies in my time, but never one that I have enjoyed so thoroughly."[6] Then he concluded his letter with more prescience than he could have known: "I may one day come to share your present convic-tions, as I apparently now share your past doubts."[7]

[4] Lunn and Joad, *Is Christianity True?* 259. —ED.
[5] Ibid., 315. —ED.
[6] Ibid., 377. —ED.
[7] Ibid., 380. —ED.

18th March, 1932

Dear Joad,

I accept your challenge to discuss Christianity in a series of letters in spite of the fact that I am supposed to be engaged on a book, somewhat similar in scope, with J. B. S. Haldane. Haldane, however, has only written one letter in the last six months, and I am beginning to suspect that he will appear before his Maker before I have succeeded in convincing him that his Maker exists. I have written to him to say that I am accepting your challenge on the understanding that we confine ourselves to Christianity in particular, rather than to the alleged conflict between science and supernaturalism which is to be the theme of my letters with Haldane if those letters are ever written.

I suggest that you and I should divide our correspondence into two parts, in the first of which you might perhaps explain why you are not a Christian, and in the second of which I explain why I am.

I accept your challenge with great pleasure.

In the first place, though we differ on fundamental issues, we are not personally antipathetic. When we first discussed this book you said that you would never agree to exchange controversial letters over a period of months with a man whom you disliked. Nor should I; and I feel that the ritualistic handshake which we shall exchange before we start hammering away at each other is not purely formal. We have certain tastes in common; the reproductions of Italian and Dutch primitives which hang round your library reassured me when I first called on you. There is always hope for a man, however perverse his views, who prefers Van Eyck[8] to the post-impressionists.

---

[8] Hubert van Eyck (1370–1426), Flemish painter. —ED.

Secondly, you are a good controversialist, with whom it will be a pleasure to cross swords. I admired your handling of Mr. Cohen[9] in your debate with that sturdy survivor of Victorian materialism. And you are not only an expert, but also a good-tempered controversialist. You give and take hard blows, as I have good reason to know, with imperturbable good-humour. It should be as easy for a controversialist to keep his temper when the argument runs against him as for a chess-player to avoid hurling the board on to the floor when mate is threatened; and good-humoured controversialists are rare. Nothing is more cramping to controversy than a sensitive opponent who construes as personal a purely impersonal attack on the arguments which he has advanced. It is a relief to feel that you and I prefer to dispense with the buttons on our foils.

In the third place, I welcome this correspondence because I admire your philosophical writings, which are lucid and well expressed.

In the fourth place, I welcome this correspondence because I do not in the least admire your religious writings, which are confused, badly expressed and plagiaristic. There is evidence of hard thinking in every line that you write on philosophy, but you give your brain a rest when you turn to the uncongenial subject of Christianity. You may console yourself, however, with the reflection that in this respect you are not unique. In your attitude towards Christianity, you are a child of your age, an age which has decided that all standards of sober criticism may be suspended when Christianity is in the dock. H. G. Wells,[10]

---

[9] Morris Raphael Cohen (1880–1947), American philosopher and educator, professor at City College of New York and author of *Reason and Nature* (New York: Harcourt Brace, 1931). —ED.

[10] H. G. Wells (1866–1946), author of novels such as *The Time Machine* (London: Heinemann, 1895), *The Invisible Man* (London: Pearson, 1897), and

Huxley[11] and many another modern prophet display in their attitude to the greatest of all problems the same distressing blend of glib assurance and ignorance. In due course I must try to diagnose the malady, but first I must convince you that you yourself are suffering from this modern complaint. My examples are all taken from your book, *The Present and Future of Religion*.[12]

You are the head of a Department of Philosophy in London University College, and I am sure that you do your best to inculcate in your students a respect for the rules which should govern all philosophic enquiry in a debate. I am convinced that you would deal faithfully with one of your pupils who based an attack on, say, Plato, on a trite misquotation from his works. Now of all trite misquotations, none is more trite than the vulgar variation of the Catechism which is so popular with people who are anxious to prove that the Church has consistently struggled to keep the underdog under. Unfortunately for the purposes of this argument the Catechism does not, as you suggest, invite the catechist to "be content with that state of life unto which it

---

The War of the Worlds (London: Heinemann, 1898). His *Outline of History* (London: Newnes, 1920) was wildly popular but so laced with anti-Catholic sentiment that Hilaire Belloc became a long-time adversary. Near the end of his life Wells wrote a virulently anti-Catholic book, *Crux Ansata* (New York: Agora Publishing, 1944), that urged the Allies to bomb Rome and thus rid the world of Catholicism. —ED.

[11] Julian Huxley (1887–1975), grandson of Thomas Huxley (1825–1895) and brother of Aldous Huxley (1894–1963), taught at Oxford and King's College, London, and served as the director general of UNESCO (1946–1948). Among his books were *Religion without Revelation* (1927), *Evolution: The Modern Synthesis* (New York: Harper, 1942), and, with H. G. Wells and G. P. Wells, *The Science of Life* (Garden City, N.Y.: Doubleday, Doran, 1931). —ED.

[12] C. E. M. Joad, *The Present and Future of Religion* (New York: Macmillan, 1930). —ED.

Compare with Vattimo & Rorty, *Future of Religion* ('06?)

has," but to do his duty (a very different matter) in that state
of life "unto which it *shall* please God to call me."

Even more surprising is your misuse of the word "substance" in your allusions to the doctrine of transubstantiation,
for in this connection it is clearly incorrect to use the word
"substance" in its vulgar rather than in its philosophical sense.
"Substance" in philosophy means, as you must know, the exact
opposite to the "substance" of vulgar speech. The "substance"
of ordinary speech corresponds to the "accidents" of philosophic discussion. The accidents of bread are its weight, shape,
taste, smell, etc. The accidents can be detected by the five
senses; the substance which underlies phenomena cannot.
Catholics believe that the substance of a consecrated wafer is
transformed into the substance of Our Lord's Body, and as
transubstantiation is not a chemical process, you have no reason
valiantly to proclaim that "we no longer hold the chemical
theory that bread, water and other objects can be changed into
substances of a different order by special processes."

I hope that when you have read this letter *you* will no
longer hold that anybody ever held such views. "An eminent
English bishop," you write, "recently issued a challenge to all
and sundry to distinguish by tasting, touching, smelling,
reducing to their ultimate chemical constituents, or subject-
ing to any other test, any difference between a consecrated
and an unconsecrated wafer. The authorities of the Church
did not take up the challenge." [13]

Of course not. It is not the duty of the Church to accept
challenges from people who have not taken the trouble to
discover the point at issue.

You are entitled to attack with vigour the doctrine of
transubstantiation, but I suggest that it is an offence against

[13] Ibid., 24. —ED.

the amenities of scholarly controversy to caricature a belief which has been held and is still held by many millions of men, among whom some few at least are not inferior to yourself in intellectual attainment. Such a travesty of a central doctrine of Catholicism makes it difficult even for those who are most charitable to attribute to your printer rather than to yourself the responsibility for the confusion between the Aryans and Arians, but perhaps it is unreasonable to expect a writer who regards all Christian dogma as absurd to waste much time in sorting out Arius the heresiarch from the Aryan race.

All you modern critics of Christianity seem to suffer from thought-shyness the moment you begin to discuss this subject. J. B. S. Haldane, for instance, is a man of outstanding intellectual gifts, and yet in all good faith he puts this sort of thing on to paper: "The old religions are full of outworn science, including the astronomical theory of a solid heaven, the chemical theory that water, bread, books and other objects can be rendered holy by special processes, and the physiological theory that a substance called the soul leaves the body at the moment of death."[14]

It is science, not Christianity, which is full of outworn science. The solidity of heaven is not a belief imposed on Christians of any denomination; and it would be easier to deal with the concluding paragraph if Haldane would define precisely what he means by "a substance called the soul."

You were apparently struck by these remarks of Haldane, for you reproduced them, almost unchanged and without quotation marks, in your book. "We no longer hold," you write, "the biological theory of man as a special creation, the astronomical theory of a solid heaven and a fixed earth, the

[14] J. B. S. Haldane, *Possible Worlds* (London: Chatto and Windus, 1928), 236. —ED.

chemical theory that bread, water and other objects can be changed into substances of a different order by special processes, or the physiological theory that a substance called the soul leaves the body at death." [15]

Lord Iddesleigh, [16] a Roman Catholic, challenged you in the *Evening Standard* to give the name of any priest who taught the doctrine of "a solid Heaven and a fixed earth." You replied by quoting from the Psalms, "Who laid the foundations of the earth that it should not be removed for ever." And the reply pleased you so much that you have repeated it in your book.

There is such a thing as poetry, and even the most ardent of Bible Christians does not maintain that the planets indulge in community singing because the Bible says that "the morning stars sang together." [17]

One of these days you must really read St. Thomas Aquinas, if only to discover that many centuries ago St. Thomas laid down certain rules for the interpretation of the Bible which, had you followed them, would have saved you from accusing the Psalmist of teaching that the foundations of the earth were irremovable. "When Scripture speaks," wrote St. Thomas, "of God's Arm, the literal sense is not that God has such a member, but only what he signifies by this member, namely, operative power . . ." It is perhaps hardly polite to continue the quotation, "The very hiding of truth in figures is useful for the exercise of thoughtful minds, and as a defence against the ridicule of the impious, according to the words, 'Give not that which is holy to dogs.'" [18]

---

[15] Joad, *Present and Future*, 56–57. —ED.

[16] Henry Stafford Northcote (1901–1970), third Earl of Iddesleigh and brother of Arnold Lunn's first wife, Mabel Northcote (died 1959). —ED.

[17] Job 38:7. —ED.

[18] Thomas Aquinas, *Summa Theologiae*, pt. I, q. 1, art. 10. —ED.

My complaint against you, Mr. Wells and Professor Julian Huxley, is that you are all so unscientific in your attitude to Christianity. It is unscientific to criticise a document without reading it; it is unscientific to bludgeon your opponent with unsupported assertions and unsubstantiated charges. All of you repeat, like a lesson learnt by rote at your mother's knee, the old, stale, stupid charge that the dogmas of the Church are at variance with science. None of you has ever deigned to give chapter and verse to this accusation. The Roman Catholic Church is usually represented as the most hostile to science of all churches, and the most reactionary. I therefore offer you these alternatives. Either name a doctrine, *de fide* for Roman Catholics, which is at variance with the proven results of scientific research, or admit that you have made charges which you cannot substantiate.

When I read the modern prophets I am impressed by their habit of passing on undocumented sneers and unsubstantiated criticism. There is a painful lack of originality about their attacks on Christianity. In your philosophical work, you are at great pains to think out things for yourself, and your work is, in consequence, interesting and original. But any stick is good enough for Christianity. The same feeble, brittle twig is passed along from hand to hand in order to save yourselves the trouble of cutting yet another decaying branch from the decaying tree. A short time ago I read, from the pen of a writer whose literary criticism is both original and brilliant, the following passage which appeared in one of those religious symposiums with which the Press favour us from time to time: "Ecclesiastics who talk about the Virgin Birth are as absurd as persons would be who, having been visited by the wisest man in the world, stopped repeating his wisdom to an audience longing to hear it and wrangled whether he had travelled to their home by a bus or a tramcar."

I was less impressed by this passage than you seem to have been, to judge from the following passage in your book: "We are regaled with disputes about the Virgin Birth. The earth, we are given to understand, was visited some two thousand years ago by a man whose wisdom was so pre-eminent that it has seemed to many to partake of the divine. The Church, it is to be presumed, is the inheritor of that wisdom, or, if not its inheritor, at least its trustee. Reverently approaching, we ask that the teaching of this great visitor to our planet should be interpreted for us in the light of the needs of our times. And his trustees meet our request with a profound discourse upon how the distinguished personage travelled to visit us!" [19]

If this planet was visited by a Martian, the first question we should ask would be how he travelled here, and I cannot see why it should be considered unreasonable for those who believe that God visited this planet to show some interest in the manner of his arrival. Be that as it may, if you want to make merry at the expense of those who attach importance to the Church's teaching on the subject of the Virgin Birth, you might at least state their views correctly. Orthodox Christians do not regard Christ as "a man whose wisdom was so pre-eminent that it has seemed to many to partake of the divine." If they did, they would not believe in the Virgin Birth. They worship Jesus as God—a very different matter.

I am convinced that if, instead of repeating silly remarks, which have already been made once too often before you reproduced them, you had taken the trouble to think out an alternative to orthodox teaching on this subject, you would have realised that whether Christ was or was not born of a Virgin, the orthodox Christian cannot be blamed for taking this question seriously.

[19] Joad, *Present and Future*, 45. —ED.

For what are the alternatives? The early enemies of Christianity circulated a foul lie to the effect that Mary was the paramour of a Roman soldier, and that Jesus was their son; nor can Christians be expected to welcome as an alternative the theory that myth and legend are embedded in the Gospel record. Those who believe that the Gospels are good history cannot regard any attack on their historical accuracy with indifference. The clerical wrangles, over which you make merry, are certainly no less significant, and are concerned with far graver issues, than those wrangles between rival philosophers which you find so interesting.

You have, I am sure, read Mr. Wells's delightful fantasy, *The Time Machine.* I should like to book a ticket for Mr. Wells himself to the thirteenth century. If only our modern prophets could spend a term at the mediaeval university of Paris, their religious writings would gain in clarity and in logic. They would certainly learn that an *ipse dixit* is no adequate substitute for an argument, nor assertion for proof, nor metaphor for thought.

"Scholasticism," as Professor Whitehead,[20] whose authority as a scientific writer is undisputed, tells us, "inculcated one valuable habit which remained long after scholastic philosophy had been repudiated—the priceless habit of looking for an exact point and sticking to that point when one found it. The Middle Ages formed one long training of the intellect of Europe in the sense of order." The ineffectiveness of the commercial travellers in modern religions is due to the fact that they are under contract not to travel theism, and are consequently compelled to supply a synthetic substitute for God. "I'm sorry, ma'am," one can imagine them

[20] Alfred North Whitehead (1861–1947), British philosopher and mathematician. With Bertrand Russell he wrote *Principia Mathematica* (1910–1913). —ED.

saying; "I can't supply you with 'God.' We don't touch those old-fashioned lines, but here's an up-to-date article guaranteed to produce the same result. We call it 'Life.' . . . Oh no, ma'am, not the common sort of life which was handed out to you when you were born, but something much more superior." And they would then proceed to read the write-up of "Life," which will be found on page 190 of your book:

> Life, then, I think of as an instinctive thrust or urge appear-ing initially in an alien environment, a dead world of chaos and blankness and matter. Life is purposive, but its purpose is at first latent, and only rises into consciousness in the course of life's evolution and development. Life evolves and devel-ops by infusing itself into the material universe. . . . In the course of its development life achieves the faculty of con-sciousness, and comes at last to a knowledge of the fact, and a glimmering of the purpose, of its evolution.

I am not clear what we have gained by dropping the word "God," which has a clear-cut meaning, and substituting the word "Life," to which you attach a private meaning of your own. St. Thomas Aquinas began, in his old-fashioned way with an axiom that nobody could dispute, the axiom that "it is certain and obvious to our senses that some things are in motion," [21] and proceeded by a series of syllogisms to deduce the existence of a personal God. You begin, not with an axiom which nobody could dispute, but with a series of wildly improbable dogmatic assertions. St. Thomas never failed to put himself in the place of an intelligent and enquiring reader; he never wrote a paragraph without asking himself what possible objection could be raised against the conclusion which he supported, or what question might be

---

[21] *Summa Theologiae*, pt. I, q. 2, art. 3. —ED.

asked by a critical reader. The paragraph I have quoted from your work is full of unanswered questions:

1. How would you define "life"? How did "life" originate?
2. How did "life" acquire an "instinctive thrust or urge"?
3. What do you mean in this connection by (a) "instinctive," and (b) "thrust"?
4. Whence did "life" obtain the motive power to "thrust"?
5. What do you mean by describing "life" as "purposive"?
6. How did "life" acquire purpose?
7. How does "life" rise into consciousness?
8. How is "life" related to personality, and how is your individual life related to "life"?
9. You say that "life" "gradually comes to a glimmering of the purpose of its evolution." Has "its evolution" a purpose, and whence came this purpose?

   This sort of thing, my dear Joad, imposes a greater strain on our credulity than the first chapter of Genesis.

   St. Thomas Aquinas, who lived in an age which believed in reason, offered severe proof for every statement in his vast array of works. We, who live in an age of faith, must be less exacting. We must take "Life" on trust; we must ask no questions; we must not seek to escape from the vague hinterland of metaphor into the clear light of thought; we must believe implicitly in the illumination granted by "life" to its interpreter, Mr. Joad.

   It has just occurred to me that one or two of my remarks might be misconstrued as aggressive, and this would be a pity, for it is precisely because I respect the high quality of your best work that I am forced, more in sorrow than in anger, to complain bitterly of your attitude to Christianity. When we first met—before the possibility of this correspondence had been broached—I suggested that we might arrange a public debate on the evidence for the Resurrection, and you replied that you had not enough time "to mug up the evidence." Now the Resurrection, if it occurred, was the most important event in the history of our planet, and while it seems strange to me that a distinguished philosopher such as yourself should never have found time "to mug up the evidence" for or against the Resurrection, it seems even stranger that you should have devoted so much of your time, in the Press and elsewhere, to condemning Christianity, whose credentials you have never examined. A distinguished Jesuit once remarked to me that he would approach the study of Buddhism, or indeed of any other religion, with vastly more reverence than you moderns vouch to Christianity. Life is clearly too short to examine the case for every creed, but there is something to be said for making a rule never to refer with contempt to any religion unless one has made an effort to investigate its claims. I happen, for instance, to regard Calvinism with contempt, but I refrained from expressing any opinion on this subject until I had taken the trouble to read Calvin's *Institutes*. And if even Calvinism should not be condemned unheard, surely the great religion of which Calvinism is an evil perversion deserves a more courteous hearing than it receives from our modern prophets. Here is a religion which has transformed the face of Europe and revolutionised the fabric of society, a religion which has profoundly affected every aspect of human activity from law to architecture. Surely it should be regarded as an integral part of a liberal education to master, at least in outline, the philosophy, history and ethics of a religion which was accepted for centuries without question by the civilised world. It is a sin against culture to ignore Christianity; and it is an offence against good breeding to adopt an attitude of contemptuous superiority towards any creed which still commands the adherence of men of undisputed intellectual attainments.

And is it not passing strange that writers who are too idle to study Christianity, and too unchivalrous to refrain from travestying a faith which has evoked such tremendous loyalties from men of every race and of every class, should never suspect that they may perhaps have missed some clue to the secret of this ancient spell?

Unfortunately, the modern world is becoming more and more thought-shy on the subject of Christianity. The mental fashion of the age prevents most people from approaching this problem with an open mind. It is an attitude of mind which recurs from age to age, for Christianity (like Charles II)[22] is an unconscionably long time in dying and (unlike Charles II) is still alive.

Our moderns are not the first to be deceived in their diagnosis of this perverse patient. "It is come, I know not how, to be taken for granted, by many persons," wrote the greatest of eighteenth-century bishops, Bishop Butler,[23] "that Christianity is not so much a subject for enquiry; but that it is, now at length, discovered to be fictitious. And accordingly they treat it as if, in the present age, this were an agreed point among all persons of discernment; and nothing remained but to set it up as a principal subject of mirth and ridicule, as it

---

[22] Charles II (1630–1685), a pleasure-loving and immoral monarch, deposed by Oliver Cromwell and then restored to the throne in 1660. —ED.

[23] Joseph Butler (1692–1752), appointed bishop of Bristol in 1738, dean of Saint Paul's in 1740, bishop of Durham in 1750. Author of *The Analogy of Religion* (London: Knapton, 1736). —ED.

were by way of reprisals, for its having so long interrupted the pleasures of the world."

I do not suggest that you are ambitious to set up Christianity as a subject for "mirth and ridicule." There are passages in your book which suggest a considerable sympathy with its aesthetic appeal and for its mystical aspects. I do not think you would have challenged me to defend Christianity unless you had begun to suspect that some sort of a case could be established for this obstinate invalid, which has refused to succumb to the displeasure of H. G. Wells, to the disapproval of Julian Huxley, and to the genial contempt of Bertrand Russell. *Equivalents today are Dawkins, Dennett, Harris + Hitchens*

And perhaps in your heart of hearts you will agree that a man writes himself down as a hopeless Philistine if he speaks with ignorant contempt of the faith which produced St. Francis, which inspired Dante, and which found expression in the canvases of Bellini[24] and in the stones of Venice. Even if I believed Christianity to be a myth, I should still salute with melancholy respect the superstition which had inspired such supreme artists in song, in paint and in stone, and should still find it difficult to understand how a mere superstition could take form in so noble a synthesis of spiritual and secular beauty. In the course of this correspondence we shall no doubt hear a great deal about the crimes of Christianity. I will not try to anticipate your attack, but I suggest that you cannot in common decency damn Christianity for the Inquisition without thanking Christianity for Chartres.

Yours ever,

Arnold Lunn

[24] Giovanni Bellini (c. 1430–1516), leading painter of the Venetian school and master of Titian, known especially for his altarpieces and many madonnas. In his later years he became a master landscape artist. —Ed.

In his letter of May 27, 1932, his fourth contribution to the exchange, Joad broaches the problem of suffering and the idea, common among intelligent sceptics, that God was created by man, not man by God. He notes that he is "bidden to accept all manner of things on the authority of revelation, provided that my reason tells me that the revealing authority is to be trusted, and it must tell me this, so the argument runs, if there is a well-disposed Deity who is responsible for the world, if Christ is His son, and if Christ established a Church. Everything then turns upon the question whether is it reasonable to believe that there is a well-disposed deity who is responsible for the world, and to this question I now address myself." [25]

Joad's argument against the existence of God is based on the state of animals, that "to be hungry or to be hunted is the universal lot of living creatures. Not, one would have thought, a pleasant pair of alternatives, nor, if we must suppose that the arrangement was devised, reflecting particular credit on its author." [26] He concludes that, to escape this reality, primitive man assigned gods, some benevolent and some malevolent, to places and to natural powers and events, and "in the course of time the multitudinous deities of the savage world are unified into a single personage, and Jehovah appears upon the scene." [27] Christianity represents the highest, or at least latest, advance on this. "Promising the poor man divine compensation in the next world for the champagne and cigars he is missing in this one, it helps him to do without the champagne and cigars; it even helps him not to envy those who have them, by assuring him that they will come to a bad end hereafter—the camel–needle business

[25] Lunn and Joad, *Is Christianity True?* 65. —Ed.
[26] Ibid., 64. —Ed.
[27] Ibid., 66. —Ed.

again—and admonishing him that, whether they do or not, luxury is a sin anyway." [28]

The arguments in this letter are representative of the arguments Joad uses throughout the correspondence. A believer is momentarily thrown off by his observations, only to realize, with Lunn's prompting, that Joad has permitted himself to descend from the philosopher's chair and to become satisfied with arguments one is likely to hear during late-night discussions in college dormitories. Lunn does not let him get away with it.

June 2nd, 1932

Dear Joad,

The first part of your letter adds nothing to your argument. The whole problem of evil is raised by the existence of one small child suffering severe pain, and you do not strengthen your case, which has already been discussed at considerable length, by the rhetorical device of piling up example after example. You are like the people whose faith was shaken by the Great War, but who had apparently contrived to reconcile the existence of God with every other war from the dawn of history up to and including the South African War. "God can get away with a lot of things," your argument seems to imply; "children smitten by incurable diseases, the agonies of battlefields, plague and volcanic eruption, but when it comes to the Ichneumonidae [29]—well, that's a bit too steep. God can't get away with them."

Dillard succumbs to a similar kind of argu. in her book on Religion

---

[28] Ibid., 73. —Ed.

[29] Joad describes the ichneumonidae as wasps "which sting their caterpillar prey in such a way as to paralyse their movements without killing them. The next step is to lay eggs in the body of the caterpillar, whose warmth in due course hatches out the young larvae. These immediately begin to feed on

There are two problems which must be kept distinct, the existence of God and the nature of God. Your jolly little wasps do not, as you yourself admit, invalidate the argument from design to a designer. Indeed, you admit the presence of design, but suggest that "it can scarcely be said to be very creditable to the author."

I wonder, by the way, how an orthodox Darwinian would explain the Ichneumonidae!

By admitting design, you have admitted the existence of an intelligent designer. Whether that designer is benevolent or malevolent will be discussed in due course.

And now anthropology comes into the picture. Anthropology is popular with the moderns because very little is known about primitive peoples, and consequently they can invent any theory they like to discredit religion and get away with it. It is so much safer than arguing about the Resurrection or Transubstantiation or any of those other "niceties of Catholic doctrine" where one is liable to be tripped up by unsporting people who will persist in referring to authorities one is too busy to consult. No such dangers attend an excursion into the realms of pre-history.

Let me begin by registering a vigorous protest against your habit of substituting the words "It is generally agreed" for the more honest "I think." In one of your recent books I counted a series of these, all of which prefaced statements for which there is no agreement, general or otherwise. This protest is necessary, for this habit of implying a background of general scientific agreement for highly controversial statements is a

still popular

---

their environment—that is, on the paralysed body of the caterpillar. Thus the forethought of the parents provides the larvae with an abundant supply of live meat. Very nice for the larvae! But one feels that from the point of view of the caterpillar the matter might have been arranged differently." Lunn and Joad, *Is Christianity True?* 65. —Ed.

recognised dodge of the omniscientists, to borrow Father Knox's admirable description of writers "who select those statements, those points of view, which tell in favour of the thesis they want to establish, concealing any statements or points of view which tell in a contrary direction, and then serve up the whole to us as the best conclusions of modern research, disarming all opposition by appeal to the sacred name of science."

It is not "generally agreed" that the origin of religion is to be found in the savage's fear of the unknown. You should read Dr. Schmidt's great work on *The Origin and Growth of Religion*.[30] Dr. Schmidt is a scientist, not an omniscientist, and his authoritative work has been translated by Professor Rose,[31] who was slightly senior to you at Balliol. Dr. Schmidt, who has devoted more years to these problems that you or I have devoted minutes, has come to the considered conclusion that it is precisely the most primitive people who retain the tradition of monotheism. He draws particular attention to the case of pigmy races, "of dwarfish people inhabiting Central Africa, the Andaman Islands, the peninsula of Malacca and the more retired parts of the Philippines." He tells us that he finds everywhere "a clear acknowledgment and worship of a supreme being . . . the supremacy of this being is so comprehensively and energetically expressed that all other supernormal beings are far inferior and invariably subject to him."

From which it would seem that monotheism does not represent, as you suggest, a later development, but, on the

---

[30] Wilhelm Schmidt (1868–1954), *The Origin and Growth of Religion: Facts and Theories*, tr. H. J. Rose (London: Methuen, 1931). —ED.

[31] H. J. Rose (1883–1961), author of several works on religions of antiquity, including *Ancient Greek Religion* (London, Hutchinson, 1946) and *Ancient Roman Religion* (London, Hutchinson, 1948). —ED.

contrary, polytheism would seem to represent a degenerate and degraded form of the purer and more primitive mono-theistic belief.

You next proceed to favour me with a spirited attack on Jehovah, who emerges, as you yourself rather reluctantly admit, more creditably than the Greek gods from your severe handling. The Jewish conception of God was undoubtedly coloured, as you suggest, by their own peculiar outlook, but the Jewish religion at its best produced some of the noblest spiritual literature in the world. If you re-read[32] the Psalms and Isaiah, you will revise your theories of Jehovah. I shall return to this point later.

We now come to an old friend, the theory which ex-plains God as a projection. Tansley, in his *New Psychology*,[33] states the case for this view very effectively. Theism, he holds, is due to "the tendency of the mind to project what is calculated to make for peace of mind. A man feels lonely and projects the idea of a loving father." It does not occur to Tansley (or to you) that projection might equally well explain the atheism of men like Samuel Butler[34] or Bernard Shaw[35] in revolt against the Calvinistic conception of God. If one had been brought up in a Calvinistic tradition, it

---

[32] Note the exquisite courtesy of "re-read".

[33] A. G. Tansley (1871–1955), *The New Psychology and its Relation to Life* (London: Allen and Unwin, 1920), chap. XIV, "Projection and Idealism", 155–162. —ED.

[34] Samuel Butler (1835–1902), English author, painter, and composer, best known for his books *Erewhon* (London: Trübner, 1872) and *The Way of All Flesh* (London: Fifield, 1903). —ED.

[35] George Bernard Shaw (1856–1950), British dramatist. Among his major plays were *Major Barbara* (1905), *Pygmalion* (1912), and *Saint Joan* (1924), commonly considered his masterpiece. In 1925 he was awarded the Nobel Prize in Literature. An early member of the Fabian Society, he became friends with Hilaire Belloc and G. K. Chesterton, once famously debating the former while the latter acted as moderator. —ED.

would certainly make for peace of mind to "project" atheism.

I wonder what wish fulfilment is realised by the belief in hell—a nice comfortable belief, hell!

These clever new psychologists begin by assuming what it is their business to prove. They ignore the proofs for the existence of God, assume that God is an illusion, and set to work to explain how this particular illusion arose. But all the facts, including the facts that you mention, are just as tolerant of a theistic as of an atheistic interpretation. If God exists, as we believe, there is no reason to suppose that the theology of primitive people will not be coloured by their primitive mentality. The views of primitive people about the sun and moon are very different to the views that we hold to-day; none the less, the sun and moon exist.

If God exists, the theory of projection merely restates the truism, first affirmed by Christian philosophers, that our human and finite conceptions of the divine must be affected by our human and finite limitations.

Your next point is that science makes us feel dreadfully insignificant. Incidentally, it is amusing to note that, whereas fifty years ago the Christian was derided for ever having supposed that this planet was the centre of the universe, and was urged to reflect on the probability of millions of inhab- ited planets circling round millions of distant suns, we are now told that our planet is probably a unique accident. "For the rest, so far as we know, the universe is without life." Why this glad news should depress or humble me, I cannot tell. On the contrary, I am pleased to note that science confirms the Christian instinct which tended to regard our planet as the scene of a unique and dramatic experiment, and man as the crown of creation. You must really think of something better if you want to make my flesh creep. Incidentally, is it not rather strange that science should inculcate modesty in one generation by assuring us that planets such as ours are scattered throughout the universe, and in the next generation by assuring us that our planet is unique?

All this worship of infinite space and astronomical light years is merely part and parcel of that snobbish worship of mere size which is such a distressing feature of the present age. Pascal has the last word on this subject:

> *L'homme n'est qu'un roseau, le plus faible de la nature; mais c'est un roseau pensant. Il ne faut pas que l'univers entier s'arme pour l'ecraser: une vapeur, une goutte d'eau, suffit pour le tuer. Mais, quand l'univers l'ecraserait, l'homme serait encore plus noble que ce qui le tue, parce-qu'il sait qu'il meurt, et l'avantage que l'univers a sur lui; l'univers n'en sait rien.*[36]

All the facts which you produce are as easy to explain on the hypothesis that God exists, and that he has revealed himself to man to guide him to heaven, to comfort him in distress and to hearten him in weakness.

I will deal with the whole subject of prayer in a subsequent letter.

Your next complaint is that Christianity has exploited the poor in the interests of the rich.

You have already been reproved in this correspondence for gross misquotation from the Catechism. You repeat the offence under the sincere impression that you are really getting it right this time. The Christian virtues, you tell us, prescribe "contentment in that state of life to which (as you

[36] Man is but a reed, the most feeble thing in nature; but he is a thinking reed. The entire universe need not arm itself to crush him. A vapour, a drop of water, suffices to kill him. But, if the universe were to crush him, man would still be more noble than that which killed him, because he knows that he dies and the advantage which the universe has over him; the universe knows nothing of this.

have corrected me) it shall please God to call them." I suppose I ought to be grateful for the fact that you have at least got the tense right this time ("shall," not "hath"), and if I hammer away long enough you may in time get the rest of the quotation right and substitute "do my duty" for "contentment."

If you are an honest controversialist, you will have the decency in your next letter to admit that you have grossly misinterpreted the Catechism, and that the resolve "to do my duty in that state of life unto which it shall please God to call me" is an unimpeachable sentiment, and might be echoed with sincerity by a navvy who was determined to become Prime Minister or by a socialist who was determined to abolish the upper classes. Please do not evade my challenge on this point; I expect an apology to the Catechism in your next letter.

Your persistent misquotation is an excellent example of the difficulties with which we Christians have to contend, of the ignorance which is literally invincible[37] and of a prejudice which continues to resist the pressure of undisputed fact.[38]

There is some truth in your statement that the Christian virtues "are precisely such as a governing class might have prescribed for the governed for the benefit of the governors." Some truth, but not the whole truth, for Christianity is a climate in which slavery cannot flourish, and a creed which

[37] "Invincible ignorance" is a term of endearment common among Catholics, and is applied to non-Catholics who are nice enough to be worth saving from Hell on the plea of "invincible ignorance" of the true faith. I fear that your chance of scraping into Purgatory on this plea is greater than mine.

[38] In his letter of July 10, 1932, Lunn would say, "The doctrine of invincible ignorance was promulgated to provide particularly for people, like yourself, who have taken a First in Greats." Lunn and Joad, *Is Christianity True?* 167. —ED.

emphasises the infinite dignity of every human soul cannot
be favourable to the cultivation of purely servile virtues. But
my real criticism of this statement is that it is incomplete. As
usual, you have been so pleased with scoring an apparent
point against Christianity that you have not bothered to
probe below the surface. You have only given us one side of
the picture. The answer is, of course, that the Christian
virtues are precisely such as the underdog might have prescribed for his governors for the benefit of the underdog. If
all masters had been inspired by the Christian virtues, there
would be precious little social discontent to-day.

I do not myself believe that the gospels provide a hopeful
quarry either for capitalists or for communists, for Christ, so
it seems to me, was concerned with the individual and his
relations to God rather than with problems of social reform.
To say: "Sell all that thou hast and give to the poor" [39] is not
quite the same thing as saying: "Take all that he hath and
distribute it among your pals." None the less, the emphasis in
all the gospels is on the tremendous danger of wealth. Had
the gospels been edited by the governing classes, they would
have been purged of many a text manifestly inspired by
sympathy with the underdog. "He hath scattered the proud
in the imagination of their hearts. He hath put down the
mighty from their seats, and exalted them of low degree. He
hath filled the hungry with good things and the rich he hath
sent empty away." [40]

Do you really suppose that this sort of thing is calculated
to inspire the lower classes with contentment, meekness and
humility?

Vaguely aware of the difficulties of your position, you try
to anticipate the obvious rejoinder by suggesting, or rather

[39] Mt 19:21. —ED.
[40] Lk 1:53. —ED.

by baldly stating that "an early governing class realist slipped the story of Lazarus into the text of St. Luke's, and the parable about the camel and the needle's eye into the mouth of Christ."

Now this sort of thing, my dear Joad, would be all very well if you were lecturing to an audience of uncritical undergraduates, who would no doubt welcome with delight anything which tells against Christianity. You and I both acquired the technique for this sort of thing in the debating societies at Oxford, but we have both grown older since those far-off Balliol days, and you must try to remember that we are engaged in a serious correspondence about the greatest of all possible issues. In this correspondence you will be expected to back up your assertions with proof, and you will not be allowed to assume that any text which is inconvenient for your theories has necessarily been interpolated.

Meanwhile will you allow me, in all courtesy, to describe your excursion into higher criticism as a museum piece of modern bosh? *Quod gratis asseritur gratis negatur.* [41]

I am prepared to admit that the governing classes have made more than one attempt to exploit Christianity in their own interests, but this proves not that Christianity favours the rich but that noble things may be prostituted by base men for base ends.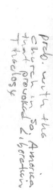

I am inclined to think that there is something to be said for Mr. Belloc's contention that Calvin was the spiritual father of modern capitalism. I come of Irish Protestant stock on my mother's side, and I have a natural understanding of Mr. Shaw's Irish Protestant background, a background which has many affinities with Calvinism. The dialogue which you quote from *Major Barbara*[42] reflects Shaw's reaction against a

---

[41] "What is gratuitously asserted may be gratuitously denied." —ED.

[42] Joad, *Present and Future*, 72. —ED.

form of Protestantism which has many virtues, but which is
certainly inclined to identify Christianity with the principles
expounded in Smiles's *Self-Help*.[43]

Few Anglicans would dispute Arthur Young's view that
Anglicanism in 1798 was far too closely identified with the
upper classes.[44] The Anglo-Catholic revival did a great deal
to destroy the smug, self-satisfied Erastianism which you
very properly criticise. It is a pity, however, that you cannot
see the sun for the sun-spots. You have spent so much time
in unearthing facts to discredit Christianity that you have
no leisure to find out the really important facts about
Christianity. Had you spent a little time in some of the East
End parishes, you would soon realise that Anglicanism has
long since ceased to be the religion of the rich. Again, you
might read what John Wesley has to say on the subject of
riches and their danger. Wesley practised what he preached.
As a young man he had an income of about fifty pounds a
year: he lived on twenty-eight pounds and gave the balance
away. As an old man he had an income of about four
hundred a year: he still lived on twenty-eight pounds and
gave the balance away.

With the exception of one quotation from Napoleon,
your examples are drawn, as usual, from Anglicanism. It is
curious that a man like you, who are cosmopolitan in your
tastes and international in your politics, should be so quaintly
insular in your outlook on religion. The Catholic Church
has been fairly successful in its struggle to curb the natural
acquisitiveness of human nature. I do not pretend that it has

[43] Samuel Smiles (1812–1904) wrote *Self Help* (London: Murray, 1859),
which emphasized Victorian values in the "gospel of work". —ED.

[44] Arthur Young (1741–1820), writer on the state of agriculture in Britain
(he served as First Secretary of the Board of Agriculture [1793]) and traveler
who wrote extensively on his journeys through France prior to the Revolution. —ED.

been completely successful in restraining the arrogance of
the rich, but at least it has consistently upheld the virtue of
"holy poverty." Eighteenth-century England glorified the
industrious apprentice as a typical product of Protestantism:
Catholicism reserves its highest honours for the saintly monk
and for the saintly nun. Again, the guild system of the
Middle Ages was a magnificent attempt, and recognised as
such by writers who, like Mr. G. D. H. Cole,[45] are completely hostile to Christianity, to realise the ideal of a society
in which profit-making was far from being the main motive.
The guildsman expected a fair return for his labour, but the
ideal of the guild was good workmanship rather than big
profits. The Middle Ages made an heroic attempt to solve
problems of social justice which still remain unsolved, and I
sometimes wonder whether the modern world would not be
a far happier place if the great doctors of the Church had
succeeded in their attempt to impose upon the world their
conception of "just price." Again, had the Church succeeded
in suppressing usury, which might be defined as interest on
unproductive loans, the present crash,[46] which Mr. Belloc
foretold in *Essays of a Catholic*, might conceivably have been
avoided. I do not wish to dogmatise on these points, but
merely to suggest to you that your discussion of the Christian
attitude to social problems is superficial and one-sided. Please
give your reference for the charter ending with the words:
"In the name of the King and the Christian Church."[47]

[45] G. D. H. Cole (1889–1959), English economist. A one-time advocate of
guild socialism, he later returned to Fabianism and headed the Fabian Society
from 1939 to 1946. His books include *The History of Socialist Thought* (six
volumes, 1953–1958). —ED.

[46] A reference to the Great Depression. —ED.

[47] See Joad's letter of May 27, 1932: "No country has felt more confidence
in its divine mission to acquire land 'in the name of the King and the Christian
Church' than our own." Lunn and Joad, *Is Christianity True?* 75. —ED.

I propose in the latter half of the book to reply in detail to your general charge that the Church has always favoured the rich against the poor, and the white man against the black.

Yours ever,

Arnold Lunn

6

Arnold Lunn vs. J. B. S. Haldane

The same year that saw the publication of Hilaire Belloc's *Essays of a Catholic*, which included the criticism of J. B. S. Haldane,[1] also saw the start of a correspondence between Haldane and Arnold Lunn. Their exchange of thirty-one letters began in October 1931 and did not conclude until November 1934. The result was *Science and the Supernatural*,[2] which appeared in 1935. When the letters began, Lunn was not yet a Catholic.[3] By the time they ended, he had been in the Church for more than a year.

Remarking, years later, on his written debates, Lunn said:

I am inclined to believe that of these debates the debate with Haldane was perhaps the most useful. It is usually a waste of time to debate with an incompetent opponent. It has happened to me more than once that those whom I had hoped to influence have conceded my victory but added, "Lunn only won because he had so much more experience of

---

[1] See chap. 2. —ED.

[2] Arnold Lunn and J. B. S. Haldane, *Science and the Supernatural* (New York: Sheed and Ward, 1935). —ED.

[3] Lunn, in his early letters to Haldane, found himself having to defend both the Catholic Church, to which he did not yet belong, and the Church of England, of which he then was a communicant. —ED.

debates and was obviously the better controversialist." Now
Haldane was not only my intellectual superior, but also a
brilliant controversialist, and his failure to defeat me inevitably raised the suspicion that I had the better case. . . . I
admired Haldane not only for his outstanding intellectual
gifts, but also for his courage. He made a series of dangerous
experiments on his body in the interest of biological research
and during the war, so I was told by one of his fellow
officers, he seemed to take positive delight in attracting
enemy fire.[4]

In 1950 Lunn undertook a long lecture tour, visiting
Egypt, Pakistan, Australia, and America. In Melbourne he
debated Glanville Cook, the secretary of the Rationalist
Society of Australia, on the theme "Is the Catholic Church
intolerant and a bar to progress?" Cook told the audience
that Lunn had won his exchange with Ronald Knox but
had been crushed in his exchange with Haldane. Lunn inquired how Cook could reconcile his thesis of Catholic
intolerance with the fact that the Lunn-Haldane book had
been a feature of the Catholic Book Club of America. "I
remember that debate", wrote Lunn, "as one of the rare
occasions when I didn't forget that the main object of a
Christian debating with an atheist is not personal victory
but to persuade his opponent and his supporters to reconsider their position. And if this be one's object one must
make every effort to refute one's opponent's arguments
without inflicting personal humiliation on him. It is important to concede everything which should be conceded because it is not only bad policy but intellectually dishonest to
defend the indefensible."[5]

[4] Arnold Lunn, *Unkilled for So Long* (London: Allen and Unwin, 1968),
98. —ED.

[5] Ibid., 104–8. —ED.

Lunn began the exchange with Haldane by saying, "It has always seemed to me a pity that the Christians and anti-Christians so seldom engage in battle on the same ground. You inform the listening world through the medium of the B.B.C. that the 'creeds are full of obsolete science' and that Christianity is dead, and the following Sunday a parson preaches a sermon on the wireless. The devout don't listen-in to you, or the undevout to the parson." [6] In his next letter to Haldane, Lunn added, "There is nothing wrong with the scientific method; indeed, I should like to see it in more general use in the scientific world. My real quarrel with the majority of scientists is that they refuse to apply the scientific method to religion." [7] Haldane, he thought, was a good example of this. Unlike Joad, who may have been more irascible, Haldane never came to embrace the Christian faith, perhaps because he never quite severed his connections with communist beliefs, for which he served, for so many years, as a prominent advocate. In his letter of July 23, 1932, Haldane wrote about the scientific method and his own lack of belief in miracles and the supernatural.[8] In Lunn's reply, which is given here, the Christian comments on the sceptic's unwillingness to be as critical about religion as he is, normally, about science. Lunn cites as an example of the "blind faith" of scientists the episode of Émile Zola's 1892 visit to Lourdes—just one

---

[6] Lunn and Haldane, *Science and the Supernatural*, 1. —ED.

[7] Ibid., 6. —ED.

[8] "I never believed in the major miracles [of Jesus], any more than (I suppose) you ever believed that Mars begat Romulus and Remus. I had plenty of Christian propaganda, and some of other beliefs, such as Judaism, materialism, and theosophy, pumped into me. None of it has convinced me." Lunn and Haldane, *Science and the Supernatural*, 17. Perhaps Haldane really thought he never imbibed any of the materialist propaganda; nevertheless, he was well known as a materialist. —ED.

of many effective examples Lunn used repeatedly in his apologetic writing.

August 14, 1932

Dear Haldane,

Your controversial style is disarming after the invective of my friend Joad. Where he shouts *Ecrasez l'infame*[9] you are content to insinuate doubt not only of God's existence but also of your own. A quarter of a century has passed since Mr. Chesterton foretold that suicide of thought which is the ultimate end of scepticism. The old sceptics began by doubting the existence of God. The modern sceptic ends by doubting his own existence. "We are on the road," wrote Mr. Chesterton, "to produce a race of men too mentally modest to believe in the multiplication table. . . . The creeds and the crusades, the hierarchies and the horrible persecutions were not organized, as is ignorantly said, for the suppression of reason. They were organized for the difficult defence of reason. Man, by a blind instinct, knew that if once things were blindly questioned, reason would be questioned first." [10]

I shall be interested to learn how you propose on the foundation of these delicate negations to erect an ethical system which shall remedy "the present alarming condition of the human race" which you deplore. But I have my doubts of the vitality of a crusade whose leader is prepared to admit that he is "nothing but a biologically and socially convenient fiction." It is certainly difficult to convince a man who is not sure that he exists that his Creator exists.

---

[9] From a letter by Voltaire to Jean d'Alembert, November 28, 1762: "*Quoi que vous fassiez, écrasez l'infâme, et aimez qui vous aime*" ("Whatever you do, crush the infamous thing [superstition], and love those who love you"). —ED.

[10] G. K. Chesterton, *Orthodoxy* (London: John Lane, 1909), 54, 57. —ED.

Your amplification of my attempt to define the "scientific method" is very welcome, for the experimental method is not peculiar to science and should be applied to religion.

I must defer for the moment any discussion of the reasons why Catholics consider that Faith is a virtue. I will content myself with stating that Catholics would not accept the distinction which you try to draw between faith and clear thinking. They hold that clear thinking leads to the Faith, and that thinking confused by defective education, sin, or conceit leads to heresy.

You have defined in a clear and interesting fashion your attitude to the supernatural. I can sympathize with you because my own attitude was once very similar. It is very difficult for men of our generation to escape from the prison of our time. The mental fashion of the age is anti-supernatural. We start with the assumption that God, if he exists, would never dream of interfering with the routine of nature. The assumption, indeed, is so embedded in our thought that we do not even realize that we are guilty of assuming as true a theory which is against all the weight of historic evidence.

It was some little time before I realized that this attitude was parochial in the extreme, for it is parochial to assume that we are in touch with no forms of consciousness higher than man. I say "in touch," for I am not concerned with the possibility that the planets may be inhabited by beings more intelligent than man.

I cannot understand why it should be considered scientific to assume that only the uneducated or old-fashioned could possibly believe in angels or evil spirits.

As that distinguished French scientist Professor Richet remarks: "Why should there not be intelligent and puissant beings distinct from those perceptible to senses? By what right should we dare to affirm on the basis of our limited senses, our defective intellect, and our scientific past, as yet hardly three centuries old, that in the vast cosmos man is the sole intelligent being, and that all mental reality always depends upon new cells irrigated by oxygenated blood?" [11]

You scientists are always urging us to cultivate a sense of proportion and to realize that man is a native of a small planet attached to an insignificant star. You yourself have preached many sermons on this cheerful text. But surely it is no more conceited to believe that the earth is the centre of the universe than to assume that man represents the climax of the evolutionary process, and that in all the vast universe there are no beings of higher spiritual worth. (Incidentally, scientists are now inclined to think that this planet may, after all, be the sole abode of consciousness in the universe, so perhaps the mediaeval cosmogony was not quite so absurd after all.)

For the life of me I cannot see any reason to suppose that we are not surrounded by a great company of invisible witnesses, and I shall continue to believe that we are until science provides me with something more than mere noisy assertions to set against the vast array of evidence for the supernatural which has been accumulated in every age and by every race from the dawn of recorded history.

> The angels keep their ancient places;—
> Turn but a stone and start a wing!
> 'Tis ye, 'tis your estranged faces
> That miss the many-splendoured thing. [12]

[11] Charles-Robert Richet (1850–1935), French physiologist and professor at the Sorbonne, was awarded the Nobel Prize for physiology or medicine in 1913. His avocation was studying spiritualism. —ED.

[12] Francis Thompson (1859–1902), "The Kingdom of God", in *The Works of Francis Thompson* (New York: Scribner's, 1913), vol. II, 226. —ED.

There is more sober scientific fact in those four lines than in half the papers read before the British Association.

The "rationalist" who rejects the supernatural is always in danger of assuming the conclusion which he is required to prove. It is, for instance, a *petitio principii* to assume, as you have done, that because miracles are admittedly unusual therefore miracles are improbable. I maintain that we have every reason to expect that God should manifest himself by miracles, and further that we have no right to expect that these miracles should be matters of common occurrence. In other words, I shall try to show that miracles are probable and that it is probable that miracles should be unusual.

The degree of evidence which we require in the case of a miracle is necessarily far stronger than the evidence which justifies a jury in bringing in a verdict of guilty in a capital charge, and I hope to satisfy you in later letters that the evidence for miracles satisfies this exacting test. Most rationalists, however, are not prepared to consider for a moment any evidence, however strong, for the miraculous. Zola,[13] unable to explain a cure at Lourdes which he had investigated, added, "I don't believe in miracles: even if all the sick in Lourdes were cured in one moment I would not believe in them!" Clearly this attitude is founded not on reason but on faith—faith in the dogma that miracles do not occur.

And indeed the inspiration of nineteenth-century rationalism was not reason but the determination to uphold a particular philosophy against the weight of historical and

[13] Émile Zola (1840–1902), French novelist and exponent of naturalism, best known for his intervention in the Dreyfus Affair. He was anticlerical and an antimiraculist. Arnold Lunn repeatedly used the story of the novelist's visit to Lourdes in 1892 as an example of the blind faith of secularists. Zola there witnessed the cure of eighteen-year-old Marie Lemarchand, one of the few whose cure has been certified by the Church as a miracle, but he nevertheless refused to acknowledge that miracles are possible. —Ed.

scientific evidence. Strauss,[14] for instance, laid down as a canon of New Testament criticism the dogma, "In the person and acts of Jesus no supernaturalism shall be allowed to remain," and he accordingly dates the gospels on the assumption that miracles must be a later interpolation. If Strauss' principles were applied in our courts of law we should doubtless be favoured with some such exchange of remarks between judge and counsel as the following:

> JUDGE: "You propose to call this witness for the defence?"
> COUNSEL: "Yes, my Lord."
> JUDGE (with a slightly puzzled air): "But the witness for the defence believes in the prisoner's innocence."
> COUNSEL: "Yes, my Lord."
> JUDGE: "Then I rule that his evidence is inadmissible. In the person and acts of the prisoner no innocent motives shall be allowed to remain."

Again, I have never been able to discover by what canon of criticism the rationalist selects his texts. Like the modernist, he assumes the accuracy of those texts which suit his particular theory, and denies the reliability of texts which support the views which he combats.

Nothing is more difficult than to report conversation accurately. Indeed, Boswell[15] is one of the few people in history who have reported with accuracy the *ipsissima verba* of their heroes. In a police court a witness who was accepted as a reliable witness of a conversation would certainly be believed if he reported some striking incident. It is therefore

[14] David Friedrich Strauss (1808–1874), German theologian and philosopher. In *Das Leben Jesu* he applied a "theory of myth" to the life of Christ and denied all supernatural elements in the Gospels. —ED.

[15] James Boswell, author of *The Life of Samuel Johnson* (1791), was known for the high degree of accuracy in his transcription of his subject's conversations. —ED.

difficult to understand why the hostile critic of the gospels assumes that the evangelists were more accurate than Boswell when they report words which the Christian may find some slight difficulty in explaining, and less accurate than a hysterical girl frightened by a ghost when they report incidents which the rationalist is anxious to explain away.

And now for miracles. To clear the ground, let me state at the outset that I do not include under the term "miracle" any form of faith healing which might conceivably be explained by scientific laws not as yet fully understood. I mean events such as the feeding of the five thousand or the Resurrection, which suggest the modification of the laws of Nature by the intrusion of supernatural will.

Please note that a miracle is neither the violation nor the suspension of a law of Nature. "When the human will," writes Dr. Harris,

> acts upon the external world, and produces a sensible effect, it does not thereby violate any law of Nature. When, for instance, a man raises a stone weighing a hundredweight, and holds it in his hands he does not in so doing violate or suspend the law of gravitation. That law continues in full force, as is proved by the continuance of the sensation of weight; but the effect of the law is counteracted by the operation of the greater force of the human muscles, directed by the human will. Similarly, when God works a miracle, it is not supposed that any of the laws of Nature are suspended, but that God counteracts or modifies some of the effects which those laws would ordinarily produce, by a process analogous to that by which the human will acts upon and influences physical Nature. This is admitted by John Mill,[16]

---

[16] John Stuart Mill (1806–1873) was a proponent of utilitarianism. He argued that all knowledge comes through empirical means. He is best known for his *On Liberty* (London: Parker, 1859). —ED.

who says: "The interference of human will with the course of Nature is not an exception to law; and by the same rule interference by the divine will would not be an exception either." [17]

If God exists, and if he is in the least interested in the human beings that he has created, it is not unreasonable to suppose that he should give men some evidence of His existence.

On the other hand, we need not be surprised that God is sparing of miracles. He does not coerce faith, for it would be inconsistent with his gift of free will to render it, humanly speaking, impossible for a man to reject God.

Very well then. I have tried to show first that the complete absence of miracles would be far more surprising than the occurrence of miracles, and secondly that we should expect miracles to be unusual occurrences, and we should expect, since God does not coerce faith, that the evidence for miracles, though strong enough to satisfy anybody who approached the subject with an open mind, would not be completely coercive for the world at large.

I am surprised that you should describe your attitude to miracles as similar to that of Hume, for I thought Hume's fallacies had been pretty thoroughly exposed. Mill, a sceptic, but a logical sceptic, rejected his "argument" as unsound. "A miracle," says Hume, "is a violation of the laws of Nature; and as a firm and unalterable experience has established those laws, the proof against a miracle, from the very nature of the fact, is as entire as any argument from experience can be." [18]

---

[17] *Pro Fide*, 269 (John Murray).

[18] David Hume (1711–1776), British philosopher, historian, and sceptic. The quotation is from his essay "On Miracles", which appeared as the tenth section in his *Enquiry Concerning Human Understanding* (Oxford: Clarendon Press, 1975 [1777]). —ED.

First, miracles are not "violations of the laws of Nature" (see above).

Secondly, it is poor reasoning to assume what it is your business to prove. We maintain that so far from the case against miracles resting on "firm and unalterable experience," there is a vast amount of unimpeachable evidence in favour of miracles. The question, as Mill rightly said, "can only be stated fairly as depending on a balance of evidence: a certain amount of positive evidence in favour of miracles, and a negative presumption from the general course of human experience against them."

And now for your bridge illustration.[19] You tell me that if I stated that I had twice seen the distribution you name you would be inclined to doubt my veracity or my sanity, or both. I am grateful for the delicate compliment of the "twice." Will you think me very rude if I reply that I should not accept your statement if you had said that you had witnessed this distribution once?

The odds against this distribution are even greater than you suppose. Inadequate shuffling does not, as you suggest, reduce, but increases, the odds against this distribution. The cards are stacked in tricks, and the majority of tricks are composed of cards of the same suit. Therefore if we re-dealt

[19] In his July 23, 1932, letter to Lunn, Haldane wrote, "I will try to make it clear by considering an event which, so far from being miraculous, is quite possible. After the cards have been well shuffled a dealer at bridge may deal out one complete suit to each player. The odds against this event are, however (unless I made a mistake, which is quite likely), about 4,470,400,-000,000,000,000,000,000,000 to one. Let us divide this figure by a billion to allow for inadequate shuffling. Now if in your next letter you tell me that you have twice observed this phenomenon I shall say, 'I have a high regard for Lunn both as a truthful man and an accurate observer; but I think it much more likely that he is lying or mad, or that he was deliberately deceived, than that the events he described really occurred." Lunn and Haldane, *Science and the Supernatural*, 12. —ED.

without shuffling, your distribution would be impossible, and is perhaps impossible without shuffling far more prolonged than is ever possible under the normal conditions in which bridge is played.

In any case the odds against this distribution are so astronomically immense that if every member of the human race had been playing bridge for six hours a day from the dawn of the Stone Age down to modern times, the odds against this distribution having occurred once would still be many billions to one. Do you know of any well-authenticated case? I know of none, and I am inclined to suspect the reported cases of one suit being monopolized by one player are the result of a practical joke.

If, then, you were to tell me that you had seen the four suits distributed, one suit to each player, I should believe that you had been deceived; whereas if, on returning from Lourdes, you told me that you had seen a completely fractured leg united in a second of time I should believe you. And I should believe you for the good reason that whereas I know of no evidence that this particular Bridge distribution has yet occurred, there is a constant stream of first-class evidence throughout the ages as to the occurrence of miracles such as those which are reported from Lourdes. I propose in later letters to summarize this evidence, and also to discuss your reasons for refusing to be impressed by "physical phenomena" as produced in séances, and I will confine myself for the moment to an attempt to show that your arguments against New Testament miracles can be refuted.

The example you give (Mark 16:17–18) is an interesting illustration of the ease with which even a clear thinker can miss the point of a passage if he reads that passage with a prejudiced mind.

In the first place you have divorced the texts you quote from the context which explains them. Let me quote the passage in full. The passage contains Christ's final exhortation to the apostles, an exhortation delivered after the Resurrection:

> And he said unto them, Go ye into all the world, and preach the gospel to every creature. He that believeth and is baptized shall be saved; but he that believeth not shall be damned. And these signs shall follow them that believe; In my name shall they cast out devils; they shall speak with new tongues; They shall take up serpents; and if they drink any deadly thing, it shall not hurt them; they shall lay hands on the sick, and they shall recover. So then after the Lord had spoken unto them, he was received up into heaven, and sat on the right hand of God. And they went forth, and preached every where, the Lord working with them, and confirming the word with signs following. Amen.[20]

You ask me, "Do you honestly believe that no believing Christian has been poisoned?" and I reply, "Do you honestly believe that the passage you have quoted suggests that believing Christians are immune from snake-bite?" Surely the passage is not a general statement applying to Christians as a whole, but a particular prophecy as to the miracles which would be associated with the missionary activities of the little group of apostles to whom Christ addressed these words: "Go ye into all the world, and preach the gospel. . . . And these signs shall follow them that believe. . . . And they went forth . . . the Lord working with them, and confirming the word with the signs following."

What could be plainer?

It is, moreover, a matter of history that these signs did follow them that believed. The apostles "spoke with new

---

[20] Mk 16:15–20. —ED.

tongues," and healed the sick; and at Melita a viper came out of the fire and fastened on St. Paul's hand, and St. Paul, to the amazement of the barbarians, received no hurt.[21]

The particular prophecy was fulfilled; but even had the prophecy been tolerant of your interpretation I should have had no difficulty in defending it. I do not believe that every "believing Christian" is immune from snake-bite, but I do believe that it is impossible to set bounds to the powers of faith. Believing Christians vary enormously in the vigour of their faith. I am quite sure that I am not immune from snake-bite. I am equally convinced that many of the saints could have handled poisonous snakes with the same casual confidence that St. Paul displayed on the "island called Melita."

You mention the discrepancies in the accounts of the Resurrection. No four witnesses reporting the same event will give exactly the same account. Had the four evangelists told the same story in identical words the hostile critic would have asserted that they had all copied the same account, and that the witnesses to the Resurrection were therefore reduced from four to one. Minor discrepancies do not invalidate the credibility of the main story in its main outlines, and may only legitimately be used, if at all, to impugn the theory that the Bible contains no error. But even this line of attack, as I found in my correspondence with Father Knox, is not particularly helpful.

"The facts to be explained," you write, "are the existence of several accounts of these events, and of organizations inculcating a belief in them." I have explained the first point, and it is for you to explain the account of the Christian Church on the assumption that the Resurrection did not

---

[21] Acts 28:3–6. —ED.

take place. The Church is no puzzle to those who believe in the Resurrection.

I am impressed by the tone of your letters, reasonable and tentative, both in what you affirm and in what you are inclined to deny, and I am puzzled to account for the contrast between your letters to me and the curt dogmatism of your published references to Christianity.

I should have been surprised had you made in this correspondence the remark which you broadcast over the wireless: "The creeds are full of obsolete science"; but it does not seem to me quite fair that you should reserve these remarks for occasions when they cannot be challenged, and for a public which accepts them at their face value, and which does not realize the very tentative nature of your views. There is, of course, no science, new or obsolete, in the creeds. The only thing that is full of obsolete science is— science. I should be interested to learn how you would begin to justify your prophecy that the Christian Churches, "if they maintain their influence, will sterilize scientific thought," and I should be glad if you would name a single scientific fact which is at variance with a defined doctrine of the Catholic Church. There is an unending conflict between science and scientists, for I need not remind you of all that scientific pioneers have had to suffer from the jealousy and obscurantism of organized science; but all this talk of the conflict between science and religion is very much beside the mark.

There is, I think, one point on which we shall be in agreement. You will unite with me in regretting the wide-spread ignorance of that which should be regarded as an integral part of culture, a knowledge of the history and philosophy of a religion which for sixteen centuries influenced every aspect of European life. In your first letter you said that you would have been mildly amused or annoyed had I accused you of writing ignorantly or in bad faith. True, like Mr. Wells and others, you have confused the Immaculate Conception with the Virgin Birth;[22] even so I make no general accusation of ignorance or bad faith, for passages such as the following are rare in your works: "The old religions are full of obsolete science, including the astronomical theory of a solid heaven, the chemical theory that water, bread, books, and other objects can be rendered holy by special processes, and the physiological theory that a substance called a soul leaves the body at death."

I will pay you the compliment of not asking you to defend this travesty of Catholic doctrine.

There is not much in your work at which a Christian could legitimately take offence. Christians, by a process of natural selection, long ago developed very thick skins, and your satisfied statement that you do not "worship a biscuit" would be met by the mild rejoinder that it is unscientific to equate the small with the trivial, as Bethmann-Hollweg discovered when he referred to a "scrap of paper." [23]

A Christian would, I think, ignore your occasional contemptuous references to the Faith, and would be most disposed to quarrel with you for your tacit assumption that your reader has no right to demand definitions of your terms or a reasoned argument in defence of your particular brand of supernaturalism. St. Thomas Aquinas would have criticized severely your tendency to rely not on reason but on faith. And he would condemn your habit of using nebulous phrases

[22] Lunn relies on Belloc's characterization of Haldane (see chap. 2, n. 20 above), but Belloc was wrong, as Lunn admits in his next letter (see n. 36 below). Lunn and Haldane, *Science and the Supernatural*, 53. —Ed.

[23] Theobald von Bethmann-Hollweg (1856–1921), chancellor of Germany 1909–1917, famed for calling the guarantee of Belgian neutrality a "scrap of paper" (1914). —Ed.

the meaning of which you have made no attempt to define. But he would make allowances for the age in which you live, an age which takes refuge from the discipline of exact thought in the mists of metaphor.

"I believe," you write, "that the scientist is trying to express absolute truth and the artist absolute beauty."

St. Thomas would never have used a phrase like "absolute truth" without defining what he meant by "absolute." All this modern talk about "values" is merely an attempt to admit the supernatural at the back door. Our generation suffers from what might be called logophobia, the fear of words. Certain words like "God" and "supernatural" are unfashionable, and so our moderns are reduced to talking about "absolute beauty" and the "realm of values." But all this is mere metaphor-mongering. How is it conceivable that eternal values can exist without an eternal God to conserve those values? You have recently affirmed your belief that "the meaning of the visible world is to be found in the invisible," and elsewhere you tell us that you have "not much use for people who are not in touch with the invisible world." What precise meaning do you attach to this phrase "invisible world"?

Now, a thinker trained in the austere school of Christian rationalism will find this vague talk about the "invisible world" unsatisfying. The Christian, like St. Thomas, insists on proof before accepting the supernatural, even though it be disguised as "absolute beauty."

Again, the Christian rationalist is perplexed by the modern attitude to immortality; for the modern sceptic does not begin by asking, as Socrates would have asked, whether life is good and therefore whether more life is better than less life. He assumes that man is mortal and proceeds to lecture those who disagree on their selfish interest in their own petty personalities.

There is nothing selfish in desiring that the whole human race should possess immortal souls, for selfishness is the search for personal happiness at the expense of other people. It would be so much easier to understand modern theology if our modern theologians would consult a good dictionary.

"I shall last out my time," you write, "and then finish. This prospect does not worry me, because some of my works will not die when I do." But your works will perish with the solar system, and if the individual is mortal his works are certainly not immortal.

In the same paper you tell us that you are proud to be a citizen of the British Empire, because the expectation of life is greatest in New Zealand, and next greatest in Australia. "I am proud to belong to a Commonwealth which has won the first and second places in the great race against death."

The Christian, then, may surely feel proud to belong to a Church which has left death standing at the post.

You are thrilled to discover that the expectation of life in New Zealand is sixty years. Why is it important for Mr. Jones to die at sixty rather than fifty-five and unimportant for Mr. Jones to continue living indefinitely beyond sixty? It would seem that it is important for us to increase our expectation of life by ten percent, but selfish of us to desire to increase it by infinity percent. I cannot quite follow the argument. Please enlighten me.

In your Conway Memorial Lecture[24] you write as follows: "Just as, according to the teachings of physiology, the unity

[24] The Conway Memorial Lecture is given annually at the South Place Ethical Society, which bills itself as "probably the oldest freethought community in the world". Founded in 1793 as a dissenting congregation, by 1888 the group had rejected the existence of God and had become an Ethical Society. In 1929 it left its original site and built a new hall named after its leader, Moncure Conway, in Red Lion Square, London. —ED.

of the body is not due to the soul superadded to the life of the cells. . . ."

Would it not have been more accurate to write: "Just as, according to some physiologists"? I do not think it is legitimate to substitute phrases such as "Science teaches" or "Physiology teaches" when you are merely voicing your own personal opinion. The quotation continues:

> So the superhuman, if it existed, would be nothing external to man, or even existing apart from human co-operation. But to my mind the teaching of science is very emphatic that such a Great Being may be a fact as real as the individual human consciousness, although, of course, there is no positive scientific evidence for the existence of such a Being. And it seems to me that everywhere ethical experience testifies to a super-individual reality of some kind. The good life, if not necessarily self-denial, is always self-transcendence.

Your confession of faith is characteristic of our age. First, because you obliterate the frontiers between religion and science. It is theology, not science, which teaches us that a Great Being exists. We can prove that God exists by pure reason without entering a laboratory or consulting modern astronomers.

Secondly, your confession is symptomatic of the growing realization that Naturalism is not enough. You have done your best to eliminate God, but—*usque recurret*.[25] Will you forgive me if I seem to detect in this passage the evidence of an *anima naturaliter Christiania*,[26] a soul unnaturally divorced

---

[25] "*Naturam expellas furca, tamen usque recurret*" ("You may drive nature out with a pitchfork, but it always will return"). Horace, *Ep.*, i, 10, 24. —ED.

[26] "A soul by nature Christian", used by Tertullian (155–c. 220) in *De testimonio animae* (*The Testimony of the Soul*), which was written in 197 shortly after and expanding upon his major work, *Apologeticum.* —ED.

by the infection of theophobia from that great religion which provides the only reasoned basis for that life of self-transcendence which you rightly admire?

Thirdly, your confession of faith is interesting, because it is modern in the sense that the moderns are abandoning all ✓ effort to ground their beliefs on reason and on evidence. To conceive of God as related to man much as man is related to his cells is an ingenious fancy, a fancy which would have delighted Fechner;[27] but it is nothing more than a fancy. It is neither probable nor plausible. By faith, and faith alone, can we even begin to believe in your synthetic God. I lack the requisite faith, for I am only a poor rationalist, a revenant from the greatest of all rationalistic centuries, the thirteenth, a century in which St. Thomas began, not with an ingenious fancy divorced from experience, but with the most obvious fact of experience, the fact that some things are in motion. And upon this irrefutable premise he proceeds to build the magnificent edifice of scholastic theology.

Certum est enim, et sensu constat, aliqua moveri in hoc mundo.[28] And upon this rock will I build my faith.

Yours ever,

Arnold Lunn

In his letter of December 14, 1932—the first few pages of which have been omitted in what follows—Lunn tried to refocus the debate onto the reasonableness of Christianity and the unreasonableness of Christianity's opponents. "Chris-

---

[27] Gustav Theodor Fechner (1801–1887), German physicist, philosopher, and psychologist. During his later years he devoted himself to natural philosophy, anthropology, and aesthetics. —ED.

[28] "It is certain, and evident to our senses, that in the world some things are in motion." Thomas Aquinas, *Summa Theologiae*, pt. I, q. 2, art. 3. —ED.

tians believe that the argument between the Christian and the non-Christian resolves itself into a duel between reason and prejudice. The case for the Church, we believe, is so strong that any man will be convinced who approaches this problem with an unprejudiced mind. . . . Your failure, then, to understand the Christian point of view cannot be ascribed either to ignorance or bad faith, and must therefore be attributable to ingrained prejudice. . . . Like most of your contemporaries, you approach this problem with a mind firmly closed to the possibility that Christianity may be true." [29]

"To begin with," writes Lunn, "the Church claims to found its case on reason. The Catholic believes that he can produce reasoned and convincing, if not coercive, arguments in support of his belief that God exists, that Christ was God, and that Christ founded a Church with authority to teach in His name." [30] There is little more frustrating for a Catholic than to be accused of leaving his mind at the door of the church. An unprejudiced man, observing the caliber of those who have entered or remained in the Church throughout the centuries, might be led to suspect that there is more to Catholicism—or to Christianity in general—than first meets the eye. If Christian beliefs seem unreasonable, yet if eminently reasonable men embrace them, then perhaps the problem is not with the beliefs but with the observer.

December 14, 1932

Dear Haldane,

By way of preface to what follows a word of personal explanation is necessary. In this correspondence we are concerned with the fundamental differences between Christianity and

[29] Lunn and Haldane, *Science and the Supernatural*, 49. —ED.
[30] Ibid., 50. —ED.

secularism and not with the minor differences between various Christian Churches. In my correspondence with Mr. Joad I had the worst of both worlds, for I did not run away from the difficulties of the Catholic position, and consequently was not free to disown, say, the Inquisition. In addition I was expected to reply to Mr. Joad's animadversions on the Church of England.

In this correspondence I propose to defend the Catholic interpretation of such doctrines as you may select for attack. I am not, as yet, a Catholic,[31] or even "under instruction," and your arguments may keep me out of the Church. Whatever be the result, I do not think I shall alter my view that the difference between a Catholic and an Anglican who is orthodox on the Incarnation is unimportant compared to the difference between those who believe in the Incarnation and those who do not.

And I hope that if I do become a Catholic I shall still be able to co-operate with all those who in this country and elsewhere are defending the basic doctrines of Christianity. And it is in defence of the beliefs which are common to all Christians that I have entered this discussion.

Having defined my position, I will now return to my criticism of yours. I share your anxiety to prevent this correspondence from developing into a "clanging match," and I see no reason why it should. I propose to criticize your recent book, *The Inequality of Man*, which I have read with the liveliest of interest; but I do so, not because I am anxious to make debating points at your expense, but because your book is a useful peg on which to hang a general criticism of the attitude of secularists to the Church.

Christians believe that the argument between the Chris-

[31] Lunn was received into the Catholic Church by Ronald Knox on July 13, 1933. —ED.

tian and the non-Christian resolves itself into a duel between reason and prejudice. The case for the Church, we believe, is so strong that any man will be convinced who approaches this problem with an unprejudiced mind. But how few do! Many years ago I wrote a book called *Roman Converts*. I should have been irritated then, as you may, perhaps, be irritated now, to be accused of prejudice. I had taken a great deal of trouble to get my facts right. I was not accused of obvious mistakes about Catholic doctrines, and yet I missed the whole point, just as you seem to me to have missed the point.

I admit that you are exceptionally placed to form an unbiased verdict. You have been trained in two great schools—philosophy and science. You have some acquaintance with Catholic literature, and you are not consciously unfair.

Your failure, then, to understand the Christian point of view cannot be ascribed either to ignorance or to bad faith, and must therefore be attributed to ingrained prejudice. You seem to start from the premise that this great philosophy, which has attracted many of the master minds of our race, is a puerile collection of absurdities. Like most of your contemporaries, you approach this problem with a mind firmly closed to the possibility that Christianity may be true.

Professor Whitehead is one of the few non-Catholic scientists in this country who have any sympathetic understanding of Catholic philosophy.

I do not want to make capital out of small points. I will therefore mention only two minor errors on points of fact which could not, I think, have been made by anybody who understood the Catholic outlook. St. Ambrose "became" a bishop when he was consecrated, not when he was offered the bishopric. A Catholic would realize instinctively that an unbaptized bishop is an impossibility. Again, Catholics do not regard "celibacy" as a pre-requisite of sanctity, as you would know if you understood the Catholic view of sanctity. These are minor points. More interesting is your failure to understand the Catholic attitude to authority and to the interpretation of the Bible, and your inability to realize what Catholics believe about transubstantiation.

To begin with, the Church claims to found its case on reason. The Catholic believes that he can produce reasoned and convincing, if not coercive, arguments in support of his belief that God exists, that Christ was God, and that Christ founded a Church with authority to teach in His name. The Church also proposes for his acceptance certain truths, such as the doctrine of the Trinity, which unaided human reason could never have discovered. It is not, however, irrational to accept these truths on the authority of the Church, provided that you can prove by reason that the Church is infallible.

The individual Catholic accepts as proven the doctrines which the Church has defined as true, but few non-Catholics realize how wide is the area open to discussion among Catholics. There is a far greater economy of definition in the Church than you seem to realize.

When, for instance, the controversy about evolution broke over Europe, the Church maintained an attitude of cautious reserve. The Church has seen too many scientific fashions rise and disappear to allow the latest scientific hypothesis to be taught in her name before it has been thoroughly examined. The Church never condemned the theory of evolution, and to-day the theory of the evolution of lower animals may be taught as a "probable hypothesis." So far as the evolution of man's body is concerned, the Church says that nobody may teach this theory in her name, but that the individual Catholic is free to hold this belief and to work for its establishment, if he wishes, by discussion and research.

There is an old saying that it is not the business of the Church to teach men how the heavens go, but to teach men how to go to heaven. The Church makes no claim to infallibility in scientific matters, but the views of churchmen on scientific matters naturally reflect those of their age.

The Church is slow to define and slow to censure, and the fact that a particular statement has not been censured no more proves that the Church made that statement her own than the fact that a particular doctrine has not been defined proves that the doctrine in question is heretical. You quote some naïve remarks by a mediaeval writer, and add a sentence which shows that you misconceive the Church's defining claims. "That is where," you write, "in the opinion of many mediaeval writers, who were not censured by the Church, your argument leads." You could produce a catena of statements by mediaeval writers who were not censured by the Church, but which no modern Catholic would accept.

Your remarks about the Bible show a similar failure to appreciate the Catholic point of view. The Church claims that her credentials can be proved from certain books in the Bible, treating them as purely human documents. The Bible itself consists of a series of books selected by the Catholic Church—books which the Catholic Church claims the right to interpret. It is for the Church to say where the Bible records objective fact and where the Bible uses metaphor and allegory, and on such points theologians differ and will differ from age to age. When the Biblical Commission, for instance, lays down certain rules for the interpretation of the first chapter of Genesis, all we can say is that the views of that Commission represent the views which, in the opinion of the Church, may safely be taught at the present moment. A future commission may take a different line.

And now for your remarks about the creeds. I read your statement about the provisional nature of your own beliefs as applying to your own confession of faith. I did not suppose that you intended these remarks to qualify your curt contempt for the creeds of other people. Nor do I think you can escape the charge of injustice to the Church merely because you began with a statement about the provisional character of your convictions. If, for instance, that statement had been followed by the assertion that the Wells-Huxley *Science of Life*[32] was "full of obsolete science"—which of course it is not—I do not think that Mr. Wells would have been much consoled by the defence that the listeners-in to this broadcast talk had been warned that all your views were provisional, and consequently could not have been misled.

Your defence of your attack on the creeds is unconvincing. Genesis is not a creed, and your allusions to Genesis have, therefore, strictly no relevance to the question as to whether the creeds are full of obsolete science. The problem as to how far Genesis is allegory, and how far fact, is still debated among Catholic theologians: there is no defined doctrine on this point. From the earliest of Christian times simple believers have thought of the heavens as solid, and have interpreted literally metaphorical statements, such as "at the right hand of God," but there have never lacked theologians to emphasize the difference between metaphor and fact. Thus St. Jerome, commenting on "foolish talking,"[33] cites as an illustration of such nonsense the fact that some Christians are foolish enough to believe that "Heaven is curved like an arch and that a throne is placed in Heaven, and that God sits upon it, and that, as if he were a commander or

[32] H. G. Wells, G. P. Wells, and Aldous Huxley, *The Science of Life* (London: Doran, 1931). —ED.

[33] Eph 5:4. —ED.

judge, the angels stand round to obey his commands and to be sent on different missions." [34]

St. Thomas Aquinas underlines the warning. "When scripture speaks," he writes, "of God's arm, the literal sense is not that God has such a member, but only what he signifies by this member, namely, operative power . . . the very hiding of truth in figures is useful for the exercise of thoughtful minds, and as a defence against the ridicule of the impious, according to the words 'give not that which is holy to the dogs.' " [35]

Controversy is tiresome if neither side is prepared to concede an obvious point. I therefore concede that Mr. Belloc was mistaken when he tentatively suggested that you had confused the Immaculate Conception with the Virgin Birth,[36] and that I should not have assumed that your failure to protest against this criticism justified me in repeating the charge. I expect in return that you will concede the point that you were wrong in stating that the creeds are full of obsolete science, a mistake which was an unconscious inheritance from your remote Protestant past. Literalism is a Protestant, not a Catholic, failing.

One small point. Neither Strauss nor Zola, so far as I know, qualified their remarks by any operative sentence at the beginning of their books as an antidote to the dogmatism of their later expression. They were both prepared to stand firmly by what they wrote. They were not, as you correctly remark, modern sceptics.

I am not particularly surprised by your failure to understand the Catholic attitude to the Bible, and, in particular, to "Literalism," for few non-Catholics are aware that these

---

[34] Jerome, *Commentary on Ephesians*, bk. III. —ED.

[35] Thomas Aquinas, *Summa Theologiae*, pt. I, q. I, art. 10. —ED.

[36] See n. 22 above. —ED.

rather elementary problems have been discussed from the earliest times; but I am frankly puzzled by your remarks about transubstantiation. Surely the whole point about transubstantiation is that it is not a change of form but of substance. Why do you persist in maintaining that transubstantiation is supposed to effect a chemical change? Surely a scientist who in certain moods affects such impressive humility can confess to an error in a branch of knowledge which is outside his normal line of research? You needn't worry. I dare say I shall make worse howlers when I begin to criticize Darwinism, though, in point of fact, at the time of writing no such patent howlers have been brought home to me. But as you apparently expect argument and resent assertion on what is, however, a simple question of fact, let me suggest that though Catholics attribute "profound effects to eating" a wafer, these effects are not, as you imply, ascribed to any chemical change in the consecrated elements. What do you make of this case? Two Catholics communicate. The first is in a state of mortal sin. The second has been absolved. The chemical constituents of the wafer are the same in both cases, and yet Catholics hold that the "profound effect of eating" the wafer are profoundly different in these two cases.

As to "bleeding hosts," it is no part of defined doctrine to believe in bleeding hosts; but if some such case could be authenticated, what would it prove? That transubstantiation is a chemical process because the host sometimes bleeds? No, but that two miracles had taken place: first the non-chemical miracle of transubstantiation; secondly, a gratuitous and additional miracle which might or might not produce a chemical change in the consecrated wafer.

But really you might allow the unfortunate Catholic to know what Catholics believe about transubstantiation. Whether transubstantiation takes place is a matter of opinion on which you are entitled to your view. Whether Catholics believe that transubstantiation involves a chemical change is a question of fact on which you are wrong and on which I am right. I shall only be prepared to qualify the curt dogmatism of this statement when you can produce in your support a recognized Catholic theologian who believes in a chemical change of accidents rather than in a non-chemical change of the substance.

Froude,[37] who hated Catholicism, had sufficient imagination to write an admirable essay on Catholic philosophy. You are content to poke fun at the sacraments, for I do not think that the following passage really represents your considered views. "If to-day," you write, "we find it difficult to imagine how so much emotion could gather round the act of eating, we must remember that the majority of Christians were so poor that they had first-hand experience of hunger. To most of them food must have presented itself, not as a source of mildly pleasant sensations, but vividly as a life-giver."

You are an adept at representing men whom Catholics revere in a slightly ridiculous light. You do not allow your reader to suspect the grandeur of that great scene when St. Ambrose held the Arians at bay—the occasion to which we owe that noble hymn the *Te Deum*. St. Ambrose emerges without distinction from your slight sketch, though you salve your historical conscience by two compliments. St. Thomas Aquinas, again, is regarded as one of the greatest intellects and greatest saints in the Catholic Church. In a few deft touches you make him ridiculous: "St. Thomas, it is said, was one of the fattest men who ever lived, and in his latter years could carry out the ritual of the Mass only at a specially constructed

[37] James Anthony Froude (1818–1894), sceptic and anti-Catholic historian whose *History of England* Charles Kingsley reviewed; younger brother of Newman's close friend Hurrell Froude (1803–1834). —ED.

legend, but one who is both a scientist and a mathematician
should be able to calculate the waist measurement which
would be necessary to prevent St. Thomas reaching the altar
with his hands. Five seconds' thought disposes of this legend.
Perhaps you have read Peter Calo's[38] life which appeared in
1300. He tells us that St. Thomas's features corresponded
with the nobility of his soul, that he was tall and of heavy
build, but straight and well proportioned. Francesca's[39] portrait at Milan confirms this impression.

Your remarks about St. Thomas occur in an essay on
"god-making," an essay which is largely taken up with a
discussion of transubstantiation.

A reviewer in *The Times Literary Supplement*, in the course
of a discerning and friendly criticism of this book, remarked
that your "animadversions on religion will cause much pain."
I was not pained, only puzzled that so much reading of
Catholic literature could produce so little understanding of
the Catholic point of view. And I think that the clue not
only to your attitude, but also to that of the intelligentsia is to
be found in one revealing sentence. "I find religions an
absorbing topic," you write. "The intellectual side of this
effort interests me mainly because of its fantastic character.
The stories of how hundreds of millions of the people came
to believe in the immaculate conception, the uncreated Ko-
ran, or the spiritual advantages of bathing in the Ganges are
fascinating both as history and psychology."

If your object be to suggest that Catholicism is only of
interest to the psychologist, you have succeeded in conveying

[38] The life of Aquinas, as written by Peter Calo, is given in Dominik
Prümmer's *Fontes Vitae S. Thomae Aquinatis* (Toulouse, 1911). —ED.

[39] Piero della Francesca (c. 1420–1492), Italian painter, master of perspective. He wrote treatises on painting and on mathematics. —ED.

Formed the
Modern Temper
in '29.

that impression of the learned man relaxing after a hard day's work in the laboratory! Feet on the fender, he dips into some weird Catholic work, and an indulgent smile steals over his lips as he muses in the rum beliefs of misguided men. Yes, you could not convey more cleverly that attitude of indulgent superiority which is so much more effective than mere argument.

I pay you the compliment of assuming that there are moments when you suspect the true scale of Catholic philosophy. The mere fact that you, a busy man, have agreed to debate these great issues is proof that you consider them worth debating. And I should be only too happy if, as the result of this correspondence, I had contrived to persuade you that it shows a certain failure of perception to bracket in the same sentence the doctrines of Catholicism and Hinduism.

Yours ever,

Arnold Lunn

In his last contribution to the correspondence (the first third of which is omitted here), Lunn sums up his argument under several points. First he lists the chief prejudices of the nonbeliever: that Christians adhere to outmoded science, that Catholics are philosophically confused on such matters as substance and accidents, that faith is fraudulent and unreasonable, and that the "Torquemada theme" undercuts Catholic claims. Then Lunn lists the propositions he has tried to convey: that faith is grounded on reason, that miracles have evidence in their favor, that evolution is at best unproved and that its advocates are disingenuous, that Thomistic arguments for the existence of God are sufficient, and that he has attacked scientists for failing to apply the scientific method.

November 14, 1934

Dear Haldane,

Life is a choice of sacrifices, and something has had to be
sacrificed for the advantages of a point-by-point discussion
between two disputants. The orderly and balanced development of an argument, which is easy enough in an *ex parte*
statement, is impossible in a correspondence of this description. I claim, however, that we have covered a great deal of
ground, and I hope our occasional digressions will be forgiven us. Moreover, this form of controversy serves at least
one valuable purpose, for it proves that the Christian has no
reason to fear debate, and no need to appeal from reason to
intuition.

The modern convert to Christianity has to fight his way
through a jungle of prejudice, and I do not therefore regret
the space which has been devoted to discussing four of the
principal prejudices which operate against an unbiased examination of the all but coercive evidence for Christianity.
Those prejudices are as follows:

First Prejudice.—That Christians are committed to pre-
Copernican astronomy, and that science has definitely disproved Christian doctrines. As you failed to reply to my
challenge to name a single authoritatively defined dogma of
the Catholic Church which has been disproved by science, I
take it that we are in agreement on this point. My quotations
from St. Thomas, St. Jerome, and St. Clement abundantly
prove that theologians were more alive to the distinction
between allegory and fact than some of their modern
critics.[40]

---

[40] The only Bishop [Ernest William Barnes, Anglican bishop of Birming-
ham] in the Royal Society appears to have contracted the habit so prevalent
among popular scientists of making stupid and unsupported statements on this

Second Prejudice.—Arising out of the first prejudice is the belief that all those who accept the Catholic doctrine of the Eucharist "worship a biscuit," to quote your phrase, and believe that a few words of hocus-pocus by a priest will produce chemical changes in the aforesaid biscuit. This vulgar error is mainly due to the fact that the word "substance" as used by philosophers means something very different from the word "substance" as used by the man in the street.

The doctrine of Transubstantiation, which I have not yet defined in these letters, is an attempt to explain the real presence of Christ in terms of that "realistic" school of philosophy which has triumphed over the "nominalist."

This great mediaeval controversy turned on the fundamental question as to the nature and reality of universals. Here is an apple. It appears red to the eye, sweet to the tongue, resilient to the touch, and silent to the ear. These qualities of the apple which are discernible by the five senses are the "accidents" of the apple. But is the apple anything more than a group of impressions? No, said the nominalists, the word "apple" is nothing but a handy name for a collection of sensations. Yes, said the realists, there is a real apple, a universal which is independent of these particular manifestations. The "substance" of an apple is the

subject. In his book, *Scientific Theory and Religion*, he tells us (page 301) that the flatness and fixity of the earth were "taken over into the Christian creeds." Which creeds? On page 420 he describes as erroneous the "authorized teaching of the Roman Church" regarding the date of creation. What date did the Church authorize? He also refers to the "doctrine of the special creation of species." There is no such doctrine. Incidentally one of the most eminent of English mathematicians, Professor Whittaker, F.R.S. [Edmund Taylor Whittaker (1873–1956), British mathematician and historian], severely criticizes the mathematical theories that are put forward in this book by Bishop Barnes.

thing "in itself" (the "real" apple, hence the term "realist"), and is imperceptible to the senses, and cannot be detected by any scientific tests. This substance—the noumenon of Kant—is the substratum which sustains phenomena. In the Mass the substance of bread is changed into the substance of our Lord's body, but the accidents, which alone are capable of chemical change, remain unaffected.

Third Prejudice.—This is due to a fundamental misunderstanding of the Catholic attitude to faith. In your second letter you made merry about our simplicity in holding that "faith is a virtue." And you proceed to draw a complaisant contrast between yourself and Father Knox, "who is bound to defend any statement found in the penny catechism." In a later letter you registered indignation because you believed, wrongly, that I had attacked your mental integrity.

You will probably be surprised that your sweeping attack on the intellectual integrity of bishops (see page 14) should provoke a rejoinder. I was not present when Christ rose from the dead, and you were not present when a reptile thought that it would be rather nice to grow wings. My belief in the Resurrection is largely based on documents which are in existence. Your belief in evolution is largely based on documents which have disappeared, those missing volumes in nature's book to which the evolutionist appeals with such sunny confidence.

The trouble with you people is that you have managed to persuade yourselves not only that your own unflattering view of Christians is correct, but that the Christian reply would be, not to deny your charge, but to defend the attitude which you falsely attribute to them. It is, for instance, a widespread illusion in your circles that Catholics have "got" to believe in certain doctrines because "faith is a virtue."

The Catholic, like other people, is bound by the rules of

the institution of which he is a member. You cannot remain a fellow of the Royal Society unless you pay your subscription, and I cannot remain a Catholic unless I continue to subscribe to the defined doctrines of the Church. I have not "got" to believe in Catholic doctrines for the good reason that I have not "got" to remain a Catholic.

You would cease to be an evolutionist if a complete human skeleton were found in Cambrian strata, and I should cease to be a Catholic if it could be proved beyond all reasonable doubt that the disciples had stolen the body of Jesus and faked the Resurrection story. But you would be very much surprised if I told you that you had "got" to believe in evolution.

True, I accept on certain authority beliefs which I am not in a position to investigate for myself, but there is nothing irrational in accepting beliefs on authority provided that one can prove by reason that the authority is reliable. I have not been to hell and I have not been to Moscow, but I believe that both these unpleasant places exist. I believe in Moscow on the authority of people who have visited it, and I believe in hell on the authority of Jesus Christ who claimed to be God, and proved his claim by rising from the dead.

Faith is a virtue not because the Christian creed is difficult to believe, but because the Christian code is difficult to accept. Self-restraint is uncomfortable, and it is therefore tempting to rationalize one's dislike of the code and represent it as an intellectual objection to the creed. "Faith," said the schoolboy, "is believing in what one knows isn't true." If this were true faith would be a vice. Faith is a virtue, for it is often difficult to believe uncomfortable truths and to reject pleasant falsehoods, and in such cases faith represents the triumph of reason over sin, silliness, and conceit.

You implied in your earlier letters that bishops continue to recite creeds which they do not believe because they are frightened of going to hell. The following quotation from the 1934 edition of Professor Karl Adam's magnificent book, *The Spirit of Catholicism*,[41] may help to lighten your darkness on this point. The italics are mine. Page 227:

> On the other hand, the Church does not compel the Catholic to shut his eyes to the religious problems which arise, nor does she even permit him to do so. The Vatican Council condemns blind faith, and stipulates with the apostle[42] that the obedience of our faith should be in accordance with reason (*obsequium rationi consentaneum*).
>
> But it is especially here, in this extremest conflict between authority and conscience, that we realize again the intense earnestness with which the Church guards the rights of conscience, even of an erroneous conscience. It can scarcely be doubted that in most cases of lapse from the Church, the ultimate causes lie not in the intellectual but in the ethical sphere. . . . But it is important to note that Catholic theologians teach plainly and unanimously that the sometime Catholic is bound to follow his new attitude of mind, so long as it is a genuine and invincible conviction of conscience. Even though the judgment of his conscience be objectively false, and even though it be not in its genesis ethically irreproachable, yet he is bound to follow conscience and conscience alone.

Fourth Prejudice.—This prejudice may be described as the Torquemada theme, which made a very early appearance in this correspondence.

"Cruelty and the abuse of absolute power," said Charles Dickens, "are the two bad passions of human nature."

---

[41] Karl Adam, *The Spirit of Catholicism* (New York: Macmillan, 1934 [1924]), 227–28. —Ed.

[42] Romans 12:1.

Dickens was more scientific than those who use these universal passions as a stick to beat any institution which they happen to dislike. Few institutions and few individuals can resist the temptations of absolute power, but if the Inquisition is an argument against Catholicism, the persecution in communist Russia is an equally valid argument against atheism.

Christ promised two things, first that his Church should endure to the end, and secondly that his Church should never teach error. He never promised that all Catholics, ecclesiastics or laymen, should be magically free from universal human passions, including the passions mentioned by Dickens.

Nothing is more irrational than to register indignation when the Church does certain things of which you disapprove, and to condone the same things when done by institutions of which you approve. Even if we Catholics were to concede as true everything that you could possibly say about the Inquisition, and every kind of libel unsupported by evidence about the Church in Ireland, or, say, Quebec, what would this prove? Merely that Dickens was right.

Severe critics have recently paid a generous tribute to the attitude of the Church during recent troubles. Our Catholic Press has whole-heartedly condemned the persecution of Jews in Germany,[43] and no less whole-heartedly supported the magnificent stand which is being made by the German Protestants for spiritual autonomy. A strong alliance between all theists, Catholics, Protestants and Jews, to protest against all forms of religious persecution would have a tremendous effect. It is a thousand pities that the left-wing Press give the

[43] Given today's allegations that Catholics and the Church took little cognizance of the Nazi persecution of Jews, it it worth noting that this correspondence occurred in 1934. —ED.

impression not of objecting to persecution as such, but merely of objecting when the victims are those with whom they are in political sympathy.

I cannot resist quoting in this connexion a leading article in the *Sunday Referee*, a paper which is not, so far as I know, in the pay of the Pope:

> The history of the Roman Catholic Church is almost the history of humanity itself. There have been periods when the Church became the instrument of tyranny and fanaticism. Now it stands in Europe as the one hope against the surging tide of dictatorship which is plunging the people into a darkness deeper than that of the feudal ages. The Pope is more than the head of the Church today. He has become the guardian and the hope of Western civilization.

If you reply that intolerance is integral to the Catholic position, you are guilty of the usual confusion between tolerance of error and tolerance of men in error. Catholics are expected, in the words of St. Augustine, "to love men and to hate error." [44] You will agree that a man need be neither a fool nor a fanatic to believe that the available evidence leads irresistibly to the conclusion that Christ proved his claim to be God by rising from the dead, and founded a Church which is supernaturally protected from teaching error. Thousands of men have sacrificed friends, position, and money to join the Catholic Church, and amongst these thousands there must be some at least who are your equal in intellectual acumen and in intellectual integrity. If, however, you once admit that a man need be neither a fool nor a fanatic to accept the Catholic claims, the claim that God speaks through his Church, you cannot deny to Catholics the right to draw logical conclusions from this

[44] Augustine, *Contra. Lit. Petil.* I, xxix, n. 31, in P.L. 23:259. —ED.

premise, or complain if they draw a distinction between the truths which God has revealed and the truths which man has discovered for himself.

You tell me that when you frame a scientific hypothesis you try your hardest to disprove it. Your writings suggest, on the contrary, that you have accepted with simple faith the fashionable dogma of the day, evolution, and made no attempt whatever to disprove it. The scepticism, however, which you preach—but do not practise—is, I agree, fully justified by the rapidity with which scientific theories are reversed and discarded. But though it is our duty to receive with scepticism every theory put forward by scientists, "Speak Lord, for thy servant heareth," [45] is the only logical attitude if we can prove by reason that God has spoken. Heresy, if the Catholic premise is correct, is rebellion against truths revealed by God. Disprove the Catholic premise if you can, but do not accuse the Catholic of intolerance merely because he draws logical conclusions from that premise. Heresy, if our premise be correct, is evil, but the individual heretic may be a near saint. May I quote again from Professor Karl Adam (page 192): "We Catholics regard this Christian life, wherever it appears, with unfeigned respect and with thankful love. . . . And not merely a Christian life, but a complete and lofty Christian life, a life according to the 'full age of Christ,' a saintly life, is possible—so Catholics believe even in definitely non-Catholic communions." So much for prejudices. And now for the main issues that divide us.

You might have chosen *The Conflict Between Science and Religion* as the title for this book, and I should have preferred *The Conflict Between Science and Atheism*, which suggests that it is time that scientists of your way of thinking

Good response to Hitchens, Dawkins, Dennett & Harris

[45] 1 Sam 3:9. —ED.

should invent some new label which we could accept to describe your sect, which achieved its greatest triumphs during the Victorian era, and which is now fighting a desperate rearguard action. And until you can suggest something better, I propose to call you people after one of your great prophets, Thomas Huxley.[46] The Victorian Huxleyites were prepared to accept any explanation, however fantastic and however unsupported by evidence, rather than admit the possibility of a supernatural explanation of apparently supernormal events. There was something heroic in their refusal to examine the evidence for facts which would have upset their theories. They had many affinities with the narrower Puritan sects, the same complaisancy and the same pulpit manner. It was no more surprising that Huxley should have published his essays under the title of *Lay Sermons* than that his grandson should preach *Religion without Revelation*.[47] Even Wells seems to have been infected for a time by Huxleyism. He wrote, you will remember, a highly comic book in which he asked us to worship a god rather like Mr. Wells. Unfortunately Mr. Wells' accommodating god did not possess a robust constitution. And Mr. Wells, who seems secretly ashamed of this episode, has yet to build an altar to the stillborn god. The true Huxleyites are disappearing. Julian Huxley has made some very sensible remarks about psychical research, and you make concessions which would have shocked his grandfather. But if you are entitled to describe yourself as a Darwinist you are no less entitled

[46] Thomas Henry Huxley (1825–1895), English biologist and avid supporter of Darwin—he was called "Darwin's bulldog". He wrote on evolution and took on Bishop Samuel Wilberforce (1805–1873), the Bishop of Oxford, in a famous exchange in 1860. He was president of the Royal Society from 1883 to 1885. —Ed.

[47] Julian Huxley (1887–1975), *Religion without Revelation* (New York: Harper, 1927). —Ed.

to describe yourself as a Huxleyite, a concession which will please you.

A debate between a Christian and a non-Christian normally begins with a sniff or two on the subject of faith, and normally ends with the non-Christian appealing to fif[48] in support of beliefs for which there is no evidence whatever. Thus Joad began good-humouredly by imploring me not to play the trump card of faith more than once, and then proceeded to play trumps throughout the rest of the book. His only reply to the evidence for the Resurrection was an appeal to his own negative faith. He claimed, for instance, that it was reasonable to reject everything in the gospels which was "antecedently improbable." It is only fair to add that Joad's mind is by no means closed to the possibility of the supernatural, and I hope and believe that the massive evidence for Christianity impressed him more than he was prepared at the time to admit.

You opened with a flagrant misunderstanding of the Church's attitude to faith, and appealed again and again to the fif which assures you that something, such as spontaneous generation, for which there is no evidence, has occurred in the past, and that the links which continue to be missing will turn up in the future.

In this book I have maintained the following propositions:

1. Faith is grounded on reason and historic documents. Huxleyism is grounded on fif, and the dogma, for which there is no shred of evidence, that everything which takes place is explicable in terms of natural law. This book might be described as the conflict between Faith and Fif.

2. I claim to have shown that the evidence for the miracles at Lourdes and for the supernormal phenomena of the séance

[48] "Funny internal feeling", a term coined by Lunn in *Now I See*, 76–83. —ED.

room which the Huxleyite rejected without examination is immeasurably stronger than the evidence for major evolution. I claim that the Huxleyite has no objective standard of truth, since he accepts the latter and rejects the former. The Huxleyite, for instance, jumped at Darwinism before the monk Mendel[49] had provided scientists with some faint vestige of an excuse for accepting that amazing theory, but refused to examine the contemporary evidence for supernormal happenings.

3. I claim to have proved that evolutionary changes do not transcend the limits of the natural family, and seldom transcend the limits of the genus. "Only rarely," writes Vialleton, "has it been found possible to trace a genus step by step without artifice into an earlier genus; moreover, when this can be done, it is never a case of two creatures essentially different in their organization, but of neighbouring forms of which the organization continues in the same line." [50]

4. I have shown that the alleged imperfection of the geological record is an invalid argument. Dewar's argument on this point[51] seems to me irresistible. The layman is apt to forget that though the odds against a particular specimen of a genus surviving in fossil form are very great, the number of specimens of any genus is also very great.

5. I accuse Huxleyites of a lack of candour. The case against theism is stated and refuted in Catholic text-books of

[49] Gregor Johann Mendel (1822–1884), Austrian botanist. He entered the Augustinians in 1843 and became known for breeding experiments with peas. —ED.

[50] Louis Vialleton (1859–1929), French zoologist, professor of comparative anatomy at Montpellier, staunch opponent of Darwin and evolution, and author of *L'Illusion Transformiste* (Paris: Plan, 1929). —ED.

[51] Douglas Dewar (1875–1957), *Difficulties of the Evolution Theory* (London: Edward Arnold, 1931). Dewar was a barrister and amateur ornithologist. After retiring from the Indian Civil Service in 1924, he turned to a critical evaluation of evolution. —ED.

natural theology. The fact that there is a case at all against evolution is suppressed in most modern books on evolution. The reader, for instance, will search contemporary evolutionary literature in vain to discover an adequate treatment of the difficulties summarized in Dewar's book *The Difficulties of the Evolutionary Theory*. You are a busy man, but you found time to read this book, and you will agree, therefore, that it cannot be dismissed as completely unimportant.

The disingenuous nature of certain favourite arguments in support of evolution might be cited by the uncharitable as evidence in support of the view that scientists were deliberately attempting to confuse the issue. But the true explanation is probably to be sought in the strange workings of crowd psychology. We have all been brought up to believe that evolution has been proved beyond all possible doubt, and this illusion muddies the springs of thought. As examples of such arguments let me mention the fact that evolutionists frequently confuse, as you have done, evidence which merely proves succession, a truth affirmed in Genesis, with the evidence which they need to prove evolution by descent. Again, evolutionists confuse, as you have done, a true lineage series with the existence of fossils difficult to classify. Finally, it is uncandid to imply, as evolutionists habitually imply, that evidence which suggests evolution within the limits of family or genus or species lends any support whatever to the belief that evolution has transcended the limits of the natural family. The fact is that your belief in evolution is mystical rather than scientific. Why don't you drop arguing and appeal quite simply to religious experience? "If you knew what archaeopteryx[52] means to me, I think you'd understand."

[52] Archaeopteryx, discovered in 1859, supposedly was a crow-sized bird of the Upper Jurassic period having reptilian characteristics. Evolutionists argue it is a transitional form between birds and reptiles. —Ed.

6. Let me sum up. There are three possible theories of evolution; first, the theory of purely natural evolution, which breaks down on the geological record; secondly, fundamentalism, that is, that the different types were created *ex nihilo* by God, a theory which raises less difficulties than that of natural evolution, but which is difficult to reconcile with the existence of vestigial remains; thirdly, there is Evo-creationism—I don't in the least like this name, but until somebody suggests a better label I shall describe as Evo-creationists all those who hold, as Vialleton for one holds that though natural evolution may explain all changes within the limits of the family, a supernatural creative force alone can account for the origin of life, and can alone offer a satisfactory explanation of the vast ragged gaps in the geological record. Direct creation out of nothing, or a supernatural and sudden mutation of existent forms, is the only reasonable explanation of the suddenness with which new forms appear. Of these two explanations, I prefer the second (Evo-creationism), for this explanation not only avoids all the difficulties of natural evolution, but also offers a perfectly satisfactory explanation of those vestigial remains which so strongly suggest evolution from simpler and earlier forms.

May I re-state in this summary that no Catholic is forbidden to believe in evolution? You probably know that the Rectorial Council of the Catholic University of Louvain sent Canon Dorlodot[53] to represent them at the Darwin centenary. He made a most eloquent speech on that occasion, and paid a generous tribute to Darwin as "the interpreter of the organic world."

7. I have met your criticisms of the Thomist arguments

[53] Henri de Dorlodot taught at the University of Louvain. His book *Darwinism and Catholic Thought* was translated into English in 1922 by E. C. Messenger.—ED

for the existence of God, and I claim to have shown that nature is not self-explanatory, and that the evidence of nature forces us to accept the hypothesis of an intelligent Creator. I do not claim in this correspondence to have proved that the Creator is either all-powerful or all good, for it is necessary to prove the existence of God before proceeding to discuss his nature.

Kreeft

8. I repeat that I have attacked neither science nor the scientific method. On the contrary, I have attacked the Huxleyites in general, and you in particular, for failing to apply the scientific method either to evolution or to religion. I believe with St. Ambrose that aspirations after truth are the workings of the Holy Spirit. The courageous experiments, for instance, which you have made on your own body are as much the product of a religious impulse as your belief in a world of absolute values.

I have tried to answer your genial pot-shots against Catholicism, but my letters must be read as a defence of theism rather than of Catholicism. I began this book just as I had completed my controversial correspondence with Father Knox, and I was not received into the Church until we had reached the middle point of our correspondence. I am just preparing a talk on "The Pleasures of Coat-Trailing," but though I enjoy enticing atheists into battle, I do not seek controversy with those who believe that the only hope for this distracted world is a return to Christ, and who worship Christ as God. I have stated, and may re-state in the future, my reasons for accepting the Catholic Faith, but I believe that this can be done without appearing to imply that the points on which Christians disagree are more important than the points on which they are in full accord. I owe a debt, greater than I can repay, to the example of Christians who are not Catholics, and I should be sorry if anything I wrote

Lewis

wounded those for whom I have such a deep affection and respect.

May I conclude by thanking you, which I do in all sincerity, for accepting my challenge, and for enabling me to put my case before your readers. We disagree on much. We agree, at least, in believing that controversy is valuable, and that hard hitting is as legitimate in verbal debate as in boxing. Our readers may have many grievances against us, but at least they will not complain that we have attempted to disguise our views.

Allow me then to subscribe myself, in the pleasant diction of the eighteenth century,

Your most humble and obliged servant,

Arnold Lunn

7

Herbert Thurston, S.J., vs. G. G. Coulton

Of the essays collected in this book, Herbert Thurston's is the most technical, the most academic, and perhaps the most devastating. His dissection of H. C. Lea's scholarship is a textbook example of the lengths to which a Catholic apologist sometimes must go to counteract falsehoods leveled against the Church. As Thurston says in his last paragraph, "Lea presents a case which to the normal reviewer, indolent or otherwise, seems entirely convincing and satisfactory. . . . The blunders only come to light when, after much toil and waste of time, one investigates the sources appealed to and finds that they say something entirely different from what the American controversialist has read into them." The problem, Thurston notes earlier, is that "he [Lea] possessed little of the scholar's devotion to accuracy for its own sake. In matters with which the literary circle he belonged to were likely to be conversant he was relatively careful, but when he was dealing with Catholic beliefs and abuses about which his friends knew nothing and cared less, he took practically no pains at all to keep his strong anti-religious bias under control."

In a letter to Ronald Knox, Arnold Lunn recounted how Thurston came to examine Lea's work:

Dr. [G. G.] Coulton was incensed by a casual remark of Father Thurston's that "it would be a safe thing probably, to say that in any ten consecutive pages" (of Dr. H. C. Lea's *Auricular Confession and Indulgences*, Vol. III) "ten palpable blunders may be unearthed." Lea was an American Coulton and Dr. Coulton was naturally concerned to increase Lea's reputation as an historian, a reputation which, like Dr. Coulton's, was largely due to the use made of his works by enemies of the Church. Dr. Coulton's faith in Lea's scholarship was so uncritical that he invited a friend to pick ten pages at random from Lea's book, threw in an extra couple of pages to prove his magnanimity, and sent the twelve pages to Father Thurston. In the course of a dictated letter he said, "I defy you to find even a single patent blunder in all these twelve pages, and I put it to you plainly that you are now in a position in which your very worse policy is that of obstinate muteism."

Father Thurston had no need to fall back upon "muteism". He produced not twelve but fifteen blunders in the twelve pages, not one of which Dr. Coulton ventured to defend. "I am forced to admit," he wrote, "that Father Thurston has damaged Lea's accuracy in these twelve pages more than I expected." [1]

Herbert Thurston, S.J. (1856–1939), is little known today, but in his time he was recognized as an expert on spiritualism. His fascination with the topic started in childhood. When he was eight or nine, his father became interested in hypnotism, which then was called "mesmerism", and the young Thurston marveled at public demonstrations of the art. "I may confess that the impression that there are mysterious forces in nature of which we understand very little has remained with me ever since, although on the other hand I

---

[1] Ronald Knox and Arnold Lunn, *Difficulties* (London: Eyre and Spottiswoode, 1952), 250. —ED.

seem to be personally quite devoid of sensibility to their subtle influence. I have never had anything which I could seriously call a psychic experience in my life, and I think that my natural bent is distinctly in the direction of scepticism." [2] It was this bent that made Thurston such a formidable scholarly adversary. He took little for granted.

Born in London, he was educated at Stonyhurst and London University. He entered the Jesuit order, served as master of Beaumont College from 1880 to 1887, and was ordained in 1890. Most of his remaining years were spent at the Farm Street Church, run by the Jesuits, and there he concentrated on writing. A frequent writer for Catholic periodicals, especially *The Month*, he also contributed articles to the *Catholic Encyclopedia*. His critical edition of Butler's *Lives of the Saints*, in twelve volumes, appeared from 1926 through 1938. This work led him into a study of mysticism, particularly the questionable kind, and resulted in several books on that topic.

Thurston's adversary in this essay, G. G. Coulton (1858–1947), studied at Cambridge and was ordained a priest in the Church of England in 1884. His faith failing him quickly, the next year he removed himself from ministerial work and began to teach in public and private schools. Around the turn of the century he decided to concentrate on medieval studies, especially the ecclesiastical system. To supplement his living he began writing books, such as *Chaucer and His England* (1908), but it was not until he was sixty-one that he was made a fellow of Saint John's College, Cambridge, and found himself with a secure income and challenging work. His reputation grew as he produced ever more articles and books based on his wide knowledge of

[2] Herbert Thurston, S.J., *The Church and Spiritualism* (Milwaukee: Bruce, 1933), xi–xii. —ED.

medieval art, architecture, and history. Considering himself a "moderate Protestant", his "strongly expressed religious views entangled him in a number of prolonged and stormy contests with Roman Catholic historians and divines and in the opinion of many raised more dust and heat than light".[3] Aidan Mackey, a bookseller who operates the G. K. Chesterton Study Centre, characterized Coulton as "an extremely gifted writer, but acrimonious in controversy, and with an obsessive hatred of the Roman Catholic Church. This, together with his unrelenting pursuit of minutiae, made him unpopular with editors and publishers, so that in his later years he was reduced to publishing his writings privately from his home in Cambridge."[4]

Hilaire Belloc engaged in repeated controversies with Coulton. Belloc's daughter, Eleanor Jebb, said her father "felt about Coulton's animosity [toward the Church] a complete despair".[5] Belloc was unabashedly an advocate of things Catholic, and he repeatedly wrote that European civilization was derived from the Catholic Church. He was candid about his underlying ideas. "Coulton never specifically admits that one of his principal aims is to minimize the Church's influence and point out its shortcomings, and therefore finds it unnecessary to substantiate the charges he makes by a thorough examination of the whole evidence."[6] H. G. Wells (against whom Belloc also frequently was in controversy) opined that on "matters of Church history Dr. G. G. Coulton is a patient, unrelenting, trustworthy guide, and no one interested in the fatal concentration of power in the hands of

---

[3] *The Dictionary of National Biography*, suppl. 1941–1950, 181. —ED.

[4] Aidan Mackey, *Hilaire Belloc and His Critics* (Bedford, England: [privately printed], 1991), 24. —ED.

[5] Eleanor Jebb and Reginald Jebb, *Belloc, The Man* (Westminster, Md.: Newman Press, 1957), 149. —ED.

[6] Ibid., 80. —ED.

the Pope since 1870 should fail to read him." [7] One must keep in mind Wells' own strident anti-Catholicism. These words of his are from *Crux Ansata*, his 1944 plea for the destruction of Catholicism as a political and cultural force.

By the time of Wells' endorsement of Coulton, Herbert Thurston had been dead five years. It already was too late to resurrect Coulton's reputation—or the reputation of his American analogue, H. C. Lea, whose reliability Thurston first undermined in 1903 and then finally demolished in the following essay, which demonstrates how uncritical Coulton was when confronted with patently anti-Catholic writing.

Two years before his own death, Coulton would write, complainingly, that Thurston had been lucky because he had had only twelve pages to work with, and those twelve pages just happened to be where Lea—uncharacteristically, implied Coulton—had fallen from his usual standards. Thurston "had time to survey this narrow ground, saw that these particular pages gave him the advantage of a narrow mountain defile in which Lea had blunderingly entangled his troops, and stuck there with devastating effect".[8] Coulton was ungenerous in defeat, even at the end.

PRELIMINARY NOTE

The contents of the two articles here reprinted from *The Month* (January and February 1937) sufficiently explain themselves, but I should like to point out that since their appearance Dr. Coulton has published a bulky pamphlet

[7] H. G. Wells, *Crux Ansata: An Indictment of the Roman Catholic Church* (New York: Agora Publishing, 1944), 106. —ED.

[8] G. G. Coulton and Arnold Lunn, *Is the Catholic Church Anti-Social?* (London: Burns and Oates, 1946), 110. —ED.

entitled *Sectarian History*, which reproduces the text of the correspondence between us and is preceded by a long and acrimonious tirade in which several other opponents besides myself are taken to task. Nevertheless, Dr. Coulton has not ventured to defend a single one of the blunders which in answer to his challenge are duly set out with exact references in the investigation which follows. On the contrary, he has even gone so far as to say: "I am forced to confess that Father Thurston has damaged Lea's accuracy in these ten [sic] pages more than I expected."

A great part of the brochure *Sectarian History*, as well as occasional references in a still more recent publication by Dr. Coulton, entitled *Divorce, Mr. Belloc, and "The Daily Telegraph,"* are devoted to past controversies, such as those, for example, which figure in my booklet, *Some Inexactitudes of Mr. G. G. Coulton* (see below, note [15]). Apart from his strictures on other opponents, Dr. Coulton charges me with "exploiting to the full my facilities for wholesale slander," with "garbling his letters," "unblushingly falsifying his conclusions," etc., not to speak of his plain insinuation that in more than one instance I have been guilty of deliberate falsehood. I have no intention of attempting any further reply to allegations which have been fully answered in the booklet just referred to, but I may mention that some comments on *Sectarian History* will be found in *The Tablet* for September 8th, 1937, and in *The Month* for October, 1937. On Dr. Lea's misrepresentation of the early history of Confession I have written further in *The Month* for January, 1938, making reference to a previous article in December, 1928, which appeared in the same periodical.

H. T.

HOW HISTORY IS MISWRITTEN

A TEST APPLIED TO THE WORK OF H. C. LEA
AT THE INSTANCE OF DR. COULTON

In the course of September 1936 I received a rather bulky letter from Dr. G. G. Coulton, the well-known assailant of mediaeval ecclesiasticism, addressed to me from Cambridge. The letter came by registered post; obviously because, in Dr. Coulton's idea, when you write to people like Jesuits you have to take such precautions; otherwise, if it suited their convenience, they would declare that the letter had never reached them. It appeared that a C.T.S. [Catholic Truth Society] pamphlet of mine on "Catholics and Divorce" had come into Dr. Coulton's hands, and that his feelings had been outraged by a sentence in which I spoke of "undocumented assertions borrowed from Dr. H. C. Lea[9] and other writers equally reckless and prejudiced." Dr. Coulton began by declaring that Catholic controversialists were making it a practice to attack Dr. Lea "now that he is dead," and to slander him as an inaccurate and untrustworthy writer. He reminded me about the good opinion of Lea's *History of the Inquisition* expressed by such scholars as Lord Acton[10] and

---

[9] H. C. Lea (1825–1909), American historian of medieval Europe whose own religious sympathies seemed to lie with the Unitarians and Quakers. Although his maternal grandfather and mother were Catholic, Lea was noted for his anti-Catholicism. He composed three volumes on the Inquisition, seven other books, and many articles during fifty years of writing. At the invitation of Lord Acton, Lea was invited to contribute an article about the eve of the Reformation to the *Cambridge Modern History*. The article received wide notice because of its anti-Catholic bias. Lea was elected president of the American Historical Society in 1903. —ED.

[10] John Edward Dalberg Acton (1834–1902), British historian. He taught at Cambridge after 1895 and was active as a Catholic liberal. —ED.

Vacandard,[11] and, as the main point of his letter, he challenged me to justify the language I had used, asking me also
to name any books or articles in which Dr. Lea's contentions
had been fairly met.

In a brief reply I pointed out that I was not attacking Lea's
Inquisition volumes, which had never specially engaged my
attention, but that I had in mind mainly his *History of Confession and Indulgences* and the *History of Sacerdotal Celibacy*.[12]
These books had sufficed to convince me that Lea was
entirely out of his depth when dealing with the internal
discipline of the Catholic Church, and that his work
abounded in reckless deductions from inadequate evidence. I
went on to mention the criticisms of Lea which formed the
substance of a small volume printed in Germany by Dr. P. M.
Baumgarten in 1908, and I referred to sundry articles of my
own,[13] published, not after Lea's death, but while he was still
in full literary activity. Amongst these was a contribution to
The American Catholic Quarterly Review for July, 1903, in
which I commented upon Lea's chapter on "The Eve of the
Reformation" in the first volume of the *Cambridge Modern
History*.

Apparently the American periodical was not accessible to
Dr. Coulton at Cambridge, but after he had found an opportunity of paying a visit to the British Museum, I received at
the beginning of November another registered packet con-

---

[11] Florent Vacandard (1849–1927), French Catholic ecclesiastical historian,
known particularly for his works on St. Bernard. —ED.

[12] On sacerdotal celibacy, see Christian Cochini, *Apostolic Origins of Priestly
Celibacy* (San Francisco: Ignatius Press, 1990), translated from the French
original, *Origenes apostoliques du célibat sacerdotal* (Paris: Éditions Lethielleux,
1981). —ED.

[13] Amongst those which I specified was an article in *The Dublin Review* for
January, 1900; three contributions to *The Tablet*, February and March, 1905;
and a note in *The Month*, March, 1908, page 311. Dr. H. C. Lea died in 1909.

taining objections and new requests for references. There were eighteen quarto pages of writing in all. Frankly, I did little more than glance at the contents. I felt that I had neither the time nor the energy to plunge into the details of a controversy which had occupied me more than thirty years ago and which I had hardly thought of since. But my attention was caught by some vehement language very characteristic of the writer, in which he commented upon my article in the American Review just named. That article ended with these words, words which I have so far found no reason to wish to modify:

> Great (I wrote) as may be the industry of Dr. Lea, I believe his capacity for misconception and misrepresentation to be even greater, and the attempts that I have occasionally made to follow up his trail and to compare his assertions with his sources, have always ended in a more deeply rooted distrust of every statement made by him. It would be a safe thing probably to say that in any ten consecutive pages ten palpable blunders may be unearthed. At any rate I should like to submit that estimate to the test of experiment. Would Dr. Lea, I wonder, be prepared to accept such a challenge and to elect to stand or fall by the third volume of his *Auricular Confession and Indulgences* or his chapter on the causes of the Reformation in the *Cambridge Modern History*?

This proposal of mine, though only read by Dr. Coulton thirty-three years after it was written, seems in its effect to have been almost as provocative as the proverbial red rag to a bull. I can only congratulate myself that I live at a safe distance. In his letter to me of November 2nd, 1936, he says: "I assert with every sense of responsibility that your challenge is libellous and false to a ludicrous and almost inconceivable degree"; and to omit other flattering amenities of the same type,[14] he writes again on November 11th desiring to know "whether you are prepared to stand by the very insulting challenge delivered to Dr. Lea."

As I explained to my assailant, I am eighty years of age, and there are other extrinsic reasons, such as a protracted illness last summer, press of work now long overdue, a sense of the futility of nearly all controversy, etc., which make me reluctant to pick up such ancient threads of which I retain little memory. But protests only led to a further multiplication of letters, and, of course, to the unpleasant insinuation that I, like his other Catholic opponents, was only intent on backing out of the encounter I had provoked. When, therefore, Dr. Coulton, without awaiting my consent, applied to Professor G. E. Moore, who (though he was, to quote his own words, "in complete ignorance of the issue") was good enough to assign at random ten definite pages in Vol. I of the *History of Auricular Confession and Indulgences*, I decided to accept the terms proposed. It might, I thought, be good for Dr. Coulton to learn once again[15] the lesson that if his opponents were reluctant to plunge into controversy in answer to his interminable challenges, that reluctance did not necessarily arise from the consciousness that they had nothing to say in reply.

I may note that the volume selected was not that which I specially indicated in my American article. Knowing the *Indulgence* volume best, I had proposed Vol. III, but as Vol. I

[14] By way of specimen, the concluding words of Dr. Coulton's letter of November 14th may suffice. He writes: "It is idle for you to plead that the slander is now thirty-three years old. If it was true then, it is equally true now; if (as I confidently assert) it is now grossly false, then you have been thirty-three years before the world with this falsehood upon your conscience."

[15] I have in view a little shilling booklet of mine, *Some Inexactitudes of Mr. G. G. Coulton*, Sheed & Ward, 1927. See especially page 41 of the booklet in question.

had been settled on, I saw no reason to quarrel with the choice made. On the other hand, Dr. Coulton, with a great display of magnanimity, in order that the section might begin and end with a complete paragraph, threw in an extra page and a half. I was free to hunt for errors from the middle of page 199 to the top of page 211. But my opponent ends his letter characteristically with these words: "I defy you to find even a single patent blunder in all these twelve pages, and I must put it to you very plainly that you are now in a position in which your very worse [sic] policy is that of obstinate muteism [sic]." Did Dr. Coulton, I wonder, intend to write "muleism"?

I am afraid that in my recoil from "muteism," it may unfortunately be necessary to discuss in some detail the crop of corrigenda which the pages assigned abundantly supply. The list of blunders may most conveniently be divided into two groups, the second being introduced with a few words of explanation.

Blunder No. 1

As Dr. Coulton in writing to me on November 14th, 1936, drew my attention, as though it were a conclusive piece of evidence, to the passage in which Dr. Lea appeals to St. Bernard's *Life of St. Malachi*, I may as well begin with this characteristic example of the American scholar's lapses. After mentioning a case in which, according to St. Bernard's report, a woman's character was completely changed when she had made her confession to St. Malachi, Lea adds:

> Apparently confession had previously not been practised in Ireland, for St. Bernard includes it among the unknown rites

introduced [c. 1130] by Malachi when he romanized the
Irish Church.[16]

There is no foundation for any such inference in the words
used by St. Bernard. The phrase he employs is *de novo
instituit*, which certainly does not mean "He introduced for
the first time." Ireland before the twelfth century had been
repeatedly ravaged by the Vikings, and what with this, the
scarcity of priests, and the internal dissensions of the people,
a deplorable neglect of religious practices had resulted in
many districts. St. Bernard, describing the reforms effected
by St. Malachi, writes as follows:

> Hence it is that to this day there is chanting and psalmody in
> these churches at the canonical hours after the fashion of the
> whole world. For there was no such thing before, not even
> in the city [Armagh]. He, however, had learnt singing in his
> youth, and soon he introduced song into his monastery
> while as yet none in the city, nor in the whole bishopric
> could or would sing. Then Malachi instituted anew the most
> wholesome usage of confession, the sacrament of confirma-
> tion, the marriage contract—of all of which they were either
> ignorant or negligent.[17]

This is from *St. Bernard's Life of St. Malachi* in the translation of Dr. H. J. Lawlor (the Protestant Dean of St. Patrick's
Cathedral, Dublin), published by the S.P.C.K.[18] Moreover,
Dean Lawlor emphasizes in a footnote the point which here
concerns us. He says: "The word 'anew' (*de novo*) seems to
indicate St. Bernard's belief that it was only in comparatively
recent times that the usages to which he refers had fallen into

---

[16] Lea, *Auricular Confession and Indulgences*, vol. 1, page 208.

[17] *St. Bernard's Life of Malachi*, pages 16–18; cf. page 37.

[18] Society for Promoting Christian Knowledge, the chief Anglican missionary organization and the Church of England's publishing house, established in 1698. —ED.

desuetude." Further, in an appendix to the same volume, we read:

> It may be true that confession had been much neglected among some classes of the people . . . but it is remarkable that the anmchara (soul-friend) or confessor is frequently mentioned in Irish literature. . . . And penance is often alluded to in the obituary notices of distinguished persons clerical and lay.[19]

So, too, it is plain from St. Bernard's words that if we suppose Malachi to have introduced confession for the first time he must also have introduced the sacrament of confirmation and the Church chant for the first time. But, as Dean Lawlor points out: "The rite of confirmation has always been used in the Irish Church though possibly neglected at some periods. St. Patrick tells us that he 'confirmed in Christ those whom he had begotten to God.' "

I may note the fact that Dean Lawlor is the author of many important works dealing with the early Irish Church and that he is also Secretary of the Royal Irish Academy. Another writer whose work has everywhere been accepted as of supreme authority in all questions bearing on the ecclesiastical history of Ireland is Dr. James F. Kenney. He happens to commend this very book of Dean Lawlor's just quoted, as probably "the best study" of the organization of the early Church in Ireland. Further, he remarks elsewhere:

> A subsidiary controversy has arisen out of the theory of Loening that private penance was originally a purely monastic practice which the Irish and Anglo-Saxon missionaries extended to the lay world. Be that as it may, it seems certain

---

[19] Ibid., page 161–162. It was a proverbial phrase that a person without a confessor was like a body without a head. See the *Martyrology of Œngus* (ed., Whitley Stokes), page 182; and cf. pages 8, 12, 64.

that one of the features of the strict and enthusiastic monastic
church of the sixth and seventh centuries which contrasted
with the more lax Christianity of the Continent was the
emphasis laid on confession and works of penance.[20]

In the light of these quotations it does not seem to me that
I am exaggerating if I describe Lea's attempt to show on St.
Bernard's sole authority that auricular confession was unknown in Ireland before the twelfth century as "a palpable
blunder."

Blunder No. 2

As we have been speaking of St. Bernard it may be convenient to turn at once to another statement made by Dr. Lea.
He writes:

> On the other hand, Abelard's great antagonist, St. Bernard,
> is never weary of extolling the virtues of confession. Yet it is
> not sacramental confession that he urges, for this had not yet
> been formulated; we hear from him nothing of absolution
> and little of penance.[21]

The assertion that St. Bernard says nothing of absolution is
simply untrue. Witness the following passage from the *Liber
ad Milites Templi*, chapter xii, which begins with a reference
to the *confessionis sacramentum et sacerdotalis ministerii mysterium*,
a phrase which seems to agree ill with Dr. Lea's contention
that in St. Bernard's time "sacramental confession had not yet
been formulated." But further on in the chapter St. Bernard
remarks:

> Wherefore it is necessary that priests who are ministers of the
> Word should keep a very careful eye on two points, viz.,

---

[20] *The Sources of the Early History of Ireland*, vol. I (New York, 1929), page
239.

[21] Lea, *Auricular Confession and Indulgences*, vol. I, page 207.

that on the one hand they should prick the hearts of sinners with such moderation of language that they on no account frighten them away from outspoken confession—in other words that they open their hearts without stopping their lips—on the other hand that they should not absolve even the conscience-stricken unless they see that he has made confession, since "with the heart we believe unto justice, but with the mouth confession is made unto salvation."[22]

There can be no question about the reading *sed nec absolvant etiam compunctum*; I have verified the passage in other editions besides that of Migne. The curious point is that in a group of references printed in a footnote on Lea's next page this very chapter of the *Liber ad Milites Templi* is prominently cited. Moreover, he has managed to forget that on page 134 of the same volume he himself admits that St. Bernard does mention absolution. The fact that the reference is brief only shows that absolution normally followed on confession. We may readily admit that an explicit mention of absolution and of the penance enjoined is of comparative rarity in St. Bernard's writings. But why should we expect these adjuncts to be alluded to? They were, long before this, an essential part of the rite, as I hope to make quite clear further on when discussing another blunder of Dr. Lea's connected with the Cistercian statutes. When Longfellow tells us of Evangeline:

But a celestial brightness, a more ethereal beauty
Shone on her face and encircled her form when, after
   confession
Homeward serenely she walked with God's
   benediction upon her[23]

---

[22] Migne, P.L., vol. 162, c. 938.
[23] Henry Wadsworth Longfellow, *Evangeline* (Boston: Ticknor, 1847), pt. I, sec. I, ll. 59–61. —ED.

the poet does not think it necessary to explain that she had received absolution and had said her penance. All the rest was included in the idea of confession. In any case, I submit that Lea's statement that "we hear from St. Bernard nothing of absolution" is a palpable blunder, and it is also a blunder which supports most conveniently the historian's theory of the very late recognition of confession as a sacrament.

Blunder No. 3

This, which is also connected with St. Bernard, may be briefly dealt with. Dr. Lea, on page 208, declares that St. Bernard "tells us that confession and true repentance are when a man so repents that he does not repeat the sin." We need not quarrel with the sentiment, and the words undoubtedly occur in the tractate *De interiore Domo* from which Lea cites them. Unfortunately, more than two and a half centuries ago, Mabillon[24] pointed out that the treatise, though printed among St. Bernard's works, was not written by him, and no scholar has since contested this verdict. The matter in itself is of no consequence, but it is entertaining to notice the scorn with which Dr. Lea, two pages further on, castigates the Catholic writers who even in the sixteenth and seventeenth centuries quoted the *De vera et falsa Poenitentia* as a genuine work of St. Augustine. If Lea in quite recent times, with a huge library and all the apparatus of modern criticism at his back, could himself be so careless, his censures on the benighted compilers of the Tridentine Catechism must sound a little ridiculous. I cannot help concluding, despite assertions to the contrary, that the American historian possessed little of the scholar's devotion to accuracy for its own

[24] Jean Mabillon (1632–1707), French Benedictine, the first scholar to treat scientifically the dating and authorship of manuscripts. —ED.

sake. In matters with which the literary circle he belonged to were likely to be conversant he was relatively careful, but when he was dealing with Catholic beliefs and abuses about which his friends knew nothing and cared less, he took practically no pains at all to keep his strong anti-religious bias under control. Even the panegyrist who wrote an account of his life and work in the *Dictionary of American Biography* (1931) permits himself the criticism: "In his [Lea's] rapidly growing library he gathered such sources as had been printed, though not always in the latest and best editions." In the present case it matters little whether Bernard or Pseudo-Bernard is cited, but when a saint like St. Ulric of Augsburg, on the sole ground of a notorious and gross forgery, is presented as inveighing against sacerdotal celibacy the case becomes much more serious.[25]

Blunder No. 4

As a result of Dr. Lea's disregard of "the latest and best editions" a passage may be noted which occurs in his book on page 205. It runs thus: "Early in the twelfth century we are told that Antwerp already was a populous city, and yet it had but one priest, who was involved in an incestuous amour and paid no attention to his duties." This, no doubt, is what we read in the Life of St. Norbert as printed in Migne's *Patrology* and elsewhere. But since the middle of the last century it has been known that there is an older and more reliable text of the same life. This was edited in 1856 for Pertz, *Monumenta Germaniae Historica*, Scriptores, Vol. XII. Consulting this, we discover that the statement that there was

[25] See on this case *The Month*, March, 1908, page 311. Dr. Lea's blunder about St. Ulric is repeated in the third revised edition of his *Sacerdotal Celibacy*.

only one priest in Antwerp is not to be found in the original
form of the biography of St. Norbert, and, as the editor,
Wilmans, points out, the insertions made by the later inter-
polator are by no means historically reliable.[26] Dr. Lea's
contention was that in the twelfth century priests were too
few to be able to hear many confessions "with the elaborate
formula then in use." There would be much to say on this
subject, but I am content to note here that the statement
about Antwerp to which he appeals is taken from an untrustworthy source and lacks any extrinsic confirmation.

Blunder No. 5

This is a much more serious matter. On page 204 Dr. Lea
remarks:

> In rendering confession obligatory, the Lateran Council
> (1215), ordered bishops to appoint penitentiaries in all con-
> ventual churches, showing that the regulars were no longer
> to be allowed to consider their chapters as sufficient, and in
> time, as we have seen in the case of the Benedictines and
> Augustinian Canons, they were required to confess oftener
> than once a year.

Dr. Lea's assumption, as anyone will see who reads the
context and follows his argument, is that this Canon 10 of
the Lateran Council was framed with the view of encouraging the practice of confession among the monks themselves,
because their chapters were no longer sufficient to maintain
discipline. But the smallest degree of attention paid to the
wording of the enactment will show that its purpose was not
to create a staff of penitentiaries for the monks, but for the

[26] See Pertz, *Monumenta Germaniae Historica*, Scriptores, vol. xii, 663, 690.

lay folk who frequented the cathedrals and great conventual churches. It was a question of providing both preachers and confessors, the former need being particularly emphasized. The bishops, we are told in the decree, because they cannot be in many places at once, and are often either overworked, old, or infirm, need help in their special duty of preaching the word of God to the people and in the administration of penance. It is consequently enjoined that both in cathedrals and in other conventual churches, suitable persons should be ordained (or appointed?) to help the bishop in his work of preaching and hearing confessions. I should have liked to quote the whole of the canon, but its length will only allow of my reproducing the more relevant words in a footnote.[27] As for Lea's gross misconception of its purport, I find it almost impossible to believe that he could ever himself have looked at the decree. A man who was capable of that sort of travesty of a perfectly plain Latin text was capable of anything. If I had stumbled upon only one such blunder as this in the ten assigned pages I should consider that the profound distrust I expressed thirty-three years ago was fully justified. The Lateran decree has absolutely nothing to do with the confessions of monks.

One might very reasonably have taxed Lea with two other exhibitions of carelessness which occur in the same paragraph on page 204. He states that Ottoboni in 1268 enacted a decree "inferring that monks should be obliged to confess monthly." This is by no means accurate. The purport of the injunction was that in the monasteries certain confessors

---

[27] "*Praecipimus tam in cathedralibus, quam in aliis conventualibus ecclesiis viros idoneos ordinari, quos episcopi possint coadjutores et co-operatores habere non solum in praedicationis officio, verum etiam in audiendis confessionibus, et penitentiis injungendis ac ceteris quae ad salutem pertinent animarum.*" The decree is printed in full in Hefele-Leclercq, *Conciles*, vol. v (1913), 1340.

should be appointed who were to report to the abbot once a month if any of the community did not often go to confession and rarely said Mass. Lea goes on to state that Aquinas "pronounces this improper," but the passage in the *Summa* to which we are referred has nothing to do with Ottoboni's English constitutions, of which St. Thomas is very unlikely to have known anything. What Aquinas is discussing is the question whether a man who has fallen into sin commits a new sin if he does not go to confession at once when he has the opportunity. St. Thomas decides in the negative, even though the offender should be a monk, but he nowhere says or hints that it would be improper to impose a law on religious requiring them to confess monthly or at any stated interval.

Blunder No. 6

A garbling of the truth in a somewhat different form occurs on page 206 when Dr. Lea writes as follows:

> Yet so vague as yet were the current notions [concerning the remission of sins] that in another passage Honorius [of Autun] describes confession as equal to baptism in remitting sins, without conditioning it on contrition and satisfaction.

The reader will infer, and is apparently meant to infer, that the laity were encouraged by Honorius and others to think that if only they confessed their misdeeds, the sin was forgiven without either sorrow or any form of penance. Anyone who looks at the *Elucidarium*[28] will at once see that this is a mischievous perversion of the writer's plain meaning. True,

---

[28] *Elucidarium*, Book II, chapter 20, in Migne, P.L., vol. 172, cc. 1150–1151. It is by no means certain that Honorius of Autun was the author of the *Elucidarium*.

the text states that as original sin is remitted by baptism so actual sin is remitted by confession. But in the few sentences immediately following we are told that there is a penance to be imposed by the confessor which is like the sentence of a judge, and that as a wound is never healed so long as the iron remains embedded in it, so no good works, not even penance, can avail to obtain the pardon of sin unless the sin itself is given up. This is surely to insist upon the need of contrition in its most practical form. Moreover, when it is stated a little further on that *peccata per penitentiam et confessionem remittuntur*[29] no one can pretend that the avowal of the lips which wins pardon is here unconditioned.

From the nature of the subject I am afraid that the further catalogue of Dr. Lea's indiscretions is bound to prove a little monotonous. There is a noticeable sameness which pervades the group of blunders now to be discussed, but they are entirely separate blunders, and in each case I would invite the reader to compare the American historian's statements with the text of the documents to which he himself makes appeal. It seems desirable, however, to preface this second list with a few words of explanation. Dr. Lea's fixed purpose to justify his own pet theories at all costs has not a little to do with the numerous perversions of fact which remain to be considered.

The eleven [sic] pages (199–211) of the *History of Confession*, selected more or less at random by Professor G. E. Moore, form part of Dr. Lea's chapter viii. This section of his work is mainly devoted to proving that auricular confession developed very slowly and very late, so much so that it cannot be regarded as coming into general use until the decree *Omnis utriusque sexus*, enacted by the fourth Council of Lateran (1215), made annual confession obligatory upon all the

---

[29] Migne, P.L., vol. 172, c. 1173, and note the emphasis laid on the power of priests to bind and loose, c. 1132.

faithful. There would be much to say on almost every aspect of this proposition, but the limits of [space] preclude its discussion here. One of Dr. Lea's main arguments in support of his theory is derived from what he alleges to have been the practice of the religious Orders. He declares that even among monks and nuns, whose lives were supposedly given up to observances of piety, private confession had no recognized place. No monastic rule enjoined it. Down to the end of the twelfth century, evidence, so he assures us, is lacking that monks and nuns went to confession at stated intervals, or that they received absolution in due course after a penance had been imposed by the confessor. On the other hand, there was an institution common to all Orders of monks which bore a somewhat close analogy to the public penance of the early centuries. When the brethren, as a rule daily, assembled in chapter, a notable part of the proceedings was concerned with the correction of offenders. In Dr. Lea's words:

> The monks thus had adopted the custom of daily chapters or assemblies in which sinners were expected to confess their faults and accept punishment, and where accusations could be brought against those who did not voluntarily accuse themselves, even as in the congregations the faithful were more or less accustomed to do the same. This answered all purposes of discipline and private confession would have been a manifest surplusage.[30]

He adds (page 197): "In their daily or weekly chapters the brethren assembled and were expected to confess their faults or to be accused, when immediate punishment, usually scourging, would be inflicted. . . . There was nothing in the slightest degree sacramental about this, but it sufficed." And

---

[30] Lea, *A History of Auricular Confession and Indulgences*, vol. I, 185.

again, a little further on, we are told (page 204) that towards the end of the twelfth century the practice of private confession began to be adopted in place of this, or, as our author puts it, "the change was probably hastened by the desire of the monks to substitute the secret confessional, with its rapidly diminishing penances, for the humiliation of self-denunciation and scourging at the discretion of the presiding prelate."

Dr. Lea is quite right in assuming that the public confession or denunciation in chapter was almost universally prevalent in religious houses, and that it was a recognized means of maintaining monastic discipline. What he fails to understand is that private confession did not aim at maintaining discipline and was in no sense a substitute for the public tribunal. The disclosure of sin to a confessor was never an observance imposed as an additional burden, a means of enforcing the rigours of cloister life, but, on the contrary, it was an alleviation, a relief for troubled consciences. For the most part auricular confession was not a matter of general discipline, but, like private prayer or the choice of spiritual reading, it was left to the discretion of the individual monk. Consequently, it is not mentioned in the Rule as are other details of uniform observance. Public self-accusation in chapter was not abrogated because sacramental confession in private became more frequent or because the latter was now explicitly provided for in later revisions of the monastic constitutions. The two had always gone on concurrently.

Consequently, when Dr. Lea talks of "surplusage" and "substitution," he is only betraying his own inability to understand the inner life of such good religious as were earnestly bent on attaining purity of conscience. Self-accusation in chapter dealt only with external faults, breaches of monastic rule, or matters giving scandal within the cloister because they were patent to all. But what really troubled the peace of mind of the more devout monk was the doubt created by evil thoughts, by temptations perhaps imperfectly resisted, by resentful and insubordinate feelings, sins of omission, broken resolutions, and above all by the more or less involuntary results of dreaming. It was never meant that these faults or misgivings should be disclosed to the brethren in chapter. Many of the fears which troubled the conscience of the scrupulous religious could not be declared in public without offence to modest ears. We know that every day the monk prayed at Compline—

> *Procul recedant somnia,*
> *Et noctium phantasmata;*
> *Hostemque nostrum comprime,*
> *Ne polluantur corpora.*

Whenever he was subject to these infirmities of the flesh he wanted confession—if possible, at once and before Mass. The need was recognized and the existing constitutions of the twelfth century, not to speak of some much earlier, show that in most cases relief was within his grasp.

With this much of general explanation, I pass on to present a further instalment of Dr. Lea's blunders, culled from the eleven pages assigned. Taking the religious Orders in turn, he professes to show that their Rule made no provision for auricular confession save possibly in the immediate anticipation of death. As against this a careful examination of the documents proves that in case after case he has grossly misrepresented, or else overlooked, all the evidence unfavourable to the theory he has propounded. The points dealt with need little comment; the facts are patent and may be left to speak for themselves.

Blunder No. 7

On pages 199–200, Dr. Lea discusses the religious observances of the Cluniac Order and amongst other things he makes these statements:

> We possess a very complete account of the discipline of the mother-house of Cluny about the year 1080, including details as to the semi-annual bathing of the monks, their stated times of blood-letting, etc. . . . We are told all the signs that were used to replace the voice, so that the holy silence of the monastery might not be broken. . . . The daily chapters for confession and accusation were duly held, but so little confidence was felt in the candour of the brethren that discipline and morals were maintained by officials known as *circatores*—spies or detectives, who had entrance everywhere and who were always moving around to observe and report offences. Yet the only prescription of auricular confession was that the novice when received confessed all the sins committed in secular life, and the monk when dying confessed again as a preparation for extreme unction. Some half a century later in the new Statutes which Peter the Venerable introduced into the Cluniac Rule, there is still no allusion to confession.

The words "still no allusion to confession" clearly imply that in the earlier code, apart from the time of entrance and of death, confession was not even referred to. But in that very code of A.D. 1080, the *Consuetudines Udalrici*, to which Dr. Lea gives copious references, Lib. II, cap. 12, bears this heading: "How he [the monk] should come to confession," and in the text of the chapter we read:

> If he has need to go to confession [*ad confessionem venire*] for something he has done amiss [*pro aliquo excessu*] he comes to the priest whom he prefers and standing before him he puts

his right hand out of his sleeve and places it on his breast, which is the sign for confession. The priest rises and the brother follows him into the chapter-house and first makes a complete prostration before him. The priest bids him rise and when he is seated the brother tells him what he has to say. If something has happened to him in the night which we, for modesty's sake, term "fragility," let him already before confession have repeated the seven penitential psalms, or the Our Father seven times if he does not know the psalms, and after he has confessed let him perform whatever penance the priest imposes. And on that day he must not kiss the text of the gospel, or come to receive the pax, or take part in the offertory.[31]

Dr. Lea seems to have overlooked this chapter in the *Consuetudines*, though he gives precise references to seven other chapters, extracting from them anything likely to throw discredit on the monks, such as their "semi-annual bathing" and the alleged "spies," etc. I can only say that, if he did overlook it, it was a piece of gross carelessness very convenient for his argument. If, on the other hand, he knew of its existence and suppressed all mention of it, such disingenuousness would fully justify a still more severe verdict.

Blunder No. 8

On page 200 we are told that "in the early Rule of the Canons Regular there was no precept of auricular confession." Whether we possess the exact wording of St. Chrodegang's original constitution or not, it is certain that we do possess texts written for the Canons Regular early in the ninth century. These direct that the Canons are to make their

[31] Migne, P.L., vol. 149, cc. 706–707.

confession twice a year to the Bishop, while at intervening times facilities were afforded that they might confess either to the Bishop or to the priest whom he should appoint, "whenever they should choose or require it." Obviously, all this can apply only to auricular confession. Moreover, in this case there was a direct precept that confession should be made at least twice in the year.[32]

Blunder No. 9

In the light of this evidence concerning the traditional observance of the Canons Regular it would in any case be difficult to credit Dr. Lea when he assures us (page 200) that about 1115 (i.e., 300 years later) "Peter de Honestis drew up an elaborate account of their discipline, including baths and blood-letting, but the only provision for private confession is on the death-bed." Here again our historian refers us boldly to the rules formulated by Peter de Honestis as they are printed in Migne, vol. 163. Now in Lib. I, cap. 30 of that code (Migne, c. 719) we have mention of a certain class of offences which, though worthy of severe punishment, it would be most undesirable to publish to the community in chapter. The offender is exhorted to confess his sin fully to the Prior, with this additional proviso:

> But if, stricken with shame or overcome by terror, he [the culprit] should be unable to bring himself to disclose this to the Prior, let him manifest it to one of the priests whom the

[32] I have translated the passage in full in *The Tablet* for March 4th, 1905. The Latin in a ninth-century copy is found in the Berne MS. 289. By W. Schmitz the text has been printed from the Leyden Codex Vossianus, Latin 94. See Schmitz's essay *Regula Canonicorum S. Chrodegangi*, Hanover, 1889, 10–11.

Prior has appointed to receive the confessions of the brethren, and let him do penance for his sin as he shall direct.

There was then, we see, some sort of staff of priests whom
the Prior had appointed to hear the confessions of the
community. What is more, we are told in Lib. III, cap. 15
(Migne, c. 738), of a method of preparing for the greater
feasts. There was a public accusation of faults in chapter and
a general penance to be performed by all. But a further
notification follows in these terms: "If, however, anyone
wishes to confess anything privately, let him confess to the
Prior, or to the priests who have been appointed by the Prior
to this office." How can we possibly reconcile these phrases
"*alicui presbyterorum quem prior fratrum confessiones suscipere
mandaverit hoc manifestet*," and "*confiteatur priori sive presbyteris
per priorem ad hoc officium deputatis*" with Dr. Lea's declaration
that in the rules of Peter de Honestis "the only provision for
private confession is on the death-bed"? Once again we seem
fully justified in declaring that a writer so scandalously neg-
ligent in studying the evidence which he himself cites forfeits
all confidence.

Blunder No. 10

Not less astonishing is Dr. Lea's reference to the rules of
the Canons at Montfort in the diocese of Saint-Malo. Although he ascribes them to the end of the twelfth century,
he assures us (page 200) that they "have no provision for
auricular confession, but the public confession and accusation in the daily chapters is in full force, when the Prior
grants absolution and adjudges the penance or punishment."
Certainly, as in nearly all the religious communities of the
Middle Ages, the public accusation of faults in chapter was

maintained, but this in no way conflicted with the practice of private confession. At Montfort full provision was made for such private confession in terms closely resembling those of the Cistercian Rule. I shall have occasion to quote the Cistercian constitution a little further on, but I may note here how the Montfort Canons are bidden (cap. 2) to spend the time between Prime and Terce "in reading, prayer, and confession"; and how in cap. 7 it is stated once more that "at any time set apart for reading before dinner, and again in the interval before Prime, those who before the first stroke of the bell make the appointed signal are free to go to confession." [33]

Blunder No. 11

Special interest attaches to Dr. Lea's inexcusable misrepresentation of the Carthusian usages, for we have confirmatory evidence of the real conditions in the practice of the great St. Hugh, Bishop of Lincoln. According to Lea (page 200) the earliest statutes of the Order were written by Abbot Guigo, about 1128, and then he goes on: "The Rule is very full, ordering the monks to shave six times a year and [be] let blood five times, but its only allusion to confession is on the death-bed, when the dying monk is expected to confess to a priest and receive absolution." Turning to the reference given, i.e., the Constitution of Guigo as printed in Migne, vol. 153, we find that the deathbed of a monk was certainly not the only occasion when confession is mentioned. In cap. 7 (Migne, loc. cit., c. 647) it is stated that: "Every Saturday we meet in the cloister [not, be it

---

[33] "*Nam omni tempore lectionis ante prandium et etiam in intervallo ante Primam, qui ante ictum fecerint signum possunt confiteri.*" See Martene, *Thesaurus*, vol. IV, c. 1220, and cf. c. 1216.

noted, in the chapter-house] and we confess our sins to the Prior or to those whom he has appointed." Again in cap. 42 we read that on the eves of festivals the *conversi* (laybrothers) come to the church of the monks where they hear an exhortation and "confess their misdoings, if such they have [*si quas habent confitentur offensas*]." Of course, the question may quite properly be raised whether this was a public or private confession. But even if Dr. Lea held it to be the former, he has no right to burke inquiry by stating categorically that the only allusion to confession was in connection with the deathbed. And, what is even more to the point, the traditions of this unchanging Order definitely affirm that the Saturday confession was private and sacramental from the beginning.[34] Thus the chaplain and biographer of the Carthusian St. Hugh of Lincoln (died 1200) assures us that "throughout life the Saint, once in the week, namely on the Saturday, had recourse to the cleansing tide of a most exact confession. This, in accord with the inviolable tradition of his Order, he on no account omitted; in fact, he would often have recourse to it more frequently, directly any scruple out of the common arose in his mind from anything he had done, said, or thought." This is recalled by his intimate friend and biographer in connection with St. Hugh's periodical visits to the Charterhouse of Witham, which the Saint had himself founded, and we are told further that when there the holy Bishop was wont over and over again to make a general confession of all the sins of his life.[35] In any case I can see no excuse for the writer who, to favour his own controversial purpose, tells us positively that in a certain document there is only one allusion to confession, whereas in point of fact there are three.

[34] See Le Couteulx, *Annales Ordinis Carthusienis*, vol. I (1887), 349.
[35] *Magna Vita St. Hugonis* (Rolls Series), 200–201.

Blunder No. 12

As we go on things get worse instead of better. There is perhaps no more flagrant example of Dr. Lea's interested misstatements veiled under a half-truth than what we find him writing about the Cistercians on page 201. He says of the *Usus Antiquiores* (c. 1134) of that Order:

> They are very prolix and minute, prescribing every detail of monastic life, even for the sudden nose-bleeding of a priest when celebrating Mass. Like other Rules they provide for accusation and self-accusation in the chapter, followed by punishment and absolution, but there is no injunction of private confession, though the abbot, prior, and sub-prior are empowered to listen to those who desire to confess such things as illusions in sleep. Even on the deathbed no formal or detailed confession is prescribed. The dying man merely said "*Confiteor*" or "*Mea culpa*, I pray you to pray for me for all my sins," [36] and the absolution was equally informal.

It is true that there is no *injunction* of private confession; it is also true that on the deathbed no formal or detailed confession is *prescribed*. These things were left to the devotion and conscience of the individual monk as he felt he needed this form of help. But nothing can be clearer than the fact that private confession was in full vigour in the Order both for those in health and for the dying, and also that other priests heard confessions besides the Prior and sub-Prior. In cap. 70, cited—but only in part—by Lea himself, we read that after the conclusion of Prime, during which the public

---

[36] Dr. Lea was probably unaware that this is just what commonly happens when Extreme Unction is administered at the present day. The rubric in the *Rituale Romanum* still stands: "*quod si ægrotus voluerit confiteri, audiat illum et absolvat.*"

confession of faults had been made and penance imposed or inflicted:

> All leave the chapter-house [*exeunt omnes*] unless someone linger behind to make his confession or because he is ill. But so long as anyone is making his confession let no one remain there unless it be someone who is similarly employed. For during all the time appointed for reading—though this applies only before dinner and in the interval preceding Prime—they can confess there [i.e., in the chapter-house].

> Accordingly, after they [the Prior and the penitent] have taken their seats, let the Prior say *Benedicite* and the other *Dominus*. The Prior rejoins with *Deus sit nobiscum*, and then let the other answer *Amen* and briefly confess the faults for which he asks forgiveness. His tale being ended, let him at once add, "Of these and all my other sins I confess myself guilty and implore pardon." Then let the Prior, after pronouncing an absolution over him [*facta super eum absolutione*], enjoin him a penance. After that he can, if he wishes, encourage him, warn him, or scold him, as he thinks most expedient, but only in a few words. If anyone, wishing to make his confession, should, after the signal for Mass is given, detain one of those who hear confessions [*aliquem eorum qui confessiones audiunt*][37] or again should call one of them away from Mass into the chapter-house, let him confess briefly while they [confessor and penitent] both remain standing.

What I complain of is that from the whole context of the passage in Lea's book the reader must inevitably infer that auricular confession among the Cistercians in 1134 was practically unrecognized, whereas an examination of the "*Usus*"

---

[37] The more accurate text published by Guignard *Monuments primitifs de la Règle Cistercienne* prints *audiunt* where Migne's edition (vol. 166, c. 1446) incorrectly gives *audivit*.

themselves shows that it formed part of the monk's daily life, and that the external ritual had been legislated for in a compendious form which rendered it thoroughly workable. Moreover, a casual proviso inserted at the close of cap. 88 makes it clear that confession at the approach of death, despite Lea's statement to the contrary, was a normal practice in the Order. Punctuality at community duties was greatly insisted upon, and those, for example, who "lost their verse," i.e., were not present in the refectory before the second versicle of the grace was pronounced, suffered a suitable penalty. But there were exceptions, and in cap. 88 we have a clause providing that the penalty does not apply to late-comers who are engaged in receiving guests or "who are taking Communion to the sick, or are anointing them, or are hearing their confession when they are at the point of death."

Blunder No. 13

On page 202 Dr. Lea states that "the only allusion to confession in the rules of Stephen of Grammont is a prohibition to confess to anyone outside of the Order; the brethren might, if they so chose, confess to each other, and, as many of them were laymen, there was no recognition of the sacramental nature of such practice." Upon this I will only remark that the reference to the words of the Epistle of St. James (5:16) does not convey the slightest suggestion that the brethren were free to confess to those who were not priests. We are bidden, Stephen says in effect, to *confess to one another* (*confitemini invicem peccata vestra*), not to people outside the Order. On the other hand, in the *Antiqua Statuta* of Grammont we have a clear indication that this ministry of penance was regarded as proper to priests alone. Cap. 5

directs that "when priests pronounce upon the brethren the judgments of penance [*cum judicia poenitentiae sacerdotes fratribus injungunt*] they must not speak of other matters which are not to the point."[38] It is, therefore, in any case, untrue that the only allusion to confession is a prohibition to confess to externs.

Blunder No. 14

I can here only point out very shortly how Dr. Lea (page 202) declares that Adam the Scot (c. 1180) knew nothing of any "precept of sacramental or auricular confession" among the Premonstratensians, but considered that the system of public self-accusation in the chapters sufficed for all needs. This, however, is ridiculous, for Adam's treatise, *Soliloquia*, proves at great length that the practice of private confession was a matter of vital interest in the Order. That the confession made to the Superior or priest was private is shown by the horror which Adam expresses at the suggestion that the Superior could possibly reveal to others the sins which had been confessed to him.[39]

Blunder No. 15

Finally, I cannot forbear adding to this list what I regard as the outrageous *suggestio falsi* conveyed in Lea's remark on page 201 that "not long after this [1134] passages in sermons of St. Bernard justify the assumption that confession and communion at Easter *were becoming customary*." I have itali-

---

[38] See Martene, *Thesaurus*, vol. IV, c. 1231.

[39] See Migne, vol. 198, cc. 865–869. Adam declares that any such revelation of confession would be an "*abominabilissimum et prorsus diabolicum scelus*" (c. 869, A.), with other strong language to the same effect.

cized the offending words which are sufficiently refuted by the quotations occurring in the earlier pages of Lea's own volume. For example, in 822, three centuries earlier than this, as our author admits (page 188), the statutes of Corbie order a holiday at the beginning of Lent "so that the labouring folk may have time to confess," and thus prepare themselves by penance for their Easter Communion.[40] References to "shrift" are of frequent occurrence in our Anglo-Saxon laws, and the normal Communion days were three, Easter, Whitsuntide, and Christmas. But the evidence, going back to the time of Archbishop Egbert, Bede, and Alcuin, is far too copious to be outlined here. Such non-Catholic authorities as Hauck, Caspari, and Liebermann fully admit its force.[41] I can only refer briefly to a passage in the contemporary Life of St. Margaret of Scotland (died 1093). The whole context shows that she found the Scottish people very barbarous and ill-instructed in the matter of Church observances. She asked them "why it was that on the festival of Easter they neglected to receive the sacrament of the Body and Blood of Christ *according to the usage of the holy and apostolic Church.*" They excused themselves by quoting St. Paul's words that he that eateth and drinketh unworthily eateth and drinketh judgment to himself. Thereupon the Queen explained:

> It is the man who, without confession and penance, but carrying with him the defilements of his sins, presumes to approach the sacred mysteries, such a one, I say it is, who eats and drinks judgment to himself.[42]

[40] "*Statuta Antiqua Abbatiae Corbiensis,*" Lib. I, cap. 2, in D'Achéry, *Spicilogium,* vol. I, 587.

[41] I have dealt with the question in some detail in *The Tablet,* February and March, 1905.

[42] *Acta Sanctorum,* June, vol. 11, page 327.

The practice, as she shows further, then and long before, was that the people confessed at Shrovetide, performed their penance (generally a much more serious matter than in later times) during Lent, and received Communion at Easter.

I submit, then, that by the exposure of the above fifteen blunders Dr. Coulton's challenge has been fairly met. What perhaps impresses me most is the fact that on the surface Dr. Lea presents a case which to the normal reviewer, indolent or otherwise, seems entirely convincing and satisfactory. Even Dr. Coulton, who has given his life to mediaeval studies, after reading the section selected, was so persuaded of its impregnable accuracy that he wrote to me in terms which awaken memories of Bombastes Furioso: "I defy you to find even a single patent blunder in all these twelve pages." The blunders only come to light when, after much toil and waste of time, one investigates the sources appealed to and finds that they say something entirely different from what the American controversialist had read into them. That was my experience thirty-six years ago when I first had occasion to study Dr. Lea's volume on Indulgences.[43] It has been my experience again during these last weeks in dealing with another aspect of his work. From one point of view I have occasion to be grateful to Dr. Coulton,[44] for he has enabled

[43] I may refer to an article of mine in *The Dublin Review*, January, 1900.

[44] I have been informed that Dr. Coulton is aggrieved because in first publishing these comments I marked with a [sic] two mistakes which occur in a letter he sent to me. I can only say that the two miswritten words occur in the last sentence of this handwritten letter, immediately above what I assume to be his own signature. How could I quote the passage otherwise, if I was to quote it at all? I am now informed that the letter in question was dictated. Be it so, but if Dr. Coulton does not take the trouble to read the letters which he signs, he is none the less responsible for their contents. I have taken little notice of Dr. Coulton's handwriting, and being rather blind and unobservant, I took it for granted that the whole was written by himself. Dictated letters are usually typed and that was not here the case. That I have not wished to

me to reaffirm with renewed conviction that such attempts as I have made to follow up Dr. Lea's trail "have always ended in a more deeply rooted distrust of every statement made by him."

---

make capital out of trivialities will be clear from the fact that I have made no reference to the misprints or slips of the pen in Dr. Lea's selected pages. On page 210 he speaks of Trithemius as living "at the close of the sixteenth century," he, of course, intended to write fifteenth century; on the same page "*aperis paradisi portus*" is printed instead of *portas*; on page 204, note 2, 1216 is given as the date of the Lateran Council, it should be 1215; and so on.

8

Arnold Lunn vs. G. G. Coulton

In late 1943 John Heenan, the future archbishop of Westminster, wrote to the *Catholic Herald* and proposed that G. G. Coulton debate Arnold Lunn on the question "Is the Catholic Church anti-social?" Coulton's acceptance was given in a letter printed the following February; Lunn's acceptance appeared in April.[1] The collected correspondence would be Coulton's last book—he died in 1946—and it was the last of the four published debates to which Lunn was a party. Lunn would live another thirty years and would continue to debate publicly, but he would not produce another such book. Perhaps he was finding it difficult to locate worthy opponents.

In Lunn's last autobiographical work, he described Coulton as "a pugnacious old gentleman" (Coulton was eighty-six when their exchange began, Lunn fifty-six) who "made a practice of issuing challenges to leading Catholic scholars to debate with him, in book form, Papal Infallibility or the social record of the Church, and when nobody accepted his challenges he proclaimed that no Catholic writer of standing 'with a real sense of responsibility'

[1] G. G. Coulton and Arnold Lunn, *Is the Catholic Church Anti-Social?* (London: Burns and Oates, 1946), v. —ED.

would agree to discuss these controversial issues with him".[2]

Lunn quotes *The Tablet*'s review of *Is the Catholic Church Anti-Social?*

> This is a rambling, discursive, inconclusive argumentation, rather thankless for the Catholic protagonist. For that very reason English-speaking protagonists are all the more indebted to Mr. Lunn for engaging in so much involved and often arid controversy, most of it on matters of Church history or theology which are the professional studies of the clergy. It was a fatiguing business engaging in controversy with Dr. Coulton and it was a very human reaction which made most seminary or college professors avoid it, even though they had taught the subject matter of his attacks. Each had his personal reason, and did not see why he needed to burden himself. But the total effect was bad, and gave the impression that the doughty old Protestant champion was sounding his trumpet and no one would venture out. Mr. Lunn was, indeed, not the first or the only accepter; Father Thurston, Father Hugh Pope, and several others engaged him, but no one, not even Father Thurston on so wide a front, nor, it may be added, with so much desire to keep the controversy—Dr. Coulton's last one—good tempered and the relationship warmly human.[3]

When Lunn wrote his supplementary letter for the second edition of *Difficulties*, which was published twenty years after the original exchange, he said to Ronald Knox, "Dr. Coulton's last book was, as you know, a controversy with me. I have a soft spot for that gallant fighter. He loved Switzerland and he could write beautiful prose and on the rare occasions

---

[2] Arnold Lunn, *Unkilled for So Long* (London: Allen and Unwin, 1968), 97. —ED.

[3] Ibid., 97–98. —ED.

when he allowed himself to look at, instead of spitting at, the Church the result was most attractive, as for instance his chapter on St. Bernard, that of Clairvaux."[4]

When planning the books with Knox, Joad, Haldane, and Coulton, Lunn and his adversary agreed to an overall word count and letters of 3,000 to 7,000 words. The quota with Coulton was to be 50,000 words each. Coulton's second letter to Lunn occupied eighty-six pages and nearly exhausted his allotment. Lunn said to him, "I have so far used 7,000 words and you 46,000 words, leaving yourself about 4,000 words to reply to 43,000 words of mine! Only lack of space prevents my replying fully to many of the points which you raise. 'I am preparing a pamphlet containing my detailed reply, copies of which may be obtained, post free, 6d.'[5] Some such sentence seems inevitable in your concluding letter if the present word-limit is observed." With the publisher's approval, Lunn offered Coulton another 10,000 words, "provided, and provided only, that you keep these for your reply to my next long letter. This leaves you 4,000 to reply to this letter." Lunn then notes that Coulton had sent him half of his long letter some weeks early, and the younger man begged him to cut it down. As it was, about 30 percent of the completed letter was not even on the agreed-upon topic.

In Lunn's last two letters to Coulton, he remarked that "you have had one tactical advantage in this correspondence. You have made so many mistakes that you have been able to edify the reader with frank and candid confessions... and by

[4] Ronald Knox and Arnold Lunn, *Difficulties* (London: Eyre and Spottiswoode, 1952 [1932]), 251. —ED.

[5] In his later years Coulton was famous for publishing pamphlets on his own, since no publisher would take up the task, and he distributed them freely. He was insistent on getting his opinions out, even at his own expense. —ED.

an odd coincidence none of your mistakes ever tell in favour of the Church." [6]

August 31, 1944

Dear Dr. Coulton,

I think it was St. Thomas Aquinas who said that no argument was possible unless one could start from an agreed premiss. You and I at least agree that this kind of controversy is of value.

I am not the first Catholic to have accepted with alacrity a challenge of this kind from a Protestant. In 1930 Father (now Monsignor) R. A. Knox defended Catholicism against my attack—I was not of course a Catholic at the time—and our book *Difficulties* [7] was the result. Since then I have defended Catholicism against C. E. M. Joad (*Is Christianity True?*) [8] and against Professor J. B. S. Haldane, F.R.S. (*Science and the Supernatural*). [9] It is also, I think, worth noting that after various Protestant publishers had declined to commission the present book it was accepted by Burns Oates, with the result that it will, I hope, be prominently displayed in Catholic bookshops. You have sometimes written as if Catholics were frightened to face the case against them, and these facts are decisive against that view.

I remember once debating with a Free-Thinker under the auspices of the Rationalist Press Association. I pointed out

[6] Coulton and Lunn, *Is the Catholic Church Anti-Social?* 234, 240. —ED.

[7] To save myself further correspondence, may I state that I cannot help those who are in search of second-hand copies of this book [referring to the first edition of Knox and Lunn, *Difficulties*. —ED.].

[8] Arnold Lunn and C. E. M. Joad, *Is Christianity True?* (Philadelphia: Lippincott, 1933). —ED.

[9] Arnold Lunn and J. B. S. Haldane, *Science and the Supernatural* (New York: Sheed and Ward, 1935). —ED.

that a Free-Thinker should be encouraged to think freely about Christianity, and that the literature displayed on R.P.A. bookstalls should, therefore, represent both sides of the case, Christian and anti-Christian. "No Catholic bookshop," said my opponent, "would sell books containing the arguments for atheism." "As a matter of fact they do," was my answer. "Haldane attacked the arguments for a personal God in our correspondence, and the book in which these attacks appear was published in America by a Catholic publisher, Sheed and Ward, and selected as the Book of the Month by the Catholic Book of the Month Club. I notice, however, that it is not on sale on your bookstalls."

The good word "propaganda" is losing its original meaning, and because there is no word which exactly expresses what we mean by "propagandist," I shall use this word to designate the kind of advocacy which is expected by a client from his counsel, in contrast to the judicial summing-up of the available evidence which we expect from a judge. You have made a great reputation as a kind of Protestant K.C.,[10] and it is not, I hope, offensive to suggest that your attitude to the Church is propagandist rather than judicial.

The treatment of context provides a criterion for distinguishing between propagandist and historian. You are fond of quoting a petulant remark of Newman's that unless one doctored all one's facts one would be thought a bad Catholic. But you omit to mention that this particular remark was first published in an article on Newman in a Jesuit paper, *The Month*. Had the editor of *The Month* doctored his facts the Newman quotation would have been deleted. Again you attack the virtual Italian monopoly of the Papacy but ignore the relevant historical context. When Italy was weak and

[10] King's Counsel. —ED.

disunited there was a strong case for preferring a candidate from some small State such as Venice or Florence to the candidate of a Great Power whose election would inevitably provoke instant resentment of rival Powers. But the situation changed when united Italy demanded the consideration due to a Great Power, and there is no further justification for a practice which weakens the prestige and influence of the Church. Incidentally the present Pope[11] was the one outstanding candidate irrespective of nationality. The same disregard for context characterizes your remarks about Malta. In Catholic Europe Protestants seldom claim to be Catholics, and Italian Cardinals find it difficult to remember the controversial implications of "Roman Catholic" as that term is employed in England. The Cardinal[12] drew an incorrect inference from Lord Strickland's action,[13] but as the infallibility of Cardinals is no part of my creed, a fact which may surprise you considering how often you quote them, I am not perturbed by the Cardinal's mistake. There has been no change since St. Augustine's day in the popular use of the "title of Catholic, which, not without cause," writes St. Augustine, "hath this Church alone, amid so many heresies, obtained in such sort, that, whereas all heretics wish to be called Catholics, nevertheless to any stranger, who asked where to find the 'Catholic' Church, none of them would dare to point to his own basilica or home." [14] Try St. Augustine's test on the nearest policeman in London, Tokyo, Chicago or Calcutta. Ask him the way to the Catholic Church

[11] Pius XII. —Ed.

[12] Pietro Gasparri (1852–1934), secretary of state under Popes Benedict XV and Pius XI. —Ed.

[13] The British Governor of Malta wanted to alter Malta's constitution so as to eliminate reference to the Catholic Church in article one. The British ruled Malta from 1814–1964. —Ed.

[14] Augustine, *Against the Letter of Mani Called "Fundamental"*, 4, 5. —Ed.

and he will direct you to a church whose congregation are in communion with Rome.

I was faintly shocked by your remarks about the bombing of Rome, for that controversy cut across all the usual religious and political lines. Civilized Leftists such as the editor and literary editor of the *New Statesman* wished to save the Rome that belongs to the world, but the philistines of the Left, like David Low,[15] wrote as if Rome belonged to Mussolini.

I should be lacking in respect for your scholarship if I took you seriously when you describe the Church as parochial and sectarian, for I refuse to believe that you are less sensitive to the cultural and cosmopolitan appeal of Catholicism than the author of *Crux Ansata*.[16]

Mr. H. G. Wells writes (italics mine):

> Protestantism, I perceived, had not done justice to Renascence Rome. Here, quite plainly, was a great mental system engaged in a vital effort to comprehend its expanding universe and sustain a co-ordinating conception of human activities. That easy word 'superstition' did not cover a tithe of it. . . . I found something congenial in the *far-flung cosmopolitanism* of the Catholic proposition. . . . Catholicism is something *greater in scope and spirit than any nationalist protestantism*. . . . I have found the ordinary Catholic controversialist a fair fighter and a civilized man—worthy of that *great cultural system* within which such minds as Leonardo and Michael Angelo could develop and find expression. He has an antiquated realist philosophy which too often gives him a pert hardness, but that is another matter. It is a question too

---

[15] David Low (1891–1963), cartoonist for the London *Evening Standard*. Lunn may have had in mind the commentaries that accompanied Low's cartoons in *The Best of Low* (London: Jonathan Cape, 1930). —ED.

[16] H. G. Wells, *Crux Ansata: An Indictment of the Roman Catholic Church* (New York: Agora Publishing, 1943), 106. —ED.

fine for me to discuss whether I am an outright atheist or an extreme heretic on the furthest verge of Christendom— beyond the Aryans (*sic*), beyond the Manicheans. But certainly I branch from the Catholic stem.[17]

If such be the impact of Eternal Rome on so prejudiced an anti-Catholic as H. G. Wells, is it surprising that Catholics should glory in their association with the See of St. Peter? It was the internationalism of Rome which appealed to me, even in the days when I was attacking the Church. At the Gregorian University students of every race and nation listened to lectures in the Latin which was once the language of all cultured Europeans. When I last visited Rome, in 1940, the General of the Jesuits was a Pole, of the Dominicans a Frenchman, and of the Benedictines a German. The "parochialism" of the Church does not seem to me to be a very hopeful controversial line for an Anglican. You were good enough to suggest that we should do well to elect an American Pope, but though American Episcopalians are in communion with Canterbury, you have yet to campaign an American Archbishop at Lambeth.

Long before I became a Catholic, in a book *Roman Converts*, which was an attack on the Church, I wrote:

> The man who can appreciate continuity of tradition will be more at ease in the European countries which have been spared that violent breach with the past which was a necessary but none the less a high price to pay for the Reformation. Ghosts of forgotten faiths still haunt those little lost hill churches in the remoter Alpine valleys, where one poor priest still serves as the only link with the culture which the Latin Church rescued from the shipwreck of Rome. . . .

[17] *An Experiment in Autobiography*, p. 573. Wells, of course, balances his praise with plenty of criticism, which you can quote in your next letter.

'Here is the old business being carried on by the old firm in the old ways; here is continuity that takes one back to the catacombs. . . .' Yes, and further back than the catacombs, back to the hidden roots of humanity and religion. Protestantism with its academic repudiation of the past has robbed us of something older than the Mass, of a communal tradition of religious instincts which goes back—who knows?—to Apollo. And among the hills it is easy to believe that Apollo has made his submission to the Church, and that the ancient worship still lingers, however much its expression may have changed.[18]

Even in those days I was attracted by the power of the Church to assimilate all that was best in the old Graeco-Roman culture. The shocked dismay with which you note certain resemblances between the organization of the Roman Empire and the organization of the Church will no doubt ring a bell with the kind of reader for whom all Italians are "Wops," but not with those who agree with Samuel Johnson that "a man who has not been in Italy is always conscious of an inferiority, from his not having seen what it is expected that a man should see. The grand object of all travelling is to see the shores of the Mediterranean . . . all our religion, almost all our law, almost all our arts, almost all that sets us above savages, has come to us from the shores of the Mediterranean." [19]

If Catholicism is parochial because of its associations with Rome, Christianity is parochial because of its "local origins" in Bethlehem and Nazareth.

You attack Catholics for "lack of clear definition," but though you devote several pages to attacking our use of the

[18] Arnold Lunn, *Roman Converts* (London: Chapman and Hall, 1924).
[19] James Boswell, *The Life of Samuel Johnson* (London: Dent, 1906), II, 25–26. —ED.

word "Catholic," you omit to give us your own definition of Catholicism. Admittedly you describe "The Catholic Church" correctly as "Christ's Church," but you do not explain whether in your view Anglicans or Free Churchmen or Unitarians are members of this Church.

Nowhere is the "lack of clear definition" more mischievous than in the case of the word "Christian." Today Unitarians camouflaged as Modernists claim the Christian name, and profess to believe in the *Divinity* of Christ, a concession the value of which is somewhat discounted by the fact that they also believe in their own divinity. For all good men, the neo-Unitarian insists, have a spark of the divine, and the difference between the divinity of Jesus and the divinity, say, of St. Francis of Assisi was a difference of degree rather than of kind. It is because the word Divinity has been degraded that I prefer to write of the *Deity* or *Godhead* of our Lord.

A man who denied the Godhead of our Lord and His *physical* resurrection would not have been considered a Christian by Luther, Calvin, John Wesley and the great Anglican divines.

I hope you will convert your fellow Modernists to your belief in the value of clear definition, for some of them resent as an impertinence the mere suggestion that they should clearly define their own beliefs.

I am the more disposed to welcome your desire for clear definition (which I hope includes a clear definition of your own Christological beliefs) because I suspect that what really divides us is not so much the infallibility of the Pope but the infallibility of Christ. It is the ethos of traditional Christianity which you dislike, the Christianity which was from the first authoritarian and dogmatic. "He that believeth and is baptized shall be saved, but he that believeth not shall be damned." [20] The primitive Christians accepted this stern saying of our Lord and regarded themselves as trustees for a precious revelation. St. Paul insisted on the respect due to ecclesiastical authority [21] and on the duty of expelling the impenitent heretic from the Church. There were no Modernists when the Church was modern. [22] The authoritarianism which you dislike is the inevitable consequence of our belief in the deity of Christ. *If* it be true that God has revealed certain beliefs, it is our duty to accept those beliefs. *If* God has imposed certain regulations of conduct, we must obey those regulations. Admittedly it is a question of "ifs" and I can understand your rejecting the Christian premiss, but it is absurd to reserve your protests for the inevitable conclusions which follow from those premisses. This is as if you were to agree that a Colonel might be allowed to believe in the existence of the King, provided that he was not such a bigot as to impose King's Regulations on his battalion.

In time of war we are as intolerant of national heresy as Torquemada of religious heresy. Hundreds of Englishmen suspected of sympathy with Nazi heresies were imprisoned without trial four years ago. Many of them are still untried and in prison.

Intolerance of error must not be equated with intolerance of men in error. St. Augustine's precept, "*diligite homines, interficite errores*," [23] should be our guiding principle. Again, his statement, "No one shall be forced to embrace the Catholic faith against his will," [24] represents the authentic

[20] Mk 16:16. —ED.

[21] I developed this argument in *Now I See*, page 207, etc.

[22] See Hebrew 13:9; 2 Timothy 1:13; Titus 1:19; Romans 16:17; 2 Thessalonians 3:6; Titus 1:10, 2 John 10:11.

[23] "Love men, slay errors" [Augustine, *Contra lit. Petil.*, I, xxix, n. 31, in P.L. 43:259. —ED.].

[24] Augustine, *Tractate* 26, 2. —ED.

voice of the Church, as is clear from the fact that Leo XIII quoted and endorsed this statement, and neither quoted nor endorsed his later aberrations. It is amusing that you should scold the Pope because he quoted what he agreed with but did not quote what he disagreed with. Your attack on the Pope is all the funnier in view of your habit of selective quotation from Catholic writers, such as Acton and Newman, in order to establish your case against the religion which they professed. But, as you rightly remark, "pharisaism is all the more mischievous in proportion as it is unconscious."

You have a sound precedent for quoting Perrone's [25] *Catechism* in this type of controversy, for I quoted Perrone against Knox in our book *Difficulties*, but being less concerned to make a case than to discover the truth, I balanced Perrone with quotations from a modern theologian less uncompromising on this question of apostasy than the Cardinal.

Perrone is stern, but so was our Lord. Nothing could be more explicit than His warning of the consequences which would follow if men rejected His revelation as preached by His accredited representatives, and it is surely inconsequential to attack those who believe that Christ speaks through the Church for drawing logical conclusions from Christ's words, "He that despiseth you despiseth me." [26] I have often thought that a minor argument for the implicit recognition of our Lord's deity by those who explicitly reject His claims is the contrast between the readiness with which Unitarians and Modernists attack the Church for bigotry, when she draws logical conclusions from the teaching and practice of our Lord, and their extreme reluctance to criticize Christ. You,

[25] Giovanni Perrone (1794–1876), Jesuit theologian. —ED.
[26] Lk 10:16. —ED.

for instance, would never dream of attacking our Lord for bigotry or intolerance.

But to return to Perrone. No Catholic would wish to deny that those (a) to whom God has given the gift of faith, and (b) who with full knowledge and consent have deliberately rejected the faith, have imperilled their hope of eternal salvation, but I believe that had you put to Cardinal Perrone a particular case of a particular apostate who had died outside the Church, he might well have replied by quoting words which he himself used in a slightly different connexion, "*Hoc enim ad Dei judicium remittimus. . . .*" [27] You know, of course, that though the Church dogmatically asserts that all those who have been canonized or beatified are in heaven, she will allow no one to assert that any particular individual is in hell.

When I became a Catholic I was puzzled by the contrast between the uncompromising severity of the Church's official pronouncements in cases such as that of the apostate, and the readiness of distinguished theologians to express in private conversation a charitable and even a hopeful view of individual cases, making every possible allowance for defective education, or for the difficulties of an environment hostile to Catholicism. But there is no inconsistency in this apparent contrast. The Church is the trustee for the eternal happiness of her children, and her task is to ensure that as many of us as possible are in a position to receive the last sacraments, and her official warnings as to peril of apostasy must necessarily be couched in language as stern as Christ's.

The Museumist Approach.—Your knowledge of the Church would seem to be derived almost exclusively from research among written documents. It is a pity you have so few personal contacts with Catholics, for you seem to me to have

---

[27] "We surely leave the judgment to God." —Ed.

no idea at all of the Church as a living society. Your knowledge of the Church might be compared to the knowledge which a man might acquire about butterflies by examining the cabinets in a natural history museum. You do not seem to have seen the Catholic butterflies on the wing. Your approach to Catholicism is essentially "museumist," to coin a necessary word.

If your approach to Catholics were less "museumist" you would not trot out all that old stuff about Catholics being "soldiers in a vast and strictly disciplined army, obedient to their officers, and subordinating their own wishes and ideas wherever conscience permits," for the fact is, as Father Martindale[28] somewhere remarks, that Catholics use up all their available unity on points of defined doctrine, and have nothing left over for anything else. Even a museumist should be able to discover this, for a few hours spent in browsing among the recent files of the Catholic press would teach you something of the wide diversity of views among modern Catholics on questions of Ecclesiastical policy. "It is not their business," you write of your hypothetical Catholics, "to criticize what the High Command is doing." It may not be their business, but it is their practice, as you could discover for yourself by reading the editorials of the *Catholic Herald*, or by listening in to the private discussions of Catholics, theological and lay, after the issue of a pastoral on a controversial subject. Incidentally most of your anti-Catholic material is quoted from the writings of "these soldiers in a vast and strictly disciplined army."

It is this illusion of mechanical and disciplined unity which explains your odd view that you have scored a telling point against the Church by quoting the attacks of an

---

[28] C. C. Martindale (1879–1963), Jesuit scholar, writer, and preacher. —ED.

Acton on the Ultramontanes. If we were to translate the controversy over Papal infallibility, defined in 1870, into political terms, Acton's party might be compared to the Liberals and the Ultramontanes to the Conservatives. You seem to think that because Acton loved the Church he could not possibly have been unfair to the Ultramontanes. Asquith[29] loved England, but it does not follow that his attacks on English Conservatives were necessarily objective and unbiased. No Catholic has much hope of a bouquet from you unless he provides you with a quotation to use against the Church. Theologians who fulfil this useful function are promptly promoted to the category of "pious and learned Churchman," and I suspect that the only Catholics whose honesty you would recognize without qualification are those who agree with your views about the dishonesty of Catholics in general.

Papal Infallibility.—We believe that the Pope is infallible (a) when he speaks *ex cathedra* as Pope; (b) when he defines a doctrine on faith or morals; (c) when the *ex cathedra* announcement is addressed to the whole world. There are only nine pronouncements by the Pope which are recognized by all theologians as fulfilling the necessary qualifications of infallibility.

It is rare for the Church to define doctrines which have not been attacked. "No doctrine," as Newman said, "is defined until it is violated." [30]

The following passage is taken from my book *Now I See*, which was translated without omissions into Italian and received the imprimatur at Rome:

[29] Herbert Henry Asquith (1852–1928), British statesman, Prime Minister 1908–1916. —ED.

[30] John Henry Newman, *An Essay on the Development of Christian Doctrine* (London: Pickering, 1878), 151. —ED.

Papal infallibility does not mean that the Pope could produce an infallible *ex cathedra* announcement at any moment
and on any subject connected with faith and morals. It is true
that the doctrines of the Catholic Church were all contained
in the original deposit of faith, but the task of rendering
them explicit involves research and study both for the Pope
and for the Episcopate. . . . Infallibility is a negative rather
than a positive gift. The Holy Ghost prevents the Church
from preaching false doctrine, but does not necessarily provide the Pope or the Episcopate with the right answer at any
given moment to any particular question. 'Supposing,' so
runs the question a priest will often put to classes of children,
'supposing that the Pope possesses the same infallibility in
algebra as he possesses in faith or morals, what would be the
least number of marks out of a possible 100 that he could
obtain in an examination on algebra?' The small boys present
usually reply, '100.' An occasional bright lad gives the right
answer, 'No marks.' Infallibility only guarantees that any
answer shown up by our hypothetical Pope in our hypothetical examination will not be incorrect. This condition
would be fulfilled if he showed up a blank piece of paper.[31]

Many people "seem to think," as Monsignor Knox remarks, "that the Pope, like the High Priest in the Old
Testament, keeps a kind of Urim and Thummim somewhere
in the Vatican, and that if he wants to know the answer to a
vexed question he just applies to the oracle and the answer is
miraculously given him."[32] This would seem to be your
view. The divine inspiration of the Book of Tobit was only
settled by the Council of Trent in the sixteenth century. "But
nothing could have been easier," you write, "than for an
infallible Pope to tell Christendom once and for all which

---

[31] Arnold Lunn, *Now I See* (New York: Sheed and Ward, 1938), 242–
43. —ED.
[32] Knox and Lunn, *Difficulties*, 124. —ED.

books could be relied upon and which could not, for inerrancy." No, nothing could have been easier if infallibility
could be equated with the kind of omniscience claimed for
the Delphic Oracle, but a guarantee that the Pope speaking
ex cathedra will never *mislead* is not the same as a guarantee
that he will always give a lead. It is odd that, in spite of your
prolonged study of the Church, you should have so completely failed to understand her doctrine of infallibility.

Your chapter on "the strange silences of the Popes" is, of
course, based on Salmon's [33] attack on "the hesitations of the
infallible guide." But the silences of the Pope are no stranger
than the silences of Christ. "Render unto Caesar the things
that are Caesar's, and to God the things which are God's," [34]
and Christians are still debating *which* things are Caesar's.
Christ never condemned slavery, and left it to His followers
to discover gradually that slavery as an institution was inconsistent with Christianity. Slavery was slowly eroded by the
Christian atmosphere. The rights of the slave to marriage
and the family were safeguarded by the precepts of the
Church, and secured by legal enactment in the Theodosian
code. The slave, a mere chattel under Roman law, was
promoted to the status of a man whom the law must protect.
The violation of a slave woman was made punishable by
death. The killing of the slave, which passed without comment in pagan Rome, was punishable as criminal homicide.
Again we find an increasing pressure in favour of emancipa-
tion and the suppression of slavery as a legal penalty. The
presumptions of the Theodosian code were deemed "in
favour of liberty." Gradually the slave was transformed into a

[33] George Salmon (1819–1904), provost of Trinity College Dublin, opponent of papal infallibility, and author of *The Infallibility of the Church* (London:
Murray, 1888). —ED.

[34] Lk 20:25. —ED.

serf, with freedom to dispose of his property. Gradually serfdom disappeared from Christian lands. In 1462 Pius II declared that slavery was a great crime,[35] and in the sixteenth century Paul III issued a tremendous condemnation of the enslavement of American Indians.[36] Exploiters of the Indians were denounced as "instruments of Satan." I have described the process at length in my book about St. Peter Claver (*A Saint in the Slave Trade*),[37] and though well aware of what you have said on this subject, I summed up the argument in the words of Chesterton: "The Catholic type of Christianity was not merely an element, it was a climate, and in that climate a slave would not grow." Revelation was never meant to be a labour-saving device. God gave us our brains to use. He guaranteed that the Church would never teach error, and would survive to the end, but He allowed Churchmen to find out many things for themselves by the ordinary human process of discussion, research, trial and error.

The Inquisition was a bad blunder, but—as in the case of slavery—the Church on her human side has learned that persecution and slavery are inconsistent with the spirit of her Divine Founder.

You will, of course, deny this and will seek to prove by a chain of syllogisms that Catholics would be bound to burn

---

[35] Pius II was writing to a missionary bishop who was on his way to Guinea. —ED.

[36] Paul III, *Sublimis Deus* (1537): "[W]e define and declare . . . that . . . the said Indians, and all other people who may later be discovered by Christians, are by no means to be deprived of their liberty or the possession of their property, even though they be outside the faith of Jesus Christ; and that they may and should, freely and legitimately, enjoy their liberty and the possession of their property; nor should they be in any way enslaved; should the contrary happen, it shall be null and of no effect." Colman J. Barry, O.S.B., *Readings in Church History* (Westminster, Md.: Christian Classics, 1985), 600. —ED.

[37] Arnold Lunn, *A Saint in the Slave Trade* (London: Sheed and Ward, 1935). —ED.

the Archbishop of Canterbury alive if ever the Church regained her medieval power. And I can no more refute you than I could refute a Catholic who believed that a revived and strengthened Anglicanism would insist on the State re-erecting the gallows of Tyburn for the execution of priests. And while we are on this subject let me question your statement that the Church "wields" (note the present tense) "even the sanction of death, if not by the priest's actual hand, at least by the irreformable command of the Pope and his ministers." Even in the days of the Inquisition this was not true, except in so far as the Pope was a temporal ruler of the Papal States, and exercised in that capacity the same rights as other temporal rulers.

Totalitarianism.—You quote the *Oxford English Dictionary* definition of totalitarianism, but reject it and invent one of your own more suitable to your thesis. " 'When I use a word,' Humpty Dumpty said in a rather scornful tone, 'it means just what I choose it to mean—neither more nor less.' " [38] Like Humpty Dumpty you dictate to words what they must mean, a very totalitarian practice. A totalitarian State, you insist, is a State "in which certain kinds of liberty are totally abolished." What kinds? This vagueness is amusing from one who opens this controversy with a demand for clear definition. Russia and Germany are totalitarian, but the Church is not totalitarian according to the O.E.D. definition—a State "which permits no rival loyalties and parties." There was no activity of life in Nazi Germany or Soviet Russia in which the totalitarian State did not interfere, from religion and science to sport. "Even in the natural sciences," writes Eugene Lyons, "there was plenty of grotesquery about 'Leninist surgery' and 'Stalinist mathematics' and ideological

[38] Lewis Carroll, *Through the Looking Glass* (New York: Heritage, 1941), 112. —ED.

deviations in biology." [39] Make the best of Galileo, the only case in nineteen centuries which would supply the most ardent of propagandists with a colourable parallel to "Stalinist mathematics."

It is not necessary to live, as I have lived, in a totalitarian country. It is not necessary to have personal experience of the evil influence of Totalitarianism as I have had in sport. Even the museumist approach suffices to establish the fact that Catholicism and Totalitarianism are poles apart.

It is no accident that the Italy of Mazzini should have ended in the Italy of Mussolini, or that those who rejected the very limited infallibility of the Pope should have ended by accepting the unlimited infallibility of Mussolini. *Mussolini a sempre ragione*—Mussolini is *always* right. The flight from Catholic authority ends in the deification of the secular tyrant. Catholic philosophy is realistic. It is firmly based on the premiss of original sin. It is neither optimistic nor pessimistic, for the Church knows that the progress and regress of nations depend on their obedience to or rejection of the commandments of God. Every individual has the same choice, salvation or damnation, but since man is fallen, few men can resist the corruption of power. Lord Acton's famous apophthegm, "Power corrupts and absolute power corrupts absolutely," [40] is a deduction from Catholic premisses, and because power corrupts, the Church has always insisted on the distribution of power as opposed to the concentration of power as demanded by a modern dictator. In Switzerland it is the Catholic cantons which are most opposed to centralization. The present Pope and his predecessors have insisted again and again that the health of the State depends on the

---

[39] *Assignment in Utopia*, p. 468.

[40] Actually, "power tends to corrupt, and absolute power corrupts absolutely", Letter to Bishop Mandell Creighton, April 5, 1887. —ED.

balance of power between the town and the country, and on resisting the ever-increasing tyranny of the bureaucracy. The Papal insistence of the importance of the family is in itself a check on totalitarianism. The Catholics believe that the State exists for the family, but many of our modern Socialists seem to think that the family exists for the State. "There is one little defect about man," writes G. K. Chesterton, "the image of God, the wonder of the world and the paragon of animals—that he is not to be trusted." And because man is not to be trusted, even Popes have been corrupted by power, and even Peter sometimes tried to trespass on the territory of Caesar; but the climate of Catholicism has proved too strong for the totalitarian ambitions of the individual.

The sentence which you quote from Boniface VIII's bull *Unam Sanctam*,[41] the only sentence binding on Catholics, means no more than that all men are spiritually subject to Christ's Vicar. The bull must be interpreted within the context of the time, and its political claims, though unjustifiable, do not approach within measurable distance with those which even good democrats are now advancing on behalf of the State. Even the most authoritarian of Popes never claimed totalitarian control, for every Pope accepts the commandment of Christ, "Render unto Caesar the things which are Caesar's." Totalitarianism was impossible in Catholic Europe, for in Catholic Europe power was not concentrated, it was *distributed*. "In the old days of conflicting authority," Aldous Huxley remarked to me, "there was always somebody to appeal to, the Emperor against the Pope, the Pope against the Emperor, the nobles against the King.

---

[41] "Moreover, we declare, assert, define, and decree that subjection to the Pontiff of Rome is an absolute necessity of salvation for every human being." Boniface VIII in *Unam Sanctam*, as translated by Coulton, *Is the Catholic Church Anti-Social?* 12. —ED.

But today we are moving towards the Moloch of a centralized totalitarian State against whose verdict there is no appeal." "Thanks to Christianity," as Mr. Walter Lippmann,[42] the famous American liberal, has admitted, "the pretensions of despots became heretical. And since that revelation, though many despots have had the blessings of the clergy, no tyranny has possessed a clear title before the tribunal of human conscience, no slave has had to feel that the hope of freedom was for ever closed. For in the recognition that there is in each man a final essence—that is, an immortal soul which only God can judge—a limit was set upon the dominion of men over men."

Henry II instigated the murder of Becket[43] and Mussolini the murder of Matteotti,[44] but Mussolini did not subsequently flog himself on the tomb of Matteotti. Do you really believe that the world has gained from the fact that the modern tyrant no longer fears those supernatural sanctions of the Catholic Church which sent one Emperor to Canossa and another to prostrate himself in Venice before the Pope whom he had previously hounded out of Italy?[45] At other times the Pope, you complain, was unduly servile to the Emperor, all of which goes to show that neither Pope nor Emperor was supreme.

In the unending attempts to define the respective limits of Ecclesiastical and Civil authority there was no finality, but there was instead a healthy determination to resist the beginnings of what we now call totalitarianism. To this spirit you

[42] Walter Lippmann (1889–1974), American journalist. —ED.

[43] Thomas Becket (1117–1170), Archbishop of Canterbury. —ED.

[44] Giacomo Matteotti (1885–1924), an early opponent of the Fascist regime, murdered in 1924. —ED.

[45] In 1077 Henry II (1050–1106) did penance at Canossa before Gregory VII (1020–1085), and in 1177 Frederick Barbarossa (1125–1190) prostrated himself before Alexander III (1105–1181). —ED.

yourself have borne witness in your letter. Even in its peak period the Papacy always recognized the limitations of Papal rights, but no such limitation is recognized by the modern dictator.

It is no accident that the beginnings of Totalitarianism coincided with the revolt against the Papacy. Marsilius,[46] whom you so much admire, sketched out a blue print for a secular tyranny, and it is a little disingenuous of you to recommend his work on the strength of a testimonial from Henry VIII and Thomas Cromwell, whose fruitful co-operation provided Hitler with ample precedents for the liquidation of Church property. It is no accident that in Nazi Germany the only effective and open resistance to Hitler comes from Catholic Bishops carrying on the great Fisher-More tradition of resistance to secular Totalitarianism. It was Luther's motto *cujus regio ejus religio* (the principle that the Prince had the right to determine the religion of his subjects) which paved the way for Nazism, and it is no accident that "private judgment" is interned in Dachau, for it is not the Lutheran principle of private judgment but the protection of the Church which alone can save men from the tyranny of secular dictatorships.

"The only open challenge to the totalitarian State," writes Walter Lippmann, "has come from men of deep religious faith." In Soviet Russia the Orthodox Church had, on the whole, a fine record. Twelve Bishops and twelve hundred priests were put to death, but the patriarch Tikhon[47] recanted under the strain of long imprisonment and the schism of the so-called "living Church" was a deplorable episode. Fortunately there was no break in the

[46] Marsilius of Padua (died c. 1342), Italian political theorist who opposed papal temporal power. —ED.

[47] Tikhon (1865–1925), Russian Orthodox Patriarch of Moscow. —ED.

Catholic ranks. "The Catholic Church," writes Captain Francis McCullagh, who witnessed the trial of the Catholics in Moscow, "remained incorruptible, invulnerable, solid as a rock. Even its laity could not be seduced. . . . The Bolsheviks could not get a single Catholic layman to act as their tool."[48] In Germany the Catholic Church has been the only power which has offered any resistance to Hitler. "Being a lover of freedom," writes Einstein,

> when the revolution came in Germany I looked to the universities to defend it, knowing that they already boasted of their devotion to the cause of Truth: but no, the universities were immediately silenced. Then I looked to the great editors of the newspapers, whose flaring editorials in days gone by had proclaimed their love of freedom: but they like the universities were silenced in a few short weeks. Then I looked to the individual writers who, as literary guides of Germany, had written much and often concerning the place of freedom in modern life, but they too were mute. Only the Church stood squarely across the path of Hitler's campaign for suppressing truth. I never had any special interest in the Church before, but now I feel a great affection and admiration because the Church alone has had the courage and persistence to stand for intellectual truth and moral freedom. I am forced, then, to confess that what I once despised I now praise unreservedly.[49]

Countess Waldeck, daughter of a Jewish banker in Mannheim, pays a similar tribute to the Church.

> But, fortunately for the anti-Nazi cause, Hitler did not succeed in suppressing all vestiges of personal courage, selflessness and perseverance in the struggle against Nazidom.

[48] Francis McCullagh, *The Bolshevik Persecution of Christianity* (London: Murray, 1924), 115–16. —ED.

[49] Quoted in *Hibbert Journal*, January, 1944.

There exist opponents to Hitler whose strength of soul and integrity is so great that, notwithstanding the calumnies with which the Nazis have tried to smear them, the Germans know that these men risk their lives and liberty, not for selfish interest, but for the spiritual protection of the Fatherland. For these men are Churchmen. Their every sermon and every pastoral letter is a political event in the Germany of today and no word by them is ever lost.

She pays a tribute to the Catholic Bishops "whose utterances are a remarkably frank denunciation of Nazi treatment of the Jews and conquered people and their contempt for individual rights. . . . To all practical intents and purposes Catholic opposition to Nazism has been much more important and articulate than Protestant opposition. . . . It is a strange fact that the few popular heroes and martyrs of anti-Nazi opposition in Germany come from Conservative Germany" (not, be it noted, from the Socialist underground movement, if there be such a movement). "The uncomfortable truth is that neither Liberal bourgeoisie nor Labour has bred any anti-Nazi opponents who enjoy even a percentage of the veneration enjoyed by Faulhaber[50] (Archbishop of Munich) and most of all Niemöller.[51] . . .

"As a matter of fact the Nazis have met their only major domestic defeat in their efforts to destroy the Christian faith. In the midst of the debris of trade unions, freemasons, lodges and of the Socialist and Communist parties which have fallen before Hitler as if they were papier mâché, organized Christianity still stands."[52]

---

[50] Michael von Faulhaber (1869–1952), Archbishop of Munich and a strong opponent of Nazism. —ED.

[51] Martin Niemöller (1892–1984), German Protestant churchman imprisoned by the Nazis 1938–1945. —ED.

[52] *Excellenz*, by Countess Waldeck, pp. 151, 167, 168.

Something stronger than modernism—the deep faith of the Catholic or the old-fashioned Lutheran—is needed to stand up against the Gestapo or OGPU.

In Italy the one force strong [enough] to resist Mussolini has been the Vatican, as is shown in *Church and State in Fascist Italy*, by D. A. Binchy, published by the Royal Institute of International Affairs.[53]

In Spain the Church made every effort to work with the Republic, for which the greater number of the clergy voted at the critical election. The Civil War was not a war between Fascism and Democracy. That myth finds no support in Madariaga's classical work on Spain,[54] though Madariaga was a determined opponent of Franco and of the Catholic Church. It was a war between two rival dictatorships, a dictatorship in whose territory the Church can live, and a dictatorship which was responsible for a persecution in which thousands of priests and nuns were murdered. Nobody expects a Jew to be wholly unbiased against Hitler, and Jews both expect and receive the practical sympathy of Catholics when they are persecuted. But for some strange reason it is supposed to be very reactionary of a Catholic to object to a regime which puts Catholics to death. The majority of British Catholics sympathized with the Spanish Nationalists in spite of Franco's alliance with Hitler, just as no British Catholic ceased to hope for the victory of his country because Britain is allied with totalitarian Russia.

In the complexity of the modern world the Church sometimes finds herself in uneasy alliance with a modern dictator. But there is an irreconcilable conflict between the principles

[53] D. A. Binchy (1899–1976), medieval historian, specialist in the Old Irish language, and editor of the six-volume *Corpus Juris Hibernici*. —ED.

[54] Salvador de Madariaga (1886–1978), *Spain* (London: Jonathan Cape, 1961 [1930]). —ED.

of the Church and the principles of Totalitarianism. The constitution of the Church is, as I have already suggested, the reverse of Totalitarianism. In theory the Pope, like our King, has tremendous powers, but in practice he seldom interferes. If the Church were totalitarian, Bishops would be completely subordinated to Archbishops and Parish Priests to Bishops. The Archbishop of Westminster, for instance, would be a kind of spiritual Gauleiter for England. In point of fact an Archbishop has virtually no power excepting in his own diocese. When Cardinal Bourne,[55] for instance, attempted to interfere in a neighbouring diocese, he suffered a defeat. Again, the irremovable Parish Priest has rights which a Bishop cannot override. A new diocese was created within the last few years in this country. The Bishop wanted to make the biggest Parish Church his Cathedral, but the Parish Priest declined to permit this. A friend of mine, Father Scantlebury, described to me a scene which he had witnessed when he was a seminary student at Nantes. In France the cathedrals belong to the State, and the State allows the Cathedral at Nantes to be used as a Parish Church. The Bishop of Nantes informed the "archpriest," who was, in effect, the Parish Priest in control of the Cathedral, that he intended to preside over the blessing of the font on Easter Saturday. "Oh no," said the archpriest, "I am going to bless the font myself."

Catholic Historians.—Responsible historians document their accusations, but propagandists have a weakness for general indictments unsupported by evidence. You state that Catholic historians are not only less accurate but less honest than Protestant historians. *Quod gratis affirmatur gratis negatur*—What you assert without evidence I need produce no evidence to deny. But it may interest you to know that the

---

[55] Francis Bourne (1861–1935), Archbishop of Westminster. —ED.

contrast between the acrimonious special pleading of your anti-Catholic propaganda and the serene confident objectivity of the best Catholic historians was one of the things which influenced my conversion. Of course some of our historians are unreliable, and I concede that in your controversy with Cardinal Gasquet[56] you were definitely in the right and he was definitely in the wrong, but your indictment of Catholic historians would be more impressive if you yourself were a competent judge of accuracy in a historian. Your anxiety to prove Catholics inaccurate is only equalled by your determination to maintain the inerrancy of anti-Catholic propagandists such as the American H. C. Lea, author of various works on the Inquisition, indulgences, etc. When Father Thurston, a *real* expert on the Middle Ages, casually remarked that "in any ten consecutive pages [of one of Lea's books] ten palpable blunders may be unearthed," you wrote (italics mine): "Take now the immense advantage of *choosing for yourself* out of the 1,600 pages which you here specify those ten which after careful study you think most vulnerable; and then indicate clearly, under cross-examination, the 'ten palpable blunders' which you fancy yourself to have discovered. You cannot be more anxious than I am to 'submit that estimate to the test of experiment,' *and to 'stand or fall' by the result*." [57]

You were so confident of Lea's scholarship that you prepared to wager his reputation, and incidentally your own, on the impossibility of finding *any ten pages* out of 1,600 named pages which averaged a blunder a page. In the sequel you invited a neutral to select ten pages at random and threw in two pages as a generous gesture. "I defy you," you wrote, "to

[56] Francis Gasquet (1846–1929), cardinal and historian. —ED.

[57] G. G. Coulton, *Sectarian History* (Taunton, England: Barnicotts, 1937), 75–77. —ED.

find even a single 'patent blunder' in all these twelve pages."
Father Thurston discovered fifteen blunders in twelve pages
selected by your friend at random, none of which you have
ventured to defend. The second test was, of course, far more
exacting than the first test which you proposed, and clearly,
if Father Thurston could satisfy your challenge on ten
pages selected at random, he could claim *a fortiori* to have
more than satisfied the original challenge on which Lea's
reputation was "to stand or fall." You clearly realized that it
was not only Lea's reputation that was at stake but your own,
for after suggesting that Father Thurston should invite the
co-operation of three of his colleagues, you added (italics
mine): "There would, indeed, be a certain piquancy if one
of those three turned out to be the providentially ordained
instrument (under you) for exploding Lea (*and incidentally
me*) once for all." [58] If I had been in the habit of referring
with immense respect to an Alpine historian, who was subsequently proved to average a blunder a page, I should have
no complaint if I was no longer accepted as an authority on
the Alps.

If you had ever seen the dead and dying being carried out
of a blitzed building you would be less censorious about the
Bishop of Rome's effort to save not only Roman stones but
also Roman citizens from bombing. As usual you ignore
the context of his protests, his consistent efforts to save the
populations of crowded areas from an aerial attack. In the
Spanish Civil War his appeal to refrain from the bombing of
towns was addressed both to Franco and to the Republicans.
In England the selective indignation of certain ecclesiastical
dignitaries was only provoked when the mastery of the air
passed from the Republicans (who began by bombing

---

[58] The entire Thurston–Coulton correspondence is reproduced in *Sectarian
History*, 63–86. —ED.

Granada in the early days of the war) to the Nationalists. Guernica, incidentally, through which troops were passing at the time, was as near the battlefield as Cassino or Caen. Your statement that the Pope "made no adequate protest even during the Polish horrors excepting in so far as the clergy and buildings of his own Roman creed suffered," is a trifle steep even for you. The Ministry of Information have published a careful record of the anti-Axis statements of the Pope and of the anti-Axis attitude of the Vatican radio and of the *Osservatore Romano*. May I commend to your attention a fragment of Euripides: "Happy is the man who knows the value of research."

By way of preface to what follows let me remind you that the Catholic claims to establish by pure reason and by the normal methods of the secular historian the existence of God, the Deity and Resurrection of Christ, and the foundation by Christ of a Church with authority to teach in His name. Once the credentials of the Church have been established by reason we may reasonably accept on her authority truths which we are in no position to verify independently. We use our reason to choose a doctor and then accept on his authority a diagnosis which we cannot independently verify.

It would be a dereliction for a Catholic historian or apologist "not to examine too closely" any objection to the Church or any historical fact which appears to tell against our claims.

It was, therefore, obvious to me that you must have misquoted the Pope when you represented Leo XIII as warning the clergy of France "not to examine too closely any historical question upon which the Church had already pronounced."

"The history of the Church," wrote Leo XIII, "is like a

mirror in which the light of the Church shines throughout the centuries, and which even more than secular and profane history demonstrates the sovereign liberty of God and His providential action on the march of events. Those who study it must never lose sight of the fact that it includes a collection of dogmatic facts which impose themselves on our faith and which nobody is permitted to call in doubt." [59]

It is not, as you falsely suggest, of history in general that the Pope writes, but of *the history of the Church*. His statement implies no more than the truism that it is impossible for the Catholic historian of the Catholic Church to reject the dogmas of the Church. There is not a word in the Pope's statement about "not examining too closely."

I should be interested to learn why you should suppose that the Catholic historian who accepts Catholic dogmas is at a disadvantage compared to those who don't. The Church, for example, maintains that Christ had two natures, divine and human, and two wills, and the Church has condemned the Monophysite and Monothelite heresies, but this fact would not cramp my style if I was writing history. Do you suppose that the Catholic historian has a large notice pinned above his desk: "N.B.—Keep off the Monophysites, don't examine too closely the Arian heresy"?

It is not the dogmas of the Church, but the sins and follies of Catholics, ecclesiastic and lay, which test the truthfulness of the Catholic historian. Is there anything in this letter of Leo XIII which suggests that we should "not examine too closely" those shadows on Church history? There is not. On the contrary, the Pope continues:

> This directing and supernatural idea which presides over the destinies of the Church is at the same time the torch whose

[59] Leo XIII, *De Puis le Jour* (1899), 25. —Ed.

light illuminates her history. Nevertheless, and because the Church which perpetuates among men the life of the Incarnate Word is composed of a divine and of a human element, this last should be expounded by scholars with great integrity ["*avec une grande probité*"]. For as it is said in the book of Job, "God has no need of our lies." [60]

You have not only misquoted the Pope, but by means of a familiar device, the truncated quotation, you omitted sentences which flatly contradict the libellous interpretation which you place on the sentences which you quote. You represent as an invitation to dishonest and evasive criticisms a passage which in point of fact is a demand to Catholic scholars to face the facts. In the paragraph just preceding the paragraph which you quote, the Pope expressly warns the historians of the Church not to conceal the faults of the Church's children, and even of her ministers.

You will now understand why Catholics who are so generous in their welcome to controversial books in which the case against the Church is stated by a non-Catholic and refuted by a Catholic are not enthusiastic about encouraging uninstructed Catholics to read anti-Catholic propaganda. A Catholic without the necessary background of knowledge would not necessarily realize that you had misquoted and misrepresented the Pope. Overawed by your footnotes and by the suggestion of accurate scholarship, he would be inclined to accept you as at least factually accurate, and he would in consequence be justly perturbed by your misrepresentation of the Pope's letter.

It is ironic that the precept which you falsely attribute to the Pope, "not to examine too closely" facts which are consistent with received dogmas, is boldly proclaimed as a

[60] Ibid., quoting Job 13:7. —ED.

fundamental principle by distinguished scientists, and by some of your own fellow modernists.

Thus many fossil remains of men of a comparatively modern type have been found in strata earlier in date than those in which the alleged ape-men—pithecanthropus—had been discovered. In fact pithecanthropus had the bad taste to be born much later than his descendants. The evolutionist prefers "not to examine too closely" these inconvenient fossils. "Were such discoveries," writes Sir Arthur Keith, "in accordance with our expectations, if they were in harmony with the theories we have formed regarding the date of man's evolution, no one would ever dream of doubting them, much less of rejecting them. . . . The majority of anatomists and geologists simply refuse to believe in the authenticity of these discoveries because they run so contrary to our preconceptions." [61] Darwinian evolution, in which incidentally Catholics are free to believe, is a quasi-religious faith, accepted as an escape from the dogma for special creation. "I am, however, thoroughly persuaded," wrote the great biologist Yves Delage in 1903, "that one is or is not a transformist (evolutionist) not so much for motives deduced from natural history as for motives based on personal philosophic opinions. If there existed some other scientific hypothesis besides that of descent to explain the origin of species, many transformists would abandon their present opinion as not being sufficiently demonstrated. If one takes his stand upon the *exclusive ground of facts* (italics mine) it must be acknowledged that the formation of one species from another has not been demonstrated at all." [62] Lemoine, an editor of the 1938

<hr>

[61] *Nineteenth Century*, cxxxvi, p. 23.

[62] Yves Delage (1854–1920), agnostic, Shroud of Turin researcher, professor of comparative anatomy at the Sorbonne, and author of *The Theories of Evolution* (1912). —ED.

edition of the *Encyclopaedie Française*, writes: "This evolution is a sort of dogma in which the priests no longer believe but which they maintain for their people." [63] Professor D. M. S. Watson informed a body of scientists at Capetown: "Evolution itself is accepted by zoologists not because it has been observed to occur or can be proved by logically coherent facts to be true, but because the only alternative, 'special creation,' is clearly incredible." [64]

Strauss, the prototype of the modernists, was a firm believer in the principles you falsely attribute to the Pope. He announced that in the life and works of Jesus no trace of the supernatural should be allowed to remain.[65] An even more interesting example of the determination not to "examine too closely" facts which conflict with preconceived dogmas is provided by Dr. Inge.

"A dramatic vindication of God's omnipotence on the world of phenomena was precisely what the contemporaries of Christ desired to see, and it was precisely what He did not come to earth to provide. 'A wicked and adulterous generation seeketh after a sign. Verily I say unto you, there shall no sign be given to this generation.'" [66] Dr. Inge omits the concluding words of St. Matthew 12:39, "*but the sign of the prophet Jonas.*" And here is the next verse. "*For as Jonas was three days and three nights in the belly of the whale; so shall the Son of man be three days and three nights in the heart of the earth.*"

---

[63] Paul Lemoine wrote the article "Introduction de L'Evolution" in the *Encyclopaedie Française*, vol. 5 (1937), 6. —ED.

[64] D. M. S. Watson (1886–1973), professor of zoology and comparative anatomy at the University of London. —ED.

[65] *Das Leben Jesu*, xv, "*und dieses Negative ist . . .*" Strauss adds, "*gerade eine—um nicht zu sagen die—Hauptsache*" ["and this negative principle is . . . one—if not to say the—essential thing." —ED.].

[66] Dr. Inge's translation of St. Matthew 12:39 only differs in unimportant details from the A.V. and R.C. (*Outspoken Essays*, Second Series, p. 50).

Thus the words which Dr. Inge omits flatly contradict the interpretation which he places on the words which he quotes. An exact parallel to your "truncated quotation" from the Pope. Moreover, the chapter from which this truncated quotation is taken contains the account *of two other miracles*. It would be interesting to learn from what private source of illumination Dr. Inge has acquired the key to his principle of selective quotation. I am sorry to bring Dr. Inge into this controversy, for I have a great respect for his integrity, for his contempt for the political fashion of the moment, and also for his mastery of the English language. His truncated quotation proves, as yours does, that it is quite possible for an honest man to employ dishonest controversial methods. While we are on the subject of truncated quotations, I wonder how you would justify quoting Newman, "Perhaps the only English writer who has any claim to be considered an ecclesiastical historian is the infidel Gibbon," without continuing the quotation, "To be deep in history is to cease to be a Protestant." [67]

May I remind you that we are limited by our agreement to 50,000 words each and no appendices. It is a pity, therefore, to waste space on irrelevancies such as the gorgeousness of Cardinals and the rudeness of some Liverpool priest who did not live up to your own high standard of courtesy to other communions. Incidentally you might have mentioned the handsome apology which he offered for the platform lapse from good taste.

If I leave any of your attacks on the Popes or other Catholics unanswered it is because I must insist on devoting half my space to a positive statement of the Catholic case. I was anxious, as you know, that we should do two books (the

[67] *Essay on the Development of Christian Doctrine*, 8. —ED.

first on infallibility) in order to cover both subjects thoroughly. You were entitled to decline that offer, but it is unfair in view of our limited space to make a series of random and disconnected attacks on the Church, each of which could be stated in a line or two, and each of which would require a letter for adequate reply. Thus you quote Quirinus[68] as *the* authority on the Vatican Council in general, and on Pius IX's alleged remarks in particular. You might as well discuss Athenian democracy on the basis of "the Old Oligarch's" [69] writings. You hand out a few texts to support a quasi-Quaker conception of the early Church and to justify your own Puritan prejudice against the colour and the beauty of Catholic ritual. Our Lord loved the service of the Temple, as ornate in their way as High Mass at St. Peter's. He came to fulfil, not to destroy the Jewish religion, and this religion, as Professor Heiler,[70] one of the most distinguished critics of Catholicism, has stated, exhibited a striking similarity to Catholicism.

The principal defect of your approach to the Church is the fact that you seem to equate the government of the Church with the Church herself, and are only interested in those aspects of Papalism which are open to criticism. This is much as if a historian of England were to ignore the life of the people and to concentrate solely on the Star Chamber, the persecution of Catholics by Elizabeth, the political corruption of the eighteenth century, 18B [71] and the British censor-

[68] "Quirinus" was the *nom de plume* of Johann Ignaz von Döllinger (1799–1890), writing about Vatican I in *Die Allgemeine Zeitung.* —ED.

[69] "The Old Oligarch" was the name given by scholars to the anonymous author of a treatise on the governance of Athens. It is preserved among the writings of Xenophon. —ED.

[70] Friedrich Heiler (1892–1957), a former Catholic who was Protestant professor of theology at Marburg University. —ED.

[71] A World War I regulation giving the British Home Secretary authority to imprison citizens without trial. —ED.

ship during the war. May I remind you of the fact that sinners sometimes sin, and that the impeccability of Catholics is no part of Catholic doctrine. Of the first twelve disciples one betrayed our Lord and one denied Him, which should have prepared for dereliction in high places.

Your method is simple. You enter into the notebooks which you have been compiling for forty years every telling example that you can find of Catholics behaving badly, and you never ask yourself whether they have behaved badly because they are Catholics or because they are human beings. "Cruelty and the abuse of absolute power," said Charles Dickens, "are the two bad passions of human nature." They are not an invention of the Catholic Church. You quote Charles Spurgeon[72] as saying: "Ours [the Baptists] is the only great Christian communion which has never persecuted, because we have never been able to." But you do not draw the deduction that the persecution of opinion (in which Catholics, Anglicans, and Presbyterians have all indulged) is something which Christianity took many centuries to eradicate rather than something for which the Church was directly responsible.

It is interesting to compare the record of the Inquisition with the record of militant atheism, for even in the ages of persecution Christianity was a brake on persecution. Some *faint* flavour of justice and of mercy tempered the injustice and cruelty of the Inquisition, of the persecution of Catholics in England, and of witches in Scotland. According to the correspondent of the *Manchester Guardian*, which supported the Republicans in Spain, the number of persons executed in Madrid was not less than 40,000. The great majority of these were murdered without trial. Anti-Republican estimates run

---

[72] C. H. Spurgeon (1834–1892), English Baptist minister and preacher. —ED.

into many hundreds of thousand; but let us compare what a friend of the Republican regime said about the Republicans with what an enemy of the Spanish Inquisition said about the Inquisition. Your friend Lea, who seldom errs on the side of generosity to the Church, accuses Llorente[73] of gross exaggeration, yet what he calls Llorente's "extravagant guesses" gives 31,912 as the grand total of victims executed by the Spanish Inquisition in 328 years, rather less than those murdered, usually without trial, in Madrid during the three years of civil war. As to Russia, the numbers murdered by militant atheists run into astronomical figures.

Complete integrity, though not unknown, is unusual among apologists for creeds, religious, scientific or political, but the kind of thing which you condemn in Catholic apologists as characteristically Catholic is, alas! characteristically human. Haeckel,[74] for instance, the great scientist, was convicted of faking diagrams in order to establish the similarity between the embryo of men and of apes. He replied: "To put an end to an unsavoury dispute I begin at once with the contrite confession that a small number (6 to 8 percent) of my embryo diagrams are really *forgeries* in Dr. Brass's sense— those, namely, for which the observed material is so incomplete or insufficient as to compel us . . . to fill in and reconstruct the missing links by hypothesis. . . . I should feel utterly condemned and annihilated by the admission *were it*

---

[73] Juan Antonio Llorente was appointed secretary to the Spanish Inquisition in 1789. In 1801 he was dismissed for alleged embezzlement. He supported the French invasion of Spain in 1808, and, after the return of the Spanish king, he retired to Paris, where in 1817 he published *The Critical History of the Spanish Inquisition*. Llorente claimed to make use of official documents to which he said he had access, but when challenged on his claims of the number of victims of the Inquisition, he said he had burned the papers on which he had relied. —ED.

[74] Ernst Haeckel (1834–1919), popularizer of Darwinism. His famous drawings of embryonic development turned out to have been faked. —ED.

not that hundreds of the best observers and most reputable biologists
lie under the same charge." [75]

If I followed your methods I should cite this as evidence of
a general indictment against the honesty of scientists.

Or, again, consider Dr. Moffatt's *The New Testament in*
Modern Speech.[76] By way of playing up to neo-Unitarians he
translates the first verse of the Fourth Gospel, "The Logos
was divine." Now St. John did not write *Theios* (divine), but
Theos (God), and Dr. Moffat's translation was a fake. An even
grosser example is his translation of St. Mark 14:22: "Take
this, it means my body." But I should never dream of suggesting that modernists could not be trusted to produce an
honest translation of the Bible, or an accurate summary of a
Papal Encyclical, in spite of your treatment of Leo XIII's
letter to the French clergy.

If you could only be induced to see the Church as a living
and developing society you would not assume that you had
made a point against the Church by quoting some uncionge-
nial utterance of a medieval theologian. You read the great
doctors of the Church not to discover how far their timeless
wisdom would help us to solve the problems of this distracted planet, but in order to pillory those sentiments and
those errors which were the sentiments and errors of their
age. And your eyes light up with all the enthusiasm of the
born collector when you discover some nice juicy bit about
the torments of the damned, or the extremely slim chances
of a heretic escaping the fires of hell. To the end of time
Catholics will believe in eternal punishment, and to the end
of time Catholics will debate the nature of eternal punishment and the conditions under which a soul is lost, and to

[75] *Münchner Allgemeine Zeitung*, January, 1909. The whole story is told in
my *Flight from Reason*, 2nd ed., p. xxv.

[76] James Moffatt (1870–1944), Protestant Scripture scholar. —ED.

the end of time there will be rigorists and moderates among Catholic theologians. You have no interest in the moderates, but you collect choice examples of rigorism in much the same spirit as other men collect rare first editions, and if we refuse to accept you as the final authority on the beliefs which we must hold, if we oppose a Karl Adam[77] to a Perrone or a Vermeersch[78] to a Billot,[79] you register signs of distress and indignation as if we were cheating. "What you say about Hell," you once wrote to me, "is mainly modern apologetics and might well have brought the authors of the *Dictionnaire Apologétique* or Father Martindale to the stake in the pre-Reformation centuries." So what?

Incidentally, I wish you would make up your mind whether writers like Father Karl Adam and Father Martindale are, as you suggest, mere decoy-ducks to entice hesitating converts across the threshold of the reactionary Church, the Church which would relight the fires of Smithfield[80] tomorrow if she got the chance, or whether, as you sometimes suggest, the Pope himself is nearer to Dr. Coulton than to St. Thomas Aquinas in his opinions about eternal punishment. Both views are, of course, wildly remote from the facts.

You have, of course, de-contexted Cardinal Billot, who was not as bigoted as might appear from your quotations, but even so I should not be prepared to defend everything which he wrote. As you are so fond of Cardinals, may I present you with two specimens for your Cardinalia. Cardinal

[77] Karl Adam (1876–1966), German Catholic theologian. —Ed.

[78] Arthur Vermeersch (1858–1936), Jesuit moral theologian, canonist, and spiritual writer. —Ed.

[79] Louis Billot (1846–1931), theologian, created cardinal by Pius X in 1911. He was sympathetic to *Action Française*, which was condemned by Pius XI in 1927. Billot then renounced his cardinalatial title. —Ed.

[80] Smithfield, near the present-day St. Paul's Cathedral, was the execution ground during Mary Tudor's reign. —Ed.

Manning[81] wrote to my father, a Protestant: "I embrace you in the soul of the Church and rejoice in all your good works"; and Cardinal Hinsley[82] said to me: "I should never use the word 'heretic' in connexion with a good man like your father who is incapable of deliberately rejecting what God proposes for our belief." The late Cardinal as you know founded the Sword of the Spirit, which has done so much to improve the relations between Catholics and Protestants. Of course, to the end of time there will be intolerant Catholics and intolerant Protestants, men who are not only intolerant of what they believe to be false but also of those whom they believe to be in error; but the common threat to Christendom is drawing Catholics and Protestants together, and the truth is that both you and Cardinal Billot are a little old-fashioned. It would be foolish to expect you to inform your readers that Cardinal Billot's sympathy with the reactionary *Action Française*[83] angered the Pope, with the result that the Cardinal was forced to resign his Hat, an incident unique, I believe, in modern times.

I should like to thank you for the vigour of your attack. It is sporting of a writer in his ninth decade to issue these fiery challenges to debates and I am happy to oblige you. We have at least two things in common, a keen enjoyment of this form of controversy and a love for that dear country Switzerland, and though I should hardly describe myself as a Coulton-fan, you will, I hope, forgive me if I say how much I enjoyed the chapter on Adelboden[84] in your attractive autobiography, *Fourscore Years*.

And now, "Over to you."

[81] Henry Edward Manning (1808–1892), English convert and cardinal. —ED.

[82] Arthur Hinsley (1865–1943), Archbishop of Westminster after 1935. —ED.

[83] Organization under the leadership of Charles Maurras (1868–1952), agnostic monarchist. It sought to overthrow the republican regime. —ED.

[84] Adelboden is a resort in the Bernese Alps. —ED.

Afterword

While shopping for an automobile a few years ago, I took the obligatory test drive. The salesman got in beside me and cranked up the radio as soon as the engine started. As he began to explain how well balanced and powerful the eleven speakers were, I stretched out my arm and pushed the off button.

"You don't want to see how good the sound system is?"

"I have no interest in the sound system. I don't plan to use it."

"You don't? What do you do on long drives?"

"I think."

He fell silent. I imagined him saying to himself, "Thinking—what a novel idea!"

It is a pity that private thinking has gone out of fashion, because that means public thinking has gone out of fashion. One consequence is that public religious discussion—what little there is of it—has lost much of its savor. No matter how lofty the topic, not much can be said if the parties fail to think things through.

The eight chapters in this book are examples of what once was common, the intelligent discussion of religious differences. Today such discussions are rare, not just because there is a disinclination to think discursively, but because of an even deeper problem: most people no longer hold that religious differences matter. For such people, each of us has a private truth, created in his own image and likeness. If my truth is right for me and yours for you, what is there to discuss? There is more sense in discussing which of us has the better automobile—mine with eleven unused speakers or yours with fewer, but well-used, speakers. My arrangement suits me, and yours suits you. There is no need to assert the other fellow is wrong when it is all a matter of *de gustibus non est disputandum*.

This attitude cannot last, because it is based on a misapprehension of man's nature. Man's soul, like any spirit, has two chief attributes: intellect and will. With the intellect we know, and with the will we love. If the two work in harmony, we know love and love knowledge. If the intellect is atrophied, the will ends up misdirected. If the will is weakened, the intellect goes astray. Some eras, such as ours, are characterized by flabby intellects, and perhaps nowhere is this more evident than in religion. America has been called the most religious country in the Western world, but that factoid reflects only how many people walk through the doors of churches on Sunday. It tells us little about Americans' intensity of faith or depth of understanding.

Around the middle of the twentieth century the idea that religion matters because it is true lost out to the idea that religion matters because it is useful. There indeed is a utility in religious truth—"The truth shall set you free"—but truth should be more than a key to a locked door. It once was valued for its own sake. For many people, truth still is a good to be pursued, but such people no longer are the ones leavening society. In terms of influence, thinkers have been supplanted by emoters, and if there is one thing that emoters shy away from, it is controversy. One may be excused for being boring, flippant, or even crass, but stepping over the line into controversy puts one beyond the pale. That is because controversy is a knife. It cuts truth from error, setting a *placet* here and a *non placet* there. We choose up sides mentally, and many people say that that is "divisive" behavior—and it is. At one time it was a compliment to call someone discriminating, as in "he is a man of discriminating tastes". Mental discrimination has gone down the memory hole, and with it has gone the notion that it is a good thing to be able to distinguish between the true and the false.

Not to worry. However much ideologies may sway us at the moment, one thing that will not change is human nature. The pendulum will swing back, striking a new balance between the intellective and the affective. Those who have shied away from thinking things through and therefore from drawing conclusions will be succeeded, in terms of influence, by those who relish mental swordplay and who appreciate it even in those with whom they disagree. Pilate's question—"What is truth?"—was delivered dismissively, but, taken in another sense, it is the key question for every man. Unless we inquire what truth is, we will not search for it. Unless we search for it, we will not find it. Unless we find it, we will not find him who is "the way, the truth, and the life". In the long run, nothing else matters.

ACKNOWLEDGMENTS

Credits

Excerpts from Arnold Lunn and J. B. S. Haldane, *Science and the Supernatural*, are reprinted with permission of Sheed and Ward, an apostolate of the Priests of the Sacred Heart, 7373 S. Lovers Lane Road, Franklin, Wisconsin 53132.

Herbert Thurston, S.J., "How History Is Miswritten", is reprinted with permission of *The Month*, a publication of the British Province of the Society of Jesus.

Excerpts from Arnold Lunn and G. G. Coulton, *Is the Catholic Church Anti-Social?* are reprinted with permission of Burns and Oates, an imprint of Continuum.

Despite due diligence, the author has been unable to determine the copyright holders of Hilaire Belloc, *Essays of a Catholic*; Ronald Knox and Arnold Lunn, *Difficulties*; and Arnold Lunn and C. E. M. Joad, *Is Christianity True?* Once the copyright holders are determined, subsequent printings will include proper credits.

Sources

CHAPTER 1, PAGES 19–21
John Henry Newman. *Apologia pro Vita Sua*. New York: Random House, 1950. Pages 388–90.

CHAPTER 1, PAGES 25–43
John Henry Newman. *Apologia pro Vita Sua*. New York: Random House, 1950. Pages 3–17.

CHAPTER 2, PAGES 49–66
Hilaire Belloc. *Essays of a Catholic*. New York: Macmillan, 1931. Pages 267–83.

CHAPTER 3, PAGES 69–73
Hilaire Belloc. *Essays of a Catholic*. New York: Macmillan, 1931. Pages 301–5.

CHAPTER 4, PAGES 84–94
Ronald Knox and Arnold Lunn. *Difficulties*. London: Eyre and
Spottiswoode, 1952. Pages 123–30.

CHAPTER 4, PAGES 95–101
Ronald Knox and Arnold Lunn. *Difficulties*. London: Eyre and
Spottiswoode, 1952. Pages 170–74.

CHAPTER 4, PAGES 102–16
Ronald Knox and Arnold Lunn. *Difficulties*. London: Eyre and
Spottiswoode, 1952. Pages 229–39.

CHAPTER 5, PAGES 120–33
Arnold Lunn and C. E. M. Joad. *Is Christianity True?* Philadelphia:
Lippincott, 1933. Pages 3–13.

CHAPTER 5, PAGES 135–46
Arnold Lunn and C. E. M. Joad. *Is Christianity True?* Philadelphia:
Lippincott, 1933. Pages 78–85.

CHAPTER 6, PAGES 150–66
Arnold Lunn and J. B. S. Haldane. *Science and the Supernatural*. New
York: Sheed and Ward, 1935. Pages 19–31.

CHAPTER 6, PAGES 167–77
Arnold Lunn and J. B. S. Haldane. *Science and the Supernatural*. New
York: Sheed and Ward, 1935. Pages 48–56.

CHAPTER 6, PAGES 177–92
Arnold Lunn and J. B. S. Haldane. *Science and the Supernatural*. New
York: Sheed and Ward, 1935. Pages 381–93.

CHAPTER 7, PAGES 197–229
Herbert Thurston. *How History Is Miswritten*. London: Catholic Truth
Society, n.d. Pages 2–32.

CHAPTER 8, PAGES 234–71
G. G. Coulton and Arnold Lunn. *Is the Catholic Church Anti-Social?*
London: Burns and Oates, 1946. Pages 19–40.